M000045857

A Guide to Happy Family Camping

A Guide to Happy Family Camping

A little help to get started
camping with kids

TAMMERIE SPIRES

Good Books®
Intercourse, PA 17534

Design by Dawn J. Ranck
Cover illustration by Cheryl Benner

A GUIDE TO HAPPY FAMILY CAMPING
Copyright © 1998 by Good Books, Intercourse, PA 17534
International Standard Book Number: 1-56148-248-X
Library of Congress Catalog Card Number: 98-11431

All rights reserved. Printed in the United States of America.
No part of this book may be reproduced in any manner,
except for brief quotations in critical articles or reviews, without permission.

Library of Congress Cataloging-in-Publication Data

Spires, Tammerie.
    A guide to happy family camping : a little help to get started camping with
kids / Tammerie Spires.
        p. cm.
    ISBN 1-56148-248-X
    1. Camping.   2. Family recreation.   I. Title.
GV191.7.S65   1998
796.54--dc21   98-11431
                                                                                CIP

Dedication

To my David, Harper, and Chandler,
who put the family in family camping for me

Acknowledgments

About a year ago I decided to leave a corporate career I loved for two other jobs I love even more: Mom and Writer. This would never have been my idea, but has proved to be an enormous blessing, so I am thankful to God for drawing me to this path.

I am deeply grateful to have grown up on a farm where I learned a love of the out-of-doors; thanks, Mom and Dad. I thank Camp Lula Sams and Camp Mystic for my early camping experiences, and my husband, David, for getting us into camping as a family.

I appreciate, too, the other families we have camped or shared ideas with: Steve and Judy Baldauf, Kim Lin and Jerry Sovich, Susan and Dan Sellers, Pat and Gary Coleman, Shannon and Rebecca Spires, Clay and Crystal Spires, and much-loved neighbors Yvonne and Clark Roberts, and Wayne and Annette Albrecht.

I am also glad to have had a cheering section vicariously hiking along this journey from Career Mom to Writer Mom with me. Their companionship and encouragement have meant a great deal: Mary Burkhead, Janee Duval, Kimberly Fairchild, Adriana Mutolo Hartley, Beth Miles, Julie Richmond, Elizabeth Bryant Robinson, and Elayne Vick.

And what a wonder it's been to work with the folks at Good Books. Merle and Phyllis Good and designer Dawn Ranck have exhibited a great deal of enthusiasm for this project and more than a little patience with me!

Lastly, to three people who have inspired and shared my love of writing: Mrs. Sammy Roiz, my sixth-grade English teacher, who tried to give me an understanding of the tools of language and writing; John Trimble, my writing professor at the University of Texas at Austin, who taught me a great respect for the reader; and finally Roger Lipsey, a wise mentor, caring compadre, and friend of the heart who has been generous in sharing his wisdom and support for many years.

— Tammerie Spires

Table of Contents

Camping With Kids . . .
WHY?

Maybe you've never camped before but think it might be something fun to do with the kids. Maybe you used to camp with your spouse, but you're just not sure it's going to work out with an infant or toddler. Maybe you've camped quite a bit with your kids, and you're curious to know if there are better ways to handle the tricky moments.

This book's for you. In it you'll discover bright ideas and basic necessities that will help novice and pro alike have more fun and less fuss outdoors. We'll cover six Happy Camper Principles, 90 handy tips, information about places to go, some stories about where we've been, and a few lists of stuff and things to remember, get, do, or see (in the real world and on the Internet). Check Section 8, Resources, for these.

What you won't find is any preconception about the "right" way to camp. If Madison Avenue has its way with you, you may think you have to be a senior citizen in an air-conditioned rolling palace or a Gen-Xer, hanging your ultra-light, four-season tent off the side of a glacier.

The fact is, you don't have to go to either of those extremes to get out of your house and out of your norm and have a great time doing it, especially if you have the nerve to take your kids and a little infrastructure with you.

What kind of infrastructure? Well, that depends on you. Which leads us to **Happy Camper Principle I:** *Camping happily requires determining what you need to camp happily.* Back seat of a car? Tent? Truck bed? Van seat? Pop-up trailer? Hard-side trailer? Big-league RV or motor home? There's a continuum here, ranging from sleeping under the stars to sleeping under the TV aerial. You decide where you need to be. And if you hear somebody snickering over how little or how much you have . . . laugh back at 'em in the secure knowledge that you have what you need to be happy.

There are lots of us in the generations between the Rolling Retired and Gen-X who sort of camped when we were kids, and who really want to sort of camp with *our* kids. Jim Shahin called it "Camping in Quotes" in an *American Way* magazine column.

Happy Camper Principle I:

Camping happily requires determining what you need to camp happily.

My husband and I both "camped" as kids: Dave in his grandmother's back pasture with other neighborhood hoodlums, during the formative years when Dinty Moore and Dr. Pepper satisfied all major food group requirements; Tam in various Girl Scout and non-Scout girl camps, with roles ranging from bookish Brownie-sized bug-tracker to quasi-adult waterfront counselor.

We started camping again soon after our daughter was born (Harper, 1993), though we didn't take her with us at first. Our first serious Camping Trip was intended to give a couple of new parents a break from the beloved four-month-old. But with a few successes under our respective belts, we soon wanted to share the fun with Harper and the new rug-rat, Chandler (1995). That's when we started learning the lessons you'll find in this book, about everything from planning to food to fun to gear.

I hope this book kindles your desire to camp with kids. If you're ready to hit the road and pitch camp, then read on, head out, and let us hear *your* adventures!

Six
Happy Camper
Principles

1. Camping happily requires determining what you need to camp happily.

2. Make and use lists.

3. Everything should be fun . . . make it so.

4. The more situations you are prepared for, the more you are prepared to enjoy.

5. Everybody over two years of age packs her own stuff.

6. Sleep is an important prerequisite to having fun on a camping trip. Make sure the kids and the adults get plenty.

1.
Planning

Most parents know that living with kids is the Great Multiplier. You're twice as late . . . or you've learned to start getting ready twice as early. Well, add camping to the mix, and you've got the Mucho Multiplier. You need four times as much underwear, but you're having four times as much fun. How can you make the Mucho Multiplier work for you? Here you go . . .

1. The key to happy camping with kids can be found in the three Ps: Planning, Packing, and Preparing. Think through where you want to go, what you'll do when you get there, and what you'll need to have with you to enjoy the experience.

    Write it down as you go, because the secret of successful planning, packing, and preparing is . . . *The List.* This one is important enough to be **Happy Camper Principle II:** *Make and use lists.* Lists save lives, hair, and marriages!

Happy Camper Principle II:

Make and use lists.

2.   I put my master list together in three columns, headed: Week Before, Day Before, and Day Of. I fold it to the appropriate time frame, and it all gets done.

Put an underline, dash, or hollow bullet next to items on your list, and check them off as they are packed or performed. Don't just cross things off by drawing a line through them. You'll forget what those items were and peer at them to see what it was you've already done.

3.   Be sure everybody is clear on who's doing what. Mark it on the list if you need to. My list also includes some blank lines at the end so I can customize my reminders for each specific trip.

Do take your list on the road with you, so you don't forget what you forgot. (When diapers are what you forgot, once is enough!)

4.   While a computer is a very expensive list-making device (in the way that a microwave is a very expensive popcorn popper), an easily revisable list is an eminently useful list. My list is on the computer, but I'd write it by hand if necessary. It's that important. (See Resources, pages 71-75 for sample lists; chances are I've already missed much of what you need!)

5.   Equally important is what not to take. Don't take crap. No brain drains (TV, video games, and pretty much everything else requiring batteries, except

Pine Whispers

Shortly after Harper was born, Dave and I took a much needed trip together sans baby (thanks, Grandmother Nan!). It was a harbinger of things to come. We hightailed it to Arkansas' Petit Jean State Park, a mountaintop camp nestled lakeside among a forest of pine trees.

I found it a great joy and relief to be set loose in the outdoors, after a few months spent mostly around the house being an over-protective, anxious first-time mom with a new baby. Dave and I happily stomped pine-shaded hiking trails and swept pine needles out of our food.

On Sunday morning before the long drive back to Texas, we sat with other campers on a row of benches in a piney grove for an early worship service. I don't remember much of what the preacher said, but I do remember the pines whispering, as they'd whispered all weekend long. "Come back," they said. "Bring the child. Come back outside where you belong." I was reminded that Spirit uses whatever means necessary to call us to where we need to be.

Harper and I started getting outside more often, and I wasn't so afraid of being a mom out in the wide, wide world.

your flashlights and weather radio). No junk food for the body (tell the kids it's their first spa weekend). No attitudes. This is the tough one. Babies don't like schedules to get out of whack . . . toddlers are bored by the drive . . . kids miss the TV . . . 'tweens think the great outdoors is geeky . . . teens believe a weekend with their parents is time off in hell. You name it, they'll whine about it. Unless they are busy.

Everybody gets a little responsibility, everybody pitches in to get the chores done, and everybody has a whole lot of fun. Keep it easygoing, and a little latitude will help the attitude.

6. Dave and I have found that the buddy system works well; we're a good team. If you're a single parent, think about doubling up. There's not much a couple of moms or a pair of dads flying in tandem can't manage. You can certainly manage everything in this book.

   Even pairs of parents may want to partner up. We have several friends we like to camp with . . . because we like them, because we're compatible campers, and because they love us and our kids enough to baby-sit during the occasional nap while Dave and I get a rare chance to mountain-bike or swim together . . . *alone!*

7. Scheduling is a big part of camp planning. This makes some of our childless friends and relatives

crazy, since they want to go and do at any hour of the day. Well, we used to do that, but we've learned it's not really fair to the kids, and it can pretty much ruin your day. (Just try setting out on a three-mile hike at nap-time.)

Nowadays, serendipity is what happens when well rested families with sufficient snacks, diapers, and dry changes of clothes meet a stream crossing to an alternative trail. Serendipity, yes, but with planning and room for error.

8. Speaking of scheduling, if you've developed a Fear of Five O'Clock, hang on to it. You need a healthy respect for the time between 5:00 p.m. and bedtime. This is *not* the time to schedule a hike, swim, or even a side trip in the car.

   Don't try to do anything but **have fun doing what *must* be done:** make dinner, feed kids, clean up kids, rig for nighttime, put kids to bed. The fact is, if you can get through the Fearful Five O'Clock hour intact, you've got it made.

9. Routine helps, but be flexible. Our system of putting both kids to bed together at the same time had to be adjusted when the youngest, Chandler, got to the gonzo giggle stage (11 months old). He and his older sister, Harper, kept each other up for hours, rocking the trailer with their laughter. We finally had to keep her up long enough for him to fall asleep first, at which time we snuck her into

The January Thaw

In the January of Chandler's first year, the weatherman forecast a weekend we couldn't resist. Even as far south as we live, January's weather is commonly raw, bitterly cold. So when we heard "highs in the 70s on Saturday," we begged and borrowed a pop-up from our neighbors Wayne and Annette and headed to nearby Mineral Wells State Park. Wayne and Annette joined us for the day, and we took turns watching the kids and mountain-biking. Then adults and children headed out for a late afternoon hike around Lake Mineral Wells, through winter-denuded trees.

At sunset, we were glad the leaves lay a-tangle on the ground, because sun and sky were putting on a show. As the sun fell toward the hills on the other side of the lake, streamers of clouds high and low turned burnished gold against a blush pink sky. The lake, rippled by the wind into wavelets, reflected a scattering of pink and gold, the pattern shifting like a tumbling blocks quilt. We stood on the hiking trail for an hour, grown-ups and children enraptured into a still wonder.

January melted our hearts that day.

her bunk. Now that Harper is four and Chandler is two, the only technique that works is to wear 'em both out before bedtime so they're too tired to giggle for long.

10. Packing is another big part of camp planning. After all, The List is primarily to help you remember what to pack, and then to actually pack it, preferably where you can remember to find it.

    A little practice and forethought will help you pack efficiently enough to justify bringing everything you know you'll need, and most of what you think you might want. Think flexible and reusable. Handy Tip #74 below explains our multiple uses for big Rubbermaid tubs, for example.

11. *Stay packed* and you'll go more often. We keep our trailer loaded with what we call *permanent stocks:* camp bedding, hiking boots, child carrier, camp chairs, towels . . . and *replenishable stocks:* non-perishable food staples, RV toilet paper, spare set of toiletries . . . You'll find other ideas in Resources, pages 72 and 73.

    We've found that the easier it is to go, the more often we go, and the more often we go, the happier we are. And the happier we are . . . well, that is the point, isn't it?

12. Work with your kids to plan and pack their backpacks: for car trips and for each hike. Help the kids

load their packs for the car trip, so each has his or her own books, blocks, and other anti-road-boredom devices.

Then, prior to the first hike, reload with hiking requirements, like water, snacks, dipes and wipes, Band-Aids . . . whatever the kid needs, within reason.

13. *Pack foods you know your family likes to eat,* and which you'll be equipped to cook and clean up after easily. Some kids like hot dogs. Ours don't. Your kids may love roasted marshmallows. Well, one of mine likes 'em raw as a foam pillow, and the other won't go near 'em (yeah, the same kid who won't eat cake icing). But they both *love* pasta with pesto, they'll pick a chicken clean, and they'll snarf S'mores ingredients a la carte.

We'll talk more about food in the next section, but the key point here is: *Pack foods you know your family likes to eat.*

14. Finally, a side benefit to family camping is how much more you will appreciate camping *without* kids. Yes, occasionally you should invest in a baby-sitter for a long four-day weekend and take your mate out for a spin.

What does this have to do with planning? Well, if you're doing the planning, sneak in a few nice surprises—a fly-fishing guide for a day, steaks instead of burgers, a luxury shampoo to wash her

Campfire Stories

One cold winter night, after putting the tired small fry to bed, Dave and I sat around a piñon bonfire with brother Shannon and sis-in-law Rebecca. We were wreathed in resinous smoke, delighting in the smells and noises of the night.

A campfire usually inspires the Spires brothers to tell tales of their childhoods and teenage lunacies. However, Dave had recently discovered the master storyteller, J. Frank Dobie. We found that Dobie's *Apache Gold and Yaqui Silver* is especially effective by firelight. Passing the book around the circle, we took turns reading out loud far into the night.

By the way, if you come upon suspected bank robbers in the deep of night out West, don't bother searching their saddlebags for the gold. It's probably buried in the last place you'd look: under their campfire. Just ask Mr. Dobie!

hair a la Redford in *Out of Africa,* Ghirardelli truffles instead of S'mores—whatever *your* beloved would prize.

2.
Roadtrip

Unless you are camping in your backyard (in which case, all other sections apply *except* this one!), you are facing a drive to your camp site. We have traveled anywhere from hours to a day to get to a camping spot and find that you need to make pretty much the same preparation for a two-hour trip as a 10-hour trip. Just be ready to cycle through your entertainment ideas a few more times, and a little extra patience and understanding doesn't hurt.

The roadtrip is your whole trip in microcosm. It can involve eating, sleeping, all the interesting body functions, little side trips, micro-hikes in parks or small town squares along the way, and it should definitely involve fun. I know parents who drug their kids with Benadryl or videos to get through a long roadtrip, but, really, that's not necessary. Try a few of these ideas, and see if they help.

15. *Get off to a good start.* A journey well begun is halfway done, someone once said, and I agree. The whole day seems to go better when we get off to a rollicking good start, but that doesn't happen by accident. Use your lists to get as much done and packed as you can in the days before the Final

Launch Countdown.

As you're finishing loading on the morning of departure, go ahead and buckle the kids in the car. This will get them out of the way, and trigger last minute issues like, "Mom, I forgot my baby-doll!," and "Dad, I have to go to the bathroom!," before the actual last minute.

16. *Getting off early helps.* When we're trying to get an obscenely early start, Dave and I get up and load while the munchkins sleep, then throw them into clean clothes (laid out the night before, natch) and strap 'em into their seats. While Dave does the final 10 minutes, I feed the kids a snack breakfast (milk, bananas, granola or Nutri-grain bars, Pop-Tarts, toast, toaster waffles, whatever), and we hit the road.

    The kids find this sort of rapid launch sequence fascinating, especially with our family yell as we head out the driveway: "Rock and roll!"

17. If you have trouble getting up early, console your-self with the thought that the time you've saved leaving at 7:00 a.m. instead of 9:00 a.m. can be spent having fun along the way, which leads me to my next point.

18. *Slow down.* The fact is, especially with small kids, you are going to have to stop and let them out to stretch, change diapers, and all that other stuff. So

Traveling in Time

We like camping in cold weather, but don't usually travel out into snowstorms on purpose. However, on one trip to the West we managed to catch a late spring snowstorm outside Albuquerque.

Coming down out of the mountains, we were sure the snow would stop or turn to rain. However, as we entered I-40, we saw a gloppy mess of an interstate, marked only by a parallel track of ruts leading east. We fell into them, proceeded around a bend in the canyon and saw . . . a parking lot. Stretching for miles ahead of us, all we saw were the taillights of stopped cars, trucks, semis, and RVs.

It didn't get better anytime soon. We took three hours to travel the next 20 miles. But after awhile, it wasn't the miles that mattered. It was the hours. As motionless reality set in, people began to climb out of their vehicles. We commiserated, hurled snowballs, sculpted snow folks, and patiently cooperated our way out of the storm.

So much for road rage. The traffic may have snarled, but the people didn't. I was proud of us all, as we proved that it's not the problem that is important, it's the perspective.

you may as well build the time for it into the schedule of whoever in your family is anal about time. Plan fun things to do when you stop, and time spent in the car will be easier.

We recently did a Springfield-to-Dallas (that includes Illinois, Missouri, Oklahoma, and Texas for those of you filling out a sticker map) run in 14 hours. Never mind that my in-laws do it in 12. I think the longer trip was actually easier on our little ones because it involved some serious rest/eat/play stops along the way.

19. If you get off at a roadside stop, bring out some chalk for hopscotch or sidewalk art. Let the kids take pictures or draw pictures. Examine weird bugs together. Read the historical markers. Play tire bingo (ask any tour bus driver how if you've forgotten). Crank up the car radio and do aerobics or the Hokey-Pokey. (See Chapter 4, "Play," page 37, for more ideas.)

    Trout Fishing in America has great kids' music that parents can stand to listen to. See who learns to count the *18 Wheels on the Big Rig* first—you or the kids!

20. *Get off the interstate* and take the back roads. Whenever we have time (and we do try to build time into our travel plans), we make getting there a big part of the fun by taking the *Blue Highways* approach.

You may remember this book by William Least Heat-Moon. He took a few months to drive a big loop around the US, taking only "blue highways" wherever he could: "On the old highway maps of America, the main routes were red and the back roads blue. Now even the colors are changing. But in those brevities just before dawn and a little after dusk—times neither day nor night—the old roads return to the sky some of its color. Then, in truth, they carry a mysterious cast of blue, and it's that time when the pull of the blue highway is strongest, when the open road is a beckoning, a strangeness, a place where a man can lose himself."

21. Women and kids like getting lost, too. Sometimes it's the roads we didn't mean to take that get us where we want to go. Try it. Once you slow down, the little towns you pass through will intrigue rather than irritate you. Try the pie at the Round Top Cafe while your kids cavort around the old roadhouse in the square at Round Top, Texas.

22. *Pack books.* We set a big box of books between the two car seats in the back, and this keeps the kids occupied until we can get out of Dallas traffic (always my husband's least favorite part of the trip). Then, periodically through the day, one or both will pick up books and entertain themselves. We especially like when Harper gets one of the

Carl books by Alexandra Day and tells us stories from what she sees. And Chandler still likes to read Dr. Seuss upside down, as if the good doctor's books weren't odd enough. We're probably going to have to get counseling for the kid someday, but for now, this works.

23. *Pack a few toys.* Pick these car toys carefully for maximum play value and ease of cleanup. A great choice for toddlers and up are the Lauri products (Call 800/451-0520 for a free catalog). Lauri makes crepe rubber learning puzzles and lacing toys. The kids have fun with them, and they are oh-so-quiet and easy to clean and put away.

     My friend Pat always kept the best car toys and a few books hidden away altogether between car trips for fresh fun.

24. *Pack car snacks,* and be prepared to vacuum. I keep trying to: (a) find snacks the kids like that make less of a mess, and (b) help Dave have a sense of humor about what he finds between and under the seats ("Honey, think of it as an archaeological dig. You're seeing the history of our trips!" "Grrr.") I fail on both counts. But the trips are happy. We do pretzel sticks, raisins, Goldfish, apples, grapes, bars, whatever works.

25. *Naps are good.* It's hard for the kids to nap in their car seats, but we keep 'em in there for safety's

Wait Five Minutes . . . It'll Change

The weather, that is.

On one of our trips, the sky poured all the first day, causing some of our party to bolt for home. We were rewarded for sticking it out with three crisp fall days of rain-washed clarity. Another trip we spied an approaching front just in time to scurry camper-wards before the storm hit with a brief but intense fury. This storm's passage left a luminescent greenish glow over land and sky and dropped the temperature 20 degrees.

But the highlight of our weather wonders has to be Dave's high energy experience. We had just set up camp in a thicket of pines, hurrying to level the trailer before threatening clouds released their deluge. Inside the camper with the kids, I saw a flash of pink concurrent with a loud CRACK of thunder. A moment later, Dave hurried into the camper, looking pale and startled. "Okay, that was close enough," he said, and went on to describe how he'd looked up for no real reason, just in time to see the pine above him struck a-sizzle with lightning. His inexplicable escape was the talk of the camp that weekend.

Close enough, indeed.

sake. Pillows and loveys from home help. Feed 'em a big lunch, and fill the vehicle with gas so you don't have to wake them by stopping. Turn down the music, and let the road sing them to sleep.

26. Every roadtrip ends with camp setup. We finally learned to pay attention to this seemingly insignificant part of the trip on our third outing. It's tricky when your children are small; big ones just help with the setup. The adults will want to work together to set up camp, and the kids will want to run wild. Not a good combination.

Install toddlers and small kids at the site's picnic table with snack and drink while you pitch the tent or level the trailer (yes, you'll need to minimize snacking on the road during the last hour or so). If you have the kind of baby swing with a spring that hangs from a doorway, you'll be glad to know it will also hang from a tree. String the kid up and he'll stay out of trouble. Teeny babies can stay in the car seat, or stretch out in the port-a-crib (you packed it last for easy access, remember?).

After setup, take a little walk to stretch the kinks out, even if you've made an evening arrival.

3.
Food

Some of you are going to want to laugh at this section. May I refer you back to the opening pages, "Camping with Kids . . . WHY?", Happy Camper Principle I: *Camping happily requires determining what you need to camp happily.*

Cooking and eating good food is one of my favorite things to do, so I minimize the work involved, but I don't eliminate it. Knowing that, you may want to look in this section for ideas and principles you can apply in your own way.

27. My kids are still at the three-squares- and three-snacks-a-day stage, so it can seem that the trip revolves around food. But by remembering the three P's of camp chow—planning, packing, and preparing—we do manage to have a little fun in between.

    Think through your trip day by day and night by night—what you'll be doing, where you'll be going, what you'll need to take to eat, and what kind of preparation and cleanup that food will require.

28. As mentioned in #13, food you know your family likes is best. Yes, you can try some campier items

than you eat in your at-home diet, but don't strand yourself in the great outdoors with nothing but camp food that only your spouse will eat (out of misguided loyalty!).

If you do want to rely on trail mix and gorp, try it a few times at home to see who's going to be a happy camper and who might need a little mac and cheese to survive.

29. *Breakfast.* We have two kinds of breakfast: break-*fast* (quick: food *prior* to entertainment) and break-fast (slow: food *as* entertainment). Breakfast is one of our favorite meals of the day, but starting off with a big breakfast can eat up half the morning. And morning is Kid Prime Time, when my kids are most rested, happy, and ready for adventure. So we toss down some granola bars and bananas, beverage of choice, and hit the trail.

But when you wake up to a rainy, foggy, or frigid day, sometimes a big breakfast is in order, with better weather by the time you're set to roll out. Big breakfast ideas include standards like pancakes and ham, and personal favorites like breakfast tacos. An added benefit: Most big breakfasts make great leftovers for snacks or lunch, thereby saving time later.

30. We take snacks *whenever* we leave camp. We can always figure on needing them mid-morning (yep, for those of you who are counting, that's *right* after

breakfast), again after nap-time in the afternoon, maybe a little snack as a late dinner comes together, or right before bed if dinner was early.

On walkabout, we take granola bars, pretzels, raisins, and apples. Crackers are good, too, but don't seem to give the kids much going power, and they shatter easily (though small crackers like Goldfish are portable and can cheer up a grumpy kid). Bananas are great snacks in camp, but too smushy for backpacking.

31. We also take water whenever we leave camp. We usually carry a squeeze bottle in every backpack and keep a couple more jugs in the back of the truck (for refilling drinking bottles, and for rinsing sandy feet or dirty hands).

32. Water is one of those things you really can't have enough of, and that includes the frozen variety. A tip: The ice-maker in our fridge at home seems to have been designed for a family of eight, which we usually are not. When it begins to overflow, we load up Zip-loc bags with ice and keep them in our extra freezer out in the garage. These ice bags go straight into the ice chest with anything we want to keep frozen or cold on the roadtrip to the camp site. Then, as the bags thaw, we can always pour clean, ice-cold water out into a cup, or lay an icy bag over a boo-boo.

My friend Pat reuses the stoppered bags her

The Eleventh Commandment

"Thou shalt not live by camp grub alone."

We heed this commandment very seriously when camped within 10 miles of a small town. We'll pick a night to decamp and head into town, looking for the crowded parking lot outside a place with character. No chain, theme, or fast-food restaurants need apply.

One of our best discoveries on the first Caprock Canyons trip was Quitaque's worst-kept secret: the restaurant with no name. During a quick provisioning stop in town, we overheard discussion that the semi-regular Friday night fajita fest was on. Where? Good question. In a tin barn on the main street through town. No name on the wall outside. Just look for a full parking lot on Friday night. And if you run out of guacamole, feel free to wander into the kitchen and get it yourself. The no-name restaurant may be short on help, but it sure is long on good food.

drink mix comes in. She freezes these ahead of time and is able to pour out ice-cold water from the stopper.

33. Lunch is the easiest meal of the day, usually sandwiches and fruit, or leftovers from breakfast or last night's dinner. The trick is to keep it quick, calm, and simple, since with little kids you want to ramp down for a nap, and for bigger kids you want to refuel for a fun afternoon. (The only reason to have a big, complicated lunch is for that to be your afternoon's entertainment, which is rare with kids.)

34. Occasionally we'll do burgers or dogs for lunch, but only if the morning fun was brief and hunger-inducing. Usually we have turkey or ham on good bread, or rolled up in a tortilla around some cheese, with one or more of the following: apples, bananas, raisins, carrots. We usually lunch at our camp site, so this is a good time for a juice box or cup of milk.

   And then it's down for the count! Nap-time, also known as adult-alone-time. Bliss.

35. Dinner can be the toughest meal of the day, because the kids are the most tired and grumpy and the hungriest and least likely to eat. I plan things for dinner that I know they'll want to eat and that will come together quickly, while they have a little snack to ward off the grumpies.

36. Pasta and rice are typical favorites. Our kids love pesto and, of course, mac and cheese, and there are lots of boil-n-serve options for rice. I usually grill some veggies (peppers, tomatoes) and put out raw vegetables (celery and carrot sticks, chopped at home) to snack on. We grill some meat: burgers, weenies, steaks. Sausage is *great* on the grill, and in your eggs the next day.

37. Pre-trip prep is key to quick and simple meat. I buy when the meat's on sale, season or marinate it, and then freeze it in big Zip-loc freezer bags. This can be weeks in advance of a particular trip. I'll plan on grilling it on the second or third night, by which time it has had a chance to thaw.

    You *can* grill chicken; I prefer to bring some baked chicken to avoid dealing with raw chicken in the wild. My baked chicken gives us meat the first night, and lunch for at least Day Two.

38. Resources, beginning on page 71, has a larder list to help you plan and pack what you'd like to prepare, but some ingredients are more important than others. I'll just mention a few of the items we like: a good, all-purpose but flavorful *cheese* (sharp cheddar is good for snacking and plain meal-enhancing), a baked *chicken* (do it yourself or from your store's rotisserie; you'll get two-to-four meals out of it), really good *bread* (make it yourself or find a local craft bakery), and your favorite, really good,

Cheap Kitchen Remodel

I always thought my kitchen was too small. It *is* small. Two people do not fit in it at once without bumping elbows or other appendages. Then I started getting really good at feeding four or more people using a two-burner camp stove, the coals in a fire-ring, and the contents of an ice chest. Plus, I had fun doing it.

It's funny how capacious my kitchen seems now whenever I come home from a camping trip. It's been a good reminder for me: abundance is a state of mind, and intentional simplicity helps keep me there.

strong *coffee*. (Pick your luxury; Starbucks Gold Coast blend is one of ours!)

The point here is that if you like food, bring a few of the things you really like. It can rescue a bad day and put the icing on a great day.

39. Don't forget the tools of the trade: we keep our camper stocked with the kitchen tools and utensils we usually need, to prepare the foods we typically bring. Think through your menu ideas to determine which utensils you'll need and put them on your list.

    Don't forget the tools you need for your luxuries; we like our coffee made in a French press, but we also bring decaf espresso for our little campfire espresso maker. We grill a lot, so we are sure to bring our long-handled tongs. A medium-sized serrated knife works best on good bread and ripe tomatoes.

    And then there are the unlikely kitchen invaluables: baby wipes can save water, a kitchen timer can save biscuits (and monitor a kid's time-out).

40. For all your meals and snacks, think extensible. You don't have to limit yourself to what your kids are having, but if you can leverage kid food into adult food, so much the easier for the cook (and the cleaner-upper).

    Stir some spicy sausage into your helping of the kids' noodles. Put some onions and extra sharp cheddar on your burger. Sprinkle some extra pine nuts and garlic on the pesto and fusilli. Pack some peppers into your hot dog's bun.

And after the kids are in bed, kick back with a fruit and cheese plate: Granny Smith apples, walnuts, Maytag bleu cheese, . . . oh, yeah! Real Life is good.

Primitive Art

My years at Camp Lula Sams in Brownsville, Texas, reached their zenith the year I turned 12, finally old enough to "Primitive Camp." The Primitives (as we were appropriately known) proved definitively that Girl Scouts are not weenies. We dug latrines, built bamboo showers, pitched Army canvas tents and cots, and cooked a slew of fire pit dinners. Steak on a Plank, anyone?

Despite being a smoke magnet, I loved fire-tending: setting the buckets of sand and water near the fire pit, digging out the ashes, building the teepee of wood, slipping tinder into the woodpile's crevices, finally coaxing the fire alight, and then, wistfully, respectfully smothering it out after the last S'more.

Canoeing ran a close second to pyromania. Our camp nestled around a *resaca*, a small body of water just big enough to challenge novice canoers. Upon reaching Primitive status and sufficient canoeing skills, we could venture out on a seven-mile canoe trip through the canals and waterways leading out of our familiar *resaca*.

I can see those Primitive joys were signposts for a road I've never wanted to leave, a wondrous blessing for our grown-ups—parents, counselors, administrators, and funders—to have given us.

4.
Play

The prize (you know, the point of camping) you are keeping your eyes on probably includes something like "Being at play in the fields of the Lord." That is, having fun being outside doing things you don't ordinarily do, seeing things you don't ordinarily see, and thinking things you don't ordinarily think about.

Unfortunately, way too many of us have completely forgotten how to have fun. We get so caught up in how something is *supposed* to be that we lose sight of the thing itself. I speak from experience; as you can tell from this book, I like to plan almost as much as I like to do. So I try to live by **Happy Camper Principle III:** *Everything should be fun . . . make it so.*

That includes the planning, the eating, the getting ready, the doing, the cleaning up, the sleeping, the remembering, the planning, and so on. How can I make chores like planning and cleaning up fun, you

Happy Camper Principle III:

Everything should be fun . . . make it so.

ask? Oh, you know. Remember when you were a kid? You were happiest when you were helping a grown-up do an important thing, and when you and the grown-up felt connected doing it.

Hiking tops a lot of lists of things to do on camping trips, and lots of us do it. So most of us know the basics, both for ourselves and for our kids: wear the right attire, avoid chigger and tick territory, take food and water, pack a first-aid kit and a lightweight blanket or ground-cloth. But, just in case, we'll talk about some ideas for how to do these things better or more easily.

Just remember, fun is contagious. Let loving fun permeate everything you do, and pretty soon it'll infect everyone around you.

By the way, we spent an entire section promoting the idea of Roadtrip as Fun. If you skipped that section, go back! Approach your roadtrips as play opportunities, and they will be. Fun, that is.

41. There are people in the world who believe camping is an end in itself. They are *not* parents. You need a prize, and to keep it in plain sight the whole time. Why *do* you want to camp? Be sure it's compelling enough to help you laugh later about chiggers, sunburns, or even rigging diapers out of coffee filters and hand towels. Think about what the kids like to do or try, or, if they're really small, what you'd like them to do or try.

42. Don't forget to be selfish. What do *you* really like to do that you never seem to find time to do at home? *Bring it,* or whatever you need to do it.

    Everybody in my family knows that when it's nap-time, the parents are taking turns baby-sitting, biking, shutterbugging, reading, showering, or just thinking about God, kids, Camping as Real Life . . .

43. In cool weather, dress in layers, and leave room in the pack to store some of those layers out of the way as the day warms up.

    Dress your kids like you dress yourself, maybe with a slightly heavier jacket or one more layer. But don't bundle 'em within an inch of their lives. They'll feel confined, and you'll be carrying a lot of excess outerwear. Kids don't need fancy hiking boots. But a properly fitting shoe with grippy-tread soles and thick socks will prevent stumbles and blisters. (Kids can pack Band-Aids and a little tube of Neosporin just in case.)

44. Speaking of chiggers, don't hike or play in tall grass, or you will be paying with your flesh for the next few weeks, if not months. I do have a couple of unsubstantiated tips: Dave's grandma used to recommend sprinkling shoes and socks with sulfur to keep the little pests away. And my mom and a pharmacist both told me the only thing you can do about chiggers—besides stay away from them—is to strip down immediately after exposure and

Perils of Urban Camping

Dave's youthful camping typically involved a crew gathering at a cow pasture camp site to sleep out. Campfires and homemade "Sterno" sufficed for light, heat, and cooking.

One weekend, after scarfing a record number of Dinty Moores and Wolf Brand Chilis, the boys' thoughts turned to dessert.

"Hey, how 'bout some apples?" And they were off. Across the pasture, over the fence, into the orchard, and up the trees. Soon exclamations of "Yeooww! That's *sour!*" filled the night air. But a wail of sirens cut laughter short, and the scene froze in a squad car's headlights.

"Okay, boys, what's going on!?!"

A moment later one of the miscreants accompanied the officer to the house. Soon guffaws erupted. It was the boy's grandfather, having a laugh at the nervous grandmother who'd called the police on her own grandson, one of the "hoodlums looting the orchard."

Clearly the moral of this story is, "Tell Grandma yourself when camping in her back pasture, because grandpas can be forgetful."

sluice off whatever portion of your anatomy may have been attacked *with rubbing alcohol.* As always, an ounce of prevention is worth pounds of cure.

45. Wear sun-block (SPF 15 or greater) on all exposed skin, and don't forget unlikely territory, such as under your chin and on the tops of your feet. Fact is, everybody has a story to tell about a weird place that got burned. Play it safe, cover it up, and, no, just a hat is not enough.

46. Kids need refueling on the trail pretty regularly. So pack lots of trail-hardy, high-energy snacks and plenty of water. We try to take a brief water break every 15 minutes and a snack break about once an hour.

    How far can kids hike? As far as they are used to. We've usually managed about a mile per year of age.

47. And it is amazing what a walk can do for other kinds of regularity, too. Since all that walking gets all those systems going, be prepared not only to change diapers and/or soiled underwear and clothes, but also to pack these dirtied items back from the trail.

    We bring along our used Zip-loc or other plastic bags, which may not be very environmentally correct, but which are better than leaving the evidence on the scene (and we have seen such evidence).

We also capture and return to camp any trashy remnants of snacks, drinks, or their packaging. Diaper wipes prove invaluable once again for on-the-trail cleanups.

48. *Do pack a first-aid kit* and a lightweight blanket or ground-cloth. The latter comes in handy for diaper changes, snack breaks, naps on unexpectedly long outings, or to protect someone who's been injured. Use common sense on the safety basics; nothing takes the fun out of a hike like getting hurt or lost.

    Use a trail map. If in doubt about the path, turn back immediately.

49. *Don't separate.* Teach the kids to hug a tree (i.e., stay put) and blow a whistle if they do get separated from the adults in the party. Assure them you will backtrack to find them so they will have the confidence to sit tight.

50. *Tuck a disposable camera in each kid's backpack.* At the very least they'll have something fun to do on the hike besides asking if it's almost over. You'll give a preschooler a legitimate show-and-tell entry. You may spur an older kid to satisfy merit badge or extracurricular requirements. You may even ensure the kid has a funny story to tell when she wins her first Pulitzer.

51. We like camping near places to swim in the summertime. Since our kids are small, we are not too

Forests of Fire

What's so amazing about fall-colored trees? Well, not much if you live in New England. But it's not exactly common where we live. Our one stand of maples is so precious that Texas has dedicated a park to them: Lost Maples State Park near the town of Vanderpool. One autumn found us there, amazed at the maple leaves still shining on the trees, the paths astrewn with fiery foliage.

And we found other wonders among the lost maples. One of the trails led to a small lake glimmering under a limestone ledge, tempting anglers and rock-skippers alike. Once downstream from the fisherkids, fishermen, and fisherwomen, Harper and Chandler spent all the precious gravel gathered along the trail. Plink, plink, plunk, and their pockets were empty. But not our memories. That fiery, tree-ringed lake ripples still in our minds.

adventurous about where we swim. We prefer to swim in places intended for swimming; no dangerous undercurrents, no trash-strewn surfaces underfoot. Wearing water shoes is a commonsense precaution. And we hang onto the kids at all times in water over their knees, since they're not swimming yet.

52. We don't like cluttering up the swimming experience with a lot of toys. The fun here is really getting to know this other environment, how it can buoy your body up, how to be safe in it, how to begin learning to make progress through the water.

    So we minimize the inflatables (no inner tubes or air mattresses giving a false sense of security) and keep the toy count down to a bucket and shovel for playing on the beach.

53. If you are camping far from water in the summertime, you just might be crazy enough to use these ideas: I actually saw a family bring an inflatable kids' pool and set it up outside their camper. Another family got creative with a sprinkler and a fan to rig their own mist system. Hey, if summer is when you can camp, you need all the help you can get!

54. Speaking of toy clutter, we have tried to minimize that altogether. We have a rainy-time bucket in the camper with a few toys that have flexible play

Canoe, Take Me Away!

Last spring we spent a long weekend at McGee Creek in Oklahoma with two other families (including a boy Chandler's age named Taylor). On the afternoon of the second day, after herding kids down the hiking trail all morning, we unleashed the canoes we'd brought along and carried them down to the rocky lakeshore.

Harper and Chandler found the canoe a little tippy for a secure ride and couldn't quite deal with having both parents paddle away at once. So the moms and the kids played on a small gravel spit near the camp while the dads took their turn. When the canoe came back, Taylor's mom, Susan, and I elected to have Mother's Day Out on the water.

Though Susan was a novice paddler, we quickly settled into a rhythm and stroked out into the lake to explore the dam and opposite shoreline. We drifted awhile in the middle of the lake, watching the settling birds, shading our eyes from the setting sun, listening to our children's laughter echoing across the lake. We got quite a reception when we paddled back into camp.

For getting away from it all, and then coming back, canoes beat Calgon any day.

value: puzzles, coloring books and colors, blocks. The great outdoors is full of entertainment, after all.

55. On one trip, Harper and her dad assembled a Bug Zoo. This particular camp site was festooned with strange, iridescent purple beetle bugs. She and Dave put one in a jar with some twigs and grass. A sprinkle of water everyday and this purple beetle was quite happy.

    Then Harper found some fuzzy caterpillars. Did you know fuzzy brown and gray caterpillars the size of your pinkie can cohabit with purple beetles? *Harper knows.*

56. One toy that's a special treat: occasionally renting a boat or other watercraft for a couple of hours. I'll never forget the sight of Chandler at 14 months, standing forthrightly in the bow of a party barge on Lake Texoma, the wind blowing his blond curls back, lake spray in his face, his fat little legs spread wide on the deck, the life jacket barely buckling around his rotund torso, toddler epiphany writ large on his face. (Yep, that's the trip I learned to put "disposable waterproof camera" on the packing list!)

57. And then there are campfires. I don't have to describe what you get out of a fire; you're either a pyromaniac or you're not. So bring seasoned firewood with you, and keep it dry.

58. On trips where all our firewood is green or damp, we've snuck in some store-bought fire-starter logs or fatwood kindling to help the fire get going. Yeah, this is cheating, but it's more fun than no fire, and certainly more effective and safer than sprinkling charcoal lighting fluid or lantern fuel on a fire.

59. An afternoon campfire is perfect for kids to help build and enjoy, besides producing perfect coals for dinner-time roasting and grilling. The flickery glow of firelight on a child's face is, well, pretty rhapsodic. Kids love gathering kindling and stacking up a firewood teepee and watching Mom and Dad light the fire.

60. Harper and I like making twig bundles of herb stems after we harvest basil or rosemary from our herb garden. These give the fire interesting smells and smokes.

61. My mom collects pinecones and dips them in cinnamon-scented wax to make firestarters (she bundles these into baskets for Christmas gifts). We have a lot of fun with these on camping trips and in our fireplace at home. They flame up like little Christmas trees. Plain pinecones found at the camp site are entertaining, too.

62. After the kids go to bed, we usually rekindle for an evening fire. Dave and I love campfires under the

Mystic Experiences

Some girls are legacy members of their mothers' sororities. I was a legacy Tonkawa. Let me explain.

I don't actually know if Mom was a Tonk. As the waterfront counselor at Camp Mystic she probably had to maintain an uneasy neutrality. I followed tradition to Mystic as a camper and, therefore, had to choose a tribe. Out of a black bowler I pulled a red slip of paper, and a Tonkawa I was.

This was heartbreaking. The one friend I had made (a day into the six-week term) was a Kiowa. A friendly foe, but An Enemy, nonetheless. Fortunately we managed to remain good friends across enemy lines.

One night near session's end, the Kiowas vanished. They went surreptitiously, until suddenly they were all gone. Then, in the distance, girls' voices. Singing friendship songs, the Kiowas strode in solemn procession back into camp, two by two. The well ordered column broke and scattered, as each Kiowa sought out a sister Tonk and led her to the last campfire of the session. My friend found me.

Candles . . . singing . . . processions . . . bonfires . . . and tears for the end of six weeks we'd remember . . . well, forever. What a night.

stars. Letting your eyes rise from firelight up to starlight will really get you thinking: "Let's see, if we cashed in the 401Ks and the mutual funds, pulled Harper out of preschool, just how long *could* we stay in Real Life ...?"

Giving Thanks

A few years ago, with time off from work in short supply, Dave and I made the risky decision to go camping over Thanksgiving. The long, four day holiday weekend beckoned, and we succumbed to the temptation.

You might be thinking, "Boy, I'd love to do that. But my [insert name here] would just kill me!" Don't be too sure.

Our first camping Thanksgiving drew Dave's brother and sister-in-law, Shannon and Rebecca, out from Albuquerque in their camper to meet us. They brought smoked turkey and fixings since I had my hands full with small kids.

Our second camping Thanksgiving drew my mom, dad, brother Curt, and his family to the town nearest our camp site, where we rendezvous'd with two sets of uncles and aunts for Thanksgiving dinner.

This year? Well, let's just say there are 21 people expected around the Thanksgiving dinner table on Thursday, with about half that number returning to their campers or tents at nearby Kerrville-Schreiner State Park, with the rest staying in nearby hotel rooms. We can hike; they can watch football. Everybody's happy.

So don't be afraid that your family will disown you for abandoning the traditional Thanksgiving. The truth is, they may want to join you!

5.
Gear

Sometimes thinking about gear makes me wonder if I own my stuff, or if my stuff owns me. But then I remind myself about my Happy Camping Principles and try to make sure we all have what we need to be happy.

My own experiences have run the gamut of gear. As a teenager, my Scout troop established a primitive camp. This was Zero Gear. Along the way, Dave and I have camped in tents, cabins, pop-up trailers, even a whale of an RV once. We've settled on a nice little hard-sided trailer, 16 feet of heaven, as far as we're concerned. Moderate Gear.

I am sure that some day Dave and I are going to backpack up into a mountain range, needing only what we can carry. Minimalist Gear. But for now, with our two little ones, our trailer offers the infrastructure that lets us camp really happily. Nobody in our family groans at the prospect of a camping trip, and neither cold nor hot weather slows us down.

So, take a look at this section for a few ideas, and then flip through some of the lists in Resources, beginning on page 71, and the catalogs listed beginning on page 77. As with the other sections, take what you need and leave the rest behind.

63. *Accommodations.* Where to rest your weary head is one of the first questions to settle when you decide to move beyond day-tripping. The good news is that you have a lot of choices whatever your budget, and most of those options can be rented or borrowed a few times before you buy.

    Over time you'll find your own comfort zone on the continuum from Spartan to deluxe. For now, start simple and see how it works. As to where to rent or buy, take a look at the list of Resources, beginning on page 77.

64. Many state parks have *cabins for rent.* Reservation policies vary, so check with the folks at your destination as far ahead of time as possible. If you're not sure where to start, check with the Parks and Wildlife Department for the state you intend to visit. A listing of these is provided in Resources, beginning on page 83.

65. *Kampgrounds of America* (KOA) now offers their trademark Kamping Kabins, which furnish basic sleeping quarters for between $20 and $40 a night (for two to four adults or children). Not all KOAs have them; check with the Kampground nearest your destination. You'll need to provide bedding, personal items, and cooking utensils. Kabins include grills and access to all KOA amenities, such as showers, restrooms, laundry, convenience store, and sometimes swimming pools or other

recreational activities. Every Kampground has its own 800 number. Call KOA at 406-248-7444 to obtain a directory.

66. *Private cabin rentals* also are available in most well traveled tourist destinations. Depending on size, location, and amenities, you can pay anywhere from $20 to over $100 a night.

67. *Tents* are where former renters often start buying. To get up to speed quickly on what's available, take at look at the L.L. Bean, Campmor, and REI catalogs. You can usually buy a very decent tent for about $100 per person (i.e., a tent that sleeps two comfortably usually costs around $200). If you are buying the tent mail-order, check the return policy.

68. Practice setting up the tent in your yard several times (do at least one night-time practice run) before heading out. If you expect kids to sleep in the tent, a few backyard sleep-outs before the main event are a good idea.

Pros: Tents are the most inexpensive camping accommodations you can own and are highly portable. You can camp anywhere you can get permission.

Cons: A really good tent may be weatherproof, but it is still an unnerving thing to get caught out in a violent storm in a tent. A bad downpour can

"They Didn't Tell Me Nothin' 'Bout No Bulb!"

It will always be known as the Summer of the (Cursed) Houseboat. Yearning for a summer flavored get-together, Dave and his two brothers and all the respective spouses pitched in to rent a houseboat on Lake Texoma, leaving the kids with loving grandmas.

What went wrong? Pretty much everything you could imagine, short of having a bad time or sinking the (Cursed) Houseboat. Our camping barge turned out to be unsinkable, as were our spirits. We managed to laugh (later) about getting stuck in a sandbank, a sheared off prop blade, shredded gas lines in the stove, the spotlight-wielding bowfishers that motored past our mooring one midnight, and, yes, even the external, running light bulb our roving mechanic neglected to bring, he of the now-infamous phrase, "They didn't tell me nothin' 'bout no bulb!"

Even more amazing than our eventual safe return is that we still happily remember the morning swims, evening landings on secluded rocky beached coves, fireworks on the Fourth, fishing off the stern, and chasing around the boat on rented SeaDoos one afternoon. So, I can recommend camping afloat. Just be sure to bring your toolbox!

make it difficult to get out and go to the bathroom, cook, or sleep.

69. *Recreational vehicles.* The basic choices here are motor homes, trailers, and pop-up trailers. Motor homes are motorized RVs that you can drive down the road. Trailers are hard-sided RVs you pull behind a tow vehicle, usually a pickup truck. Pop-up trailers are soft-sided RVs that fold down into a lightweight, compact size you can pull easily with a car or minivan.

   Price and comparison info is beyond the scope of this book, but be aware that there is an available supply of used RVs. Check your newspaper's want ads, and start scanning issues of *Trailer Life* and *Motor Home* magazines, or their Web sites (see Resources, beginning on page 77, for more info on these publications).

70. Our main justification for getting a modest, little, hard-sided trailer was protection from sudden weather (well, that and simplifying midnight potty runs for a recently trained little girl). But in addition to thunderstorms and cold snaps, we've also been beset by sudden swarms of flies and gusts of dust at meal-time. The trailer has enabled us to escape all airborne pestilences, while cooking and eating.

   You can achieve the same outcome with your camp stove under a tent flap with a little mosquito netting, or a net-and-nylon dining canopy over a

> ## Happy Camper Principle IV:
>
> The more situations you are prepared for, the more you are prepared to enjoy.

picnic table. Just remember **Happy Camper Principle IV:** *The more situations you are prepared for, the more you are prepared to enjoy.*

71. *Backpacks.* You probably already have a day-pack, and it's probably all you need. If not, check out the Army-Navy surplus store, your local sporting goods store, or a college bookstore if you live in a college town.

    Think through what you need to take and the kinds of places you'll be hiking, and you'll have a requirements list together in no time. A waterproof (or at least water-resistant) pack is a good idea, but no need to pay extra for it. Just Scotchgard your pack yourself. An outside pocket or two is handy, whether solid or mesh.

72. The most important point on packs? **Happy Camper Principle V:** *Everybody over two years of age packs her own stuff.* The goal is for any kid who's old enough to walk part or all of the hike to carry his own weight (and munchies!). My daugh-

The Luggable Child

"He ain't heavy, he's my . . . " Child, actually. I still vividly remember a Virginia Blue Ridge day-hike that a toddling Harper finished asleep on my back, her drooping body lolling in the carrier, her breath hot on my neck. She even snoozed right through a semi-perilous stream crossing.

Even now that the kids have outgrown the backpack carrier, we still occasionally find ourselves lugging a tired child over hill and dale to continue or conclude a hike. Don't tell your chiropractor this, but if you loosen the straps of your daypack, you can sling a kid onto your back in just such a way that the backpack helps cradle the precious load.

Now don't get me wrong. I do not want two-year-old, 42-pound Chandler to get used to the idea of Mom as Pack Mule. But, truth be told, there is something awfully sweet about carrying a little somebody who's old enough to say "Thanks, Mom."

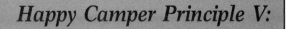

Happy Camper Principle V:

Everybody over two years of age packs her own stuff.

ter, Harper, hiked her little butt off at 18 months, and my son, Chandler, is a hiking bandit now at two. *And* he carries his own pack with diapers, wipes, spare T-shirt, and shorts. Go, boy!

73. *Camp chairs.* You'll find several models available, ranging in style from very upright chairs that prop you up at table height to more casual lounging chairs that keep you closer to the ground in a more relaxed position. Most of the places we camp have picnic tables, so we've opted for the low-to-the-ground type. They work well for grown-ups and kids; very comfy around a campfire. Get a couple to spare; they beat sitting on the ground.

74. *Rubber tubs.* We don't go anywhere without our big Rubbermaid tubs. We keep one full of firewood (it doubles as a dirty clothes hamper on the home-bound trip), and the other stows hiking boots, water shoes, lanterns, and various other bits of small gear.

75. *Camp stoves.* We have a basic Coleman stove we purchased before we got the camper (which is equipped with a nice little kitchen setup), and we

still use it when we want to cook outside, at home and on camping trips. We think getting a "dual-fuel" model is a good idea. These can run on unleaded gasoline or kerosene.

76. *Lanterns.* You can obtain these in electric or liquid fuel models. We purchased a small Coleman dual-fuel lantern, which we hang in a handy tree or on the lantern stand some campgrounds provide. We also purchased a couple of candle lanterns for the table, which cast a very nice soft glow over dinner and protect the flame from moths and wayward evening breezes.

77. *Shovel, hatchet, and knife.* Your local Army-Navy surplus store is a good place to look for these items. A folding shovel is handy for digging a fire pit or emptying a charcoal grill, and hatchets are great for chopping kindling. You can get these with leather blade guards that help keep them safe around small children.

   Multifunctional Swiss Army knives are nice to have in your pack, since they can solve so many small but annoying problems.

78. *Water shoes.* You can pay a bunch of money for these. Don't. Every discount retailer carries them now for less than $10 a pair. We got ours at Wal-mart for less than $6, and three years later they are still wading strong.

Sandal-style water shoes are fine for pool-side, but the slipper-style shoes are much better for spending time in the water, especially where you might have unstable footing, as in a rocky beach or shoreline. Strap sandals don't offer enough support in those situations. The slipper-style also gives more protection from hot sand at the beach.

79. *Hiking boots.* As with all other camping gear, you can get basic, economically priced hiking boots, or pay for extra features. For kids, lightweight uppers and sturdy, lugged soles are the key features to look for. High ankle support and Achilles' heel cuts are helpful.

Waterproof is nice for adults who won't outgrow their boots in a year, but too expensive for kids' boots (just put trash bags over their boots and tie off with rubber bands. Little kids think this is cool!).

The Campmor and Sierra catalogs described in "Resources," page 77, have some great bargains on kids' and adults' boots.

80. If you have friends or family who camp with their kids, get in line for used boots. My daughter has worn a pair of her older cousin's boots for the last year, and my son has been wearing my daughter's work boots for hiking. These shoes tend to be durably made, so going the "pre-owned" route will save you money.

Star Spying in the Canyonlands

What do the words "West Texas" bring to mind? Well if you were driving across the plains south of Amarillo, you might think "Flat. Cow pastures. Dry and dusty. Too warm and too boring." A warning: Don't limit yourself to what you think you know, based on what you think you see.

If you happened to detour through prairie and pasture to Turkey, Texas (Bob Wills' hometown) and the nearby town of Quitaque ("kitty-kay" to the locals), you'd find verdant fields yielding to weather-etched red bluffs capped with limestone. When you catch your first glimpse of Caprock Canyons, you might think you've fallen off Texas into New Mexico.

It was on our first trip to Caprock that we discovered Harper could *hike*. Not quite two-and-a-half years old, Harper strode the two-mile Eagle Point trail with abandon, examining mysterious poops, warily eyeing cactus and yuccas, and clambering up trail-side rocks with Mom.

Quite frankly, though, the most amazing thing about West Texas is what it doesn't have: light pollution. Naked-eye stargazing is astounding, and a Celestron puts you in telescope heaven. You may find yourself torn, as we were, between fire-gazing and heaven-watching, ember-stirring and satellite-counting.

West Texas. Warm, yes . . . boring, no.

When shopping for new, if you intend to hand down a pair of boots eventually, look for gender-neutral colors. Cousin Julie's boots are purple and black, so Chandler will be wearing them this fall.

81. Got a baby? Do yourself a favor. Get yourself a stout, backpack-style, child carrier. Some people start out with front carriers for little infants, but you're probably not going to take Baby on that many hikes before five months of age or so. At that point she can hold her head well enough to sit up in the backpack carrier, which is useful a lot longer. Which is why I am not kidding about stout. You're going to be using the carrier for at least the next two years, or longer if you get suckered into kid number two, or—bless your heart—three, four . . .

82. In shopping for a backpack carrier, look for sturdy shoulder straps, a hip belt to transfer the child's weight to the hips of the person doing the carrying, and shoulder and lap belts inside the carrier to hold the kid securely.

    Several models have little packs that stow in the frame below the kid's seat. This is a nice feature, but I wouldn't bother with the "rain-hood." (Oh, right, like I'm going to lug 30 pounds of kid out into a rainstorm, or even a threat of rain!)

83. *Mountain bikes.* Most areas with good biking trails have a local outfitter who will rent bikes to you.

Some companies even specialize in bike trips where you're ferried to a starting point (no need to leave your vehicle at the trailhead), fed and watered along the route, and trundled back to your car.

If you find yourself biking more than three or four times a year, start shopping. If you are interested in riding some around town as well, check out the hybrid trail/city bikes. These have slightly less knobby tires but all the appeal of the trail bike (like grip-shifters, a dream come true for the balance-challenged among us!).

84. *Canoes* and other small, transportable watercraft also are excellent candidates for rentals (unless you frequently camp near water warm enough to enjoy three-fourths of the year, in which case you might want to buy). Most sizable lakes with tourist populations have outfitters renting canoes and personal watercraft like SeaDoos, ski boats, and sailboats.

Camper's Prayer

Creator of this earth, we give thanks to You.
It is in the cathedral of the wild
That we feel closest to You.
We feel your Spirit moving when the breeze
  touches our faces.
We see your care in the tiny details of the
  wildflowers by the trail.
We know your strength when we wonder at the
  might of the high places,
    and rest in the gentleness of the low valleys.
We hear your joy in life when soaring birds cry
  out, and song birds whistle.
We taste the freshness of your creation in the
  simple meals we make and ask You to bless.
We sing your praise when we bring our
  children up and out into the wildness of your
  making.
We feel you here with us in the place you made
  for us,
    and we are glad. We give thanks.

Amen.

6.
Sleep

My kids on a full night's sleep are different kids than when sleep-deprived. In fact, I have a theory that most juvenile delinquents getting into trouble today are just feeling the effects of years of sleep deprivation. Maybe if we just put them all to bed for 10 hours a day for a few years . . . oh well. Back to the point at hand. **Happy Camper Principle VI:** *Sleep is an important prerequisite to having fun on camping trips. Make sure the kids and the adults get plenty.*

85. Schedule is important for my kids' sleep habits. Fact is, they *have* sleep habits, which I have carefully reinforced over the years with rituals and schedules. I maintain those rituals and schedules as nearly as possible on camping trips, for both naps and bedtime.

Happy Camper Principle VI:

Sleep is an important prerequisite to having fun on camping trips. Make sure the kids and the adults get plenty.

86. Nap follows hard on the heels of lunch, and we usually don't have a problem with it, since the kids are tuckered out from the morning's activities, and their bellies are full. So they get that nice logy feeling, and Mom tucks them in . . . and then it's party-time! Well, for the adults anyway.

87. At night we have what we call the Big Slide to bedtime: the progression flows from dinner, to bath, into jammies, with bedtime stories, prayers, hugs and kisses, and then lights out. Of these, the bath is the most tempting to skip, but we always try to get one in, since it seems to really cue my kids' subconscious that it's bedtime.

    Of course, sometimes we derail our own best laid plans by lingering overlong 'round the campfire, reading bedtime stories . . . but hey, that's what camping is for, right?

88. Build enthusiasm ahead of time for whatever the sleeping arrangements are going to be, to help create a fun adventure. Our camper has a full-size foldout bed for the grown-ups, a slide-out twin-size bed, and a foldout shelf of a twin bed above the full-size bed.

    To help Harper (three years old at the time) get into the foldout bed (mentally and physically), we let her pick out a kid sleeping bag with her favorite Disney character on it and talked about it for weeks before our first trip. She was so excited she

Amazing Grace at Cedar Lake

A recent camping trip deliberately close to home ended up taking me many miles and years away.

Camped at Cleburne State Park on tiny Cedar Lake, we were enjoying an evening bonfire, debating whether to mosey over to the natural amphitheater to hear Cowboy Poetry Night.

Suddenly a humming intake of air broke the evening's calm with a boisterous blow. Our neighbors across the road included a bagpiper, and he'd begun an evening serenade.

We drew closer in the dark, each with a child on hip, listening with shivers and tingles to the stirring music, skillfully played. We spoke of feeling transported to a distant isle, sentimental and green at dusk.

Then the piper started a new song with a strong breath, and things got personal. It was "Amazing Grace," my grandmother's favorite hymn. I hadn't heard it since her funeral less than a year ago. I couldn't stop the tears that came, but I sang the song to Chandler, who carries her maiden name: Wilma Lura Chandler. I told him that was Grannybopper's favorite song.

As the song faded into the night, we returned to the fire and stirred the embers alight. That was poetry enough.

almost flew up into the bed. Dave built a bed rail to help her stay in, and stay she does. She loves her little aerie.

89. When we first started using the trailer, Chandler was 14 months old and still needed confinement to get to sleep. We put his portable crib on the slide-out twin bed and put him in it. However, by 18 months we had him in a twin bed at home with a bed rail. So now we bring the bed rail with us and slide the bed out partway, and he has a cozy little nest of his own. He stays in it for the most part. We just try to wear him out during the day so he's too pooped to stir up much trouble at night.

90. One little trick that helps us at nap- and night-time is to keep things the adults might need while the kids are sleeping *outside* the trailer, tent, or cabin, including jackets, firewood, cooler of ice and/or drinks, books, lanterns, camping chairs. That way we can let sleeping babies lie, which leads to all sorts of interesting evenings. But that's another book . . .

7.
Conclusion

Sounds easy enough, doesn't it? Sure it does. Go on, now that you've got some kindling together, put a big log on the fire!

Don't forget to send me a postcard to tell me who went where, how much fun you had, and what you learned. I can't wait to hear.

8.

Resources: Additional Information You Might Find Useful

The Lists: Planning, Packing, and Preparing

As mentioned in Tip #2, my primary list has three columns: Week Before, Day Before, and Day of Trip. I keep it in a three-column format so I can fold it to the appropriate view. It looks like this. (See below for detail on list contents.)

Week Before	Day Before	Day Of Trip
❑ Xxxxxxxxxxxxxx	❑ Xxxxxxxxxxxxxx	❑ Xxxxxxxxxxxxxx
❑ Xxxxxxxxxxxxx	❑ Xxxxxxxxxxxxx	❑ Xxxxxxxxxxxx
❑ Xxxxxxxxxxxxxxxxx	❑ Xxxxxxxxxxxxxxxxx	❑ Xxxxxxxxxxxxxxxxx
❑ Xxxxxxxxxxxx	❑ Xxxxxxxxxxxx	❑ Xxxxxxxxxxxx
❑ Xxxxxxxxxxxxxx	❑ Xxxxxxxxxxxxxx	❑ Xxxxxxxxxxxxxx
❑ Xxxxxxxxxxxxx		❑ Xxxxxxxxxxxxx
❑ Xxxxxxxxxxxx	❑ Xxxxxxxxxxxxxxxxxxx	❑ Xxxxxxxxxxxx
❑ Xxxxxxxxxxxxxxxxxxxxx	❑ Xxxxxxxxxxxxx	❑ Xxxxxxxxxxxxxxxxxxxxx
❑ Xxxxxxxxxxxx	❑ Xxxxxxxxxxxxxx	❑ Xxxxxxxxxxxx
❑ Xxxxxxxxxxxxxx	❑ Xxxxxxxxxxxxx	❑ Xxxxxxxxxxxxxx
❑ Xxxxxxxxxxxxxx	❑ Xxxxxxxxxxxxxxxxx	❑ Xxxxxxxxxxxxx
❑ Xxxxxxxxxxxxxxxxx		❑ _____
❑ Xxxxxxxxxxxxxx	❑ Xxxxxxxxxxxxxxxxx	❑ _____
❑ Xxxxxxxxxxxxx	❑ Xxxxxxxxxxxxx	❑ _____
❑ Xxxxxxxxxxxxx	❑ Xxxxxxxxxxxxxxxxx	❑ _____
❑ Xxxxxxxxxxxxxx	❑ Xxxxxxxxxxxxxx	❑ _____
❑ Xxxxxxxxxxxxx	❑ Xxxxxxxxxxxxxxxxx	❑ _____
❑ Xxxxxxxxxxxxxxxxx		❑ _____

Week Before

Week Before includes "permanent" and "consumable" stocks. *Consumables* include non-refrigerated and refrigerated food, listed separately to aid in packing.

Permanent stocks are those items we usually keep packed to go, but sometimes "borrow" out of camp storage or bring in for a thorough cleaning. Before the trip, I make sure these items are in the camper, and replace them if necessary.

- ❏ kid cups
- ❏ towels
- ❏ camping chairs
- ❏ Lexan utensils
- ❏ camera
- ❏ binoculars
- ❏ weather radio
- ❏ small cutting board
- ❏ backpack carrier

Consumable stocks are the things we always use up eventually. Every trip I check to see what we've used up on the last trip and need to replenish. Non-food items include:

- ❏ wipes, dipes
- ❏ toilet paper
- ❏ RV toilet chemicals
- ❏ trash bags (big, small)
- ❏ firewood
- ❏ fire starters
- ❏ charcoal
- ❏ foil
- ❏ batteries (AA, D)
- ❏ Zip-locs
- ❏ paper towels, plates
- ❏ camera film

We list food under *Consumables* as well. This list includes a lot of optional items as idea triggers. What we take on each trip varies and may include:

Non-refrigerated
- ❏ bread
- ❏ salt/pepper
- ❏ olive oil
- ❏ pasta
- ❏ rice-in-bags
- ❏ canned potatoes
- ❏ canned beans
- ❏ cereal
- ❏ juice boxes
- ❏ evaporated or dry milk
- ❏ crackers, chips
- ❏ chocolate bars
- ❏ graham crackers
- ❏ marshmallows
- ❏ Nutri-grain bars
- ❏ granola bars

Refrigerated
- ❏ coffee
- ❏ club soda
- ❏ fruit, veggies
- ❏ cheese
- ❏ eggs
- ❏ butter
- ❏ mayo, mustard
- ❏ pesto
- ❏ ice cream (quarts)
- ❏ roasted chicken
- ❏ steaks, hamburger
- ❏ lunch meat, hot dogs
- ❏ milk
- ❏ tortillas
- ❏ sandwich pickles, relish

Day Before

The Day Before list is primarily organized to get everything packed and as much loaded and done as possible the day before departure.

Check tire pressure
- ❏ truck
- ❏ trailer

Fill truck with premium gas

Get cash

Pack duffels
- ❏ clothes
- ❏ underwear, socks
- ❏ jammies
- ❏ hiking boots
- ❏ water sandals
- ❏ camper shoes
- ❏ jackets
- ❏ long underwear

Pack kit bags
- ❏ shampoo
- ❏ contact stuff
- ❏ sunscreen
- ❏ kid medicine
- ❏ grown-up medicine
- ❏ glasses
- ❏ hair bands, clips
- ❏ deodorant

Pack road-trip backpacks
- ❏ dipes, wipes
- ❏ changing pad
- ❏ snacks
- ❏ books
- ❏ coloring books, colors
- ❏ brush, hair bands

Day of Trip

The Day of Trip list helps you get out the door and on the road without forgetting the things you really can't or don't want to do till the last minute. For us, that includes:

Load trailer
- ☐ duffels
- ☐ sleeping bags, sheet
- ☐ pillows
- ☐ cold food in fridge
- ☐ ice, drinks in cooler or freezer
- ☐ doormat
- ☐ Chandler's bed rail

Take out trash

Load truck
- ☐ backpacks
- ☐ book box
- ☐ road snacks
- ☐ road cups/drinks
- ☐ Coleman stove
- ☐ Coleman lantern
- ☐ compressor, gauges
- ☐ tool kit
- ☐ firewood box
- ☐ bikes, helmets
- ☐ maps, other directions

Magazines, Catalogs, and Web Sites

Family Camping. This newish magazine by Rodale Press has a nice mix of stories on family oriented camping gear, places to stay, things to do, ways to save money. Must have some parents on the staff! The downside is it's only published twice a year and is not available by subscription. If they get enough new readers, maybe they'll start bringing it out more often and offering subscriptions. Call 800-480-1110 for information about retailers that carry it.

Backpacker. Aimed at "wilderness travelers." Not family-specific, but lots of useful knowledge for all campers. Published nine times a year by Rodale Press. For subscription information call 800-666-3434.

Trailer Life and *Motor Home.* Aimed at retired adults, these magazines are, nonetheless, good sources of information about pull-behind trailers, towing vehicles and motor homes, as well as after-market items (items you might buy to repair or enhance your trailer or motor home) RVers of any age might need. You can find some destination ideas as well. For subscription information on *Trailer Life* or *Motor Home,* call 800-825-6861. *Trailer Life* also has a Web page; see www.trailerlife.com.

StarDate is the name of the radio show and magazine put out by the McDonald Observatory Public Information Office, associated with the University of Texas at Austin. Each magazine includes star charts for the two months covered by the bimonthly issue, in addition to articles of interest to amateur astronomers and more casual stargazers. You can also find StarDate on the Web at http://stardate.utexas.edu. For more information check the Web site, where there's lots to do and look at, including a form to order a sample issue of the magazine, or call 800-STARDATE.

REI. We've rented equipment several times from REI, a co-op retailer specializing in outdoor gear and clothing. Call 800-426-4840 for the location nearest you, or to obtain a catalog.

Get a membership the first year you start camping. You may be getting quite a bit of stuff, and the membership gets you a rebate of 10 percent on everything you buy (except sale items). Do watch for the sales. We got a good deal on a couple of nice mountain bikes one Christmas.

L.L. Bean. Has several outdoor, sporting specialty, mail-order catalogs of clothing (for all ranges of weather), equipment (everything from mountain bikes to canoes), and gear (for everybody from the yuppies to the real mountaineers), including L.L. Bean Kids, Camping, season-specific Sports, Women's, etc.

Periodically throughout the year, each catalog discounts slow-moving or overstocked merchandise, so keep a sharp eye out. (We have compared prices between L.L. Bean, Sierra Trading Post, Campmor and local discount retailers on things we want to buy. When L.L. Bean discounts an item, they are competitive with the others. However, day-in, day-out prices are higher.)

They are known for excellent customer service and product quality, and we've always had good dealings with them.

You probably already receive one or more of their catalogs. If not, or if you don't get one that has what you want, call 800-221-4221, or visit them on the Web at www.llbean.com.

Campmor. Another discount mail-order catalog specializing in sporting gear, clothing, and equipment. Huge selection with pretty good prices, including a range of tent styles and sizes for those of you going light on infrastructure.

They carry kids' stuff, and many of the same brand names as L.L. Bean, usually with lower prices (sometimes a lot lower). Call 800-CAMPMOR (800-226-7667) for a catalog, or visit their Web site at www.campmor.com.

Sierra Trading Post. Discount mail-order catalog of sporting gear, clothing, and equipment. Sierra offers overstocks and closeouts they've picked up from name-brand marketers like Merrell, Hind, New Balance, and others; some seconds with minor blemishes. Limited selection, but discounts are significant, from 35-70 percent. Sierra has two outlet stores, one in Reno and one in Cheyenne. The rest of us can get their catalog by calling 800-713-4534.

After the Stork. Mail-order catalog (one company store at headquarters in Albuquerque) specializing in cotton kids' clothing. The Stork offers a good value on kids' long underwear basics in plain or thermal cotton knit, in a rainbow of colors and sizes. Good selection of sturdy shoes and boots, too. Call 800-441-4775 for a catalog.

The Stork also has begun holding Warehouse Sales around the country, where they offer discontinued and overstock items in a variety of sizes and styles. You can get some *outrageous* bargains. I once got a $15.00 long-sleeve, full-leg thermal romper for my son for $3.00.

Call the Warehouse Sale Hotline at 800-826-0619 for more

information. Their email address is storkmail@ afterthestork.com. See their Web page at www.afterthe stork.com.

Texas Parks and Wildlife. The Web site for this state agency is outstanding. Take a look at http://www. tpwd.state.tx.us/tpwd.htm. You'll find descriptions of all state parks, including available attractions, amenities, and lodging options. You can also reach the TP&W agency at its general information line number: 800-792-1112. (Note: Names and addresses of other state agencies of this type can be found in Resources, beginning on page 83.)

World Wide Wilderness Directory. This on-line public access forum, located at www.wbm.ca/wilderness, provides information regarding all kinds of outdoor services. You can find information about many outdoor adventure opportunities, including wilderness eco-tourism treks, whitewater rafting, canoeing, camping, family and corporate packages, hunting and fishing outfitters, even luxurious five-star resorts. This Web service gives adventure outfitters everywhere in the world the capability to list their offerings.

The directory service is available to adventure camps, outfitters, camp owners or their agents (including group associations), and regional, provincial/state, and federal tourism authorities.

US National Park Service. Aka Parknet: The National Park Service Place on the Net is located at www.nps.gov. This Web site offers a lot more than camping information. The opening screen offers hotlinks not only to information about every park in the system, but also special sections on Links to the Past: America's Histories and Cultures; Park Smart: Education and Interpretation; Info Zone: Service-wide Information; and Nature Net: Nature Resources in the Parks.

Parknet also links to the National Park Foundation's online **Park Store,** connecting you to an increasingly wide array of Park-related products and services that you can order or purchase over the Internet, or by phone or fax. The Park Store is designed as a gateway to the best National Park publications, maps, videos, tours, collectibles, and a wealth of other products to help you plan, enjoy, and remember your National Park adventures.

Now available: *The Complete Guide to America's Parks,* a traveler's guide to all 369 units in America's National Park System, and *Trails Illustrated Maps,* high quality, richly detailed maps of the National Parks for a wide range of uses, from hiking to sightseeing.

US Fish and Wildlife also has a page, more oriented toward fish and game management than camping and hiking, but, if you are interested, take a look at www.fws.gov.

United States Geological Survey. Established by the US Department of the Interior, the USGS is the nation's largest earth science research and information agency. You can visit their page at www.usgs.gov. The USGS provides "geologic, topographic, and hydrologic information in the form of maps, databases, descriptions, and analyses of the water, energy, and mineral resources, land surface, underlying geologic structure, natural hazards, and dynamic processes of the earth."

If you've never seen a USGS topo map, try ordering one for your area, or a place you know and love. Look in your phone book's Yellow Pages, or call 800-HELP-MAP, or write: USGS Information Services, Box 25286, Denver Federal Center, Denver, CO 80225.

Parks Canada. This is the management organization for the national parks system in Canada. You can reach them by phone at (819) 997-0055. Their TDD number is (819)994-4957, and their email address is parks_webmaster@pch.gc.ca. You can write to the national office at: Parks Canada National Office, 25 Eddy Street, Hull, Quebec, Canada, K1A 0M5.

Parks Canada's Web site is simply phenomenal; point your browser at http://parkscanada.pch.gc.ca/. This site offers a wealth of information in English and French (you can switch languages on many of the pages). At the main screen, you can select *Visit Us*; this displays listings on Cultural Heritage, Natural Heritage, and Cooperative Heritage Initiatives. Click on *National Heritage* to select National Parks; on this page, you can choose whether you want to see an alphabetical list of all the parks, or an alphabetical list of parks by province. Once at this list, you can select any park and visit its dedicated page, which will display options for just about anything you want to know, including how to reach the park by mail or phone, how to travel to it, what its featured attractions are, description of its historical background, among other options.

Great Outdoor Recreation Pages. This on-line-only resource is not to be missed; see www.gorp.com. According to the publishers, Diane and Bill Greer, GORP is a Web site packed with valuable information of interest to outdoor recreationists and active travelers. You'll find information on traveling the world.

Attractions lists national parks, forests, wildernesses, wildlife refuges, historic sites, and more, describing where to go and what to do on lands throughout the United States.

Activities helps the outdoor enthusiast in pursuit of just about anything: hiking, biking, fishing, paddling, skiing, birding.

Locations lets you throw a dart at the world map and learn about whatever distant corner the point hits. Books, gear, tours, recipes, art . . . if it has an outdoor and active travel theme, it's fair game for GORP.

Alphabetical List of U.S. Parks and Wildlife Departments and Canadian National Parks

For more information on places to go and things to do, you may want to contact the department of parks and wildlife for the state or province you are interested in visiting.

Alabama Department of Game and Fish
64 N. Union St.
Montgomery, AL 36130
(205) 261-3486

Alaska Department of Fish and Game
P.O. Box 3-2000
Juneau, AK 99802
(907) 465-4100

Arizona Game and Fish Department
Arizona State Parks
2222 W. Greenway Road
Phoenix, AZ 85023
(602) 942-3000

Arkansas Game and Fish Commission
2 Natural Resources Drive
Little Rock, AR 72205
(501) 223-6300

California Department of Fish and Game
1416 Ninth Street
Sacramento, CA 95814
(916) 445-3531

California Department of Parks and Recreation
1416 Ninth Street
Sacramento, CA 95814
(916) 653-6995

Colorado Department of Natural Resources
1313 Sherman Street, Room #718
Denver, CO 80203
(303) 866-3311

Connecticut Department of Environmental Protection
165 Capitol Avenue
Hartford, CT 06106
(203) 566-5599

Delaware Division of Fish and Wildlife
P.O. Box 1401
Dover, DE 19903
(302) 736-4431

Delaware Division of Parks and Recreation
89 Kings Highway
P.O. Box 1401
Dover, DE 19903
(302) 739-4413

Florida Game and Freshwater Fish Commission
620 S. Meridan Street
Tallahassee, FL 32399-1500
(904) 488-1960

Florida Marine Fisheries Commission
2540 Executive Center, Circle West
Tallahassee, FL 32301
(904) 447-0554

Georgia Department of Natural Resources
205 Butler Street
Atlanta, GA 30334
(404) 656-3510

Hawaii Department of Land and Natural Resources
1151 Punchbowl Street
Honolulu, HI 96813
(808) 548-4000

Idaho Fish and Game Department
Idaho Department of Parks and Recreation
600 South Walnut Street
P.O. Box 25
Boise, ID 83707
(208) 334-3700

Illinois Department of Conservation
524 S. Second Street
Springfield, IL 62701
(217) 782-6302

Indiana Department of Natural Resources
402 W. Washington Street
Indianaplis, IN 46204
(317) 232-4020

Iowa Department of Natural Resources
Wallace State Office Building
E. Ninth and Grand Ave.
Des Moines, IA 50319
(515) 281-5145

Kansas Department of Wildlife & Parks
RR 2, Box 54A
Pratt, KS 67124
(316) 672-5911

Kentucky Department of Fish and Wildlife
1 Game Farm Road
Frankfort, KY 40601
(502) 564-3400

Kentucky Department of Parks
Capital Plaza Tower, 500 Mero St., Suite 1100
Frankfort, KY 40601-1974
(800) 255-PARK

Louisiana Department of Wildlife and Fisheries
P.O. Box 98000
Baton Rouge, LA 70898
(504) 765-2800

Maine Department of Inland Fisheries and Wildlife
284 State Street Station #41
Augusta, ME 04333
(207) 289-2766

Maryland Department of Natural Resources
Tawes State Office Building
580 Taylor Avenue
Annapolis, MD 21401
(301) 974-3990

**Massachusetts Department of Fisheries,
Wildlife and Environmental Law Enforcement**
100 Cambridge Street
Boston, MA 02202
(617) 727-1614

Michigan Department of Natural Resources
P.O. Box 30028
Lansing, MI 48909
(517) 373-1220

Minnesota Department of Natural Resources
Division of Fish and Wildlife
500 Lafayette Road
St. Paul, MN 55155
(612) 296-6157

Mississippi Department of Wildlife Conservation
P.O. Box 451
Jackson, MS 39205
(601) 362-9219

Missouri Department of Conservation
P.O. Box 180
Jefferson City, MO 65102
(314) 751-4115

Montana Department of Fish and Wildlife
1420 E. Sixth
Helena, MT 59620
(406) 444-2535

Nebraska Game and Parks Commission
2200 N. 33rd Street
P.O. Box 30370
Lincoln, NE 68503
(402) 464-0641

Nevada Department of Wildlife
P.O. Box 10678
Reno, NV 89520
(702) 789-0500

New Hampshire Fish and Game Department
2 Hazen Drive
Concord, NH 03301
(603) 271-3421

New Jersey Division of Fish, Game, and Wildlife
401 E. State Street CN402
Trenton, NJ 08625
(609) 292-2695

New Mexico Game and Fish Department
Villagra Building
Santa Fe, NM 87503
(505) 827-7899

New York Deparment of Fish and Wildlife
50 Wolf Road
Albany, NY 12233
(518) 457-5690

North Carolina Wildlife Resources Commission
Archdal Building
512 N. Salisbury Street
Raleigh, NC 27611
(919) 733-3391

North Dakota State Game and Fish Department
100 N. Bismark Expressway
Bismark, ND 58501
(701) 221-6300

Ohio Department of Natural Resources
Division of Wildlife
Fountain Square
Columbus, OH 43224
(614) 265-6565

Oklahoma Department of Wildlife Conservation
P.O. Box 53465
1801 N. Lincoln
Oklahoma City, OK 73152
(405) 521-3851

Oregon Department of Fish and Wildlife
P.O. Box 59
Portland, OR 97207
(502) 299-5551

Pennsylvania Game Commission
2001 Elmerton Avenue
Harrisburg, PA 17110
(717) 787-4250

Rhode Island Department of Environmental Management
22 Hayes Street
Providence, RI 02908
(401) 277-2774

South Carolina Department of Natural Resources
P.O. Box 167
Columbia, SC 29202
(803) 734-3888

South Dakota Game, Fish, and Parks
445 E. Capitol
Pierre, SD 57501
(605) 773-3888

Tennessee Wildlife Resources Agency
Ellington Agricultural Center
P.O. Box 40747
Nashville, TN 37204
(615) 781-6500

Texas Parks and Wildlife
4200 Smith School Road
Austin, TX 78744
(512) 389-4800

Utah State Department of Natural Resources
1596 W. North Temple
Salt Lake City, UT 84116
(801) 538-4700

Vermont Fish and Wildlife Department
103 S. Main Street
Waterbury Complex
Waterbury, VT 05676
(802) 244-7331

Virginia Department of Game and Inland Fisheries
4010 W. Broad Street
P.O. Box 11104
Richmond, VA 23230
(804) 367-1000

Washington Department of Fish and Wildlife
600 Capitol Way N.
Olympia, WA 98501-1091
(206) 753-5700

Washington State Parks and Recreation Commission
P.O. Box 42650
Olympia, WA 98504-2650
(800) 233-0321

West Virginia Department of Natural Resources
1900 Kanawha Boulevard E.
Charleston, WV 25305
(304) 348-2754

Wisconsin Department of Natural Resources
P.O. Box 7921
Madison, WI 53707
(608) 266-2621

Wyoming Game and Fish Department
5400 Bishop Boulevard
Cheyenne, WY 82006
(307) 777-4600

Canadian National Park Service Centers and Parks

Calgary Service Centre
Room 552
220-4th Avenue S.E.
Calgary, Alberta
Canada T2G 4X3
Telephone: (403) 292-4401 or 1-800-748-7275
Fax: (403) 292-6004
Email (Manitoba, Saskatchewan, Alberta, Northwest
Territories): NatlParks-AB@pch.gc.ca
Email (British Columbia): py_infocentre@pch.gc.ca

Alberta national parks include:

Banff National Park. UNESCO World Heritage Site
and Canada's first National Park (1885).

Elk Island National Park. Alberta plains oasis for rare
and endangered species.

Jasper National Park. UNESCO World Heritage Site
and glacial jewel of the Rockies.

Waterton Lakes National Park. International Peace
Park near the Rocky rises from grasslands.

Wood Buffalo National Park. UNESCO World
Heritage Site larger than Switzerland.

British Columbia national parks include:

Glacier National Park. British Columbia's lush interior rainforest and permanent glaciers.

Gwaii Haanas National Park Reserve. Haïda culture and coastal rainforest on Queen Charlotte Islands.

Kootenay National Park. UNESCO World Heritage Site featuring the famous Radium Hot Springs.

Mount Revelstoke National Park. Rainforest of 1,000-year-old cedars and spectacular mountains.

Pacific Rim National Park Reserve. Pacific Coast Mountains make up this marine and forest environment.

Yoho National Park. UNESCO World Heritage Site in Rockies.

Manitoba national parks include:

Riding Mountain National Park. Protected "island" area in the Manitoba Escarpment.

Wapusk National Park. One of the largest polar bear denning areas in the world.

Northwest Territories national parks include:

Aulavik National Park. Over 12,000 square kilometers of arctic wilderness on Banks Island.

Auyuittuq National Park Reserve. Baffin Island landscapes containing northern extremity of Canadian Shield.

Ellesmere Island National Park Reserve. Most remote, fragile, rugged and northerly lands in North America.

Tuktut Nogait National Park. Calving ground for the Bluenose caribou herd.

Nahanni National Park Reserve. Northwest Territories' UNESCO World Heritage Site.

Wood Buffalo National Park. UNESCO World Heritage Site larger than Switzerland.

Saskatchewan national parks include:

Grasslands National Park. Saskatchewan's rare prairie grasses, dinosaur fossils, and badlands.

Prince Albert National Park. Protects slice of northern coniferous forest and widlife.

Halifax Service Center
Historic Properties
1869 Upper Water Street
Halifax, Nova Scotia
Canada B3J 1S9
Telephone: (902) 426-3436 or 1-800-213-7275
Fax: (902) 426-6881
Email: atlantic_parksinfo@pch.gc.ca

Nova Scotia national parks include:

Cape Breton Highlands National Park. Home to
Cabot Trail, a land blessed with spectacular cliffs.

Kejimkujik National Park. Nova Scotia's inland of historic canoe routes and portages.

Quebec Service Center
3 Passage du Chien d'Or
P.O. Box 6060,
Haute-Ville
Quebec City, Quebec
Canada G1R 4V7
Telephone: (418) 648-4177 or 1-800-463-6769
Fax: (418) 649-6140
TDD: (418) 648-5099
Email: webinfo@sunqbc.
risq.net

Quebec national parks include:

Forillon National Park. The "Jewel of the Gaspé"
where land meets sea.

La Mauricie National Park. Lakes winding through forested hills for canoe and portage activities.

Mingan Archipelago National Park Reserve. A string of islands carved out by wind and sea.

Ontario Service Center
111 Water Street East
Cornwall, Ontario
Canada K6H 6S3
Telephone: 1-800-839-8221
Fax: (613) 938-5729

Ontario national parks include:

Bruce Peninsula National Park. Landscapes including the northern end of Niagara Escarpment.

Georgian Bay Islands National Park. Captivating islands representing Lake Huron's landscape.

Point Pelee National Park. Most southerly point on Canadian mainland.

Pukaskwa National Park. Canadian Shield's ancient landscape on Superior's North Shore.

St. Lawrence Islands National Park. Canada's smallest national park located in Ontario.

Yukon Service Centre
Suite 205 - 300
Main Street
Whitehorse, Yukon
Canada Y1A 2B5
Telephone:1-800-661-0486
Fax: (867) 393-6701
Email: whitehorse_info@
  pch.gc.ca

Yukon national parks include:

Ivvavik National Park. Calving ground for the
Porcupine caribou herd.

Kluane National Park Reserve. Yukon's UNESCO
World Heritage Site contains Canada's highest peak.

Vuntut National Park. Northern Yukon's unique non-
glaciated landscape.

*Additional national parks are located in New Brunswick,
Newfoundland, Labrador, and Prince Edward Island. Check
the Web pages for these parks, or contact the national office.*

New Brunswick national parks include:

Fundy National Park. Atlantic's sanctuary with
world's highest tides.

Kouchibouguac National Park. Intricate Acadian
blend of coastal and inland habitats.

Newfoundland and Labrador national parks include:

Gros Morne National Park. UNESCO World Heritage Site amid Newfoundland's wild natural beauty.

Terra Nova National Park. Remnants of the Eastern Newfoundland Ancient Appalachian Mountains.

Prince Edward Island is the location of the:

Prince Edward Island National Park. A protected area with spectacular coast.

Camping Notes

Camping Notes

_____

_____

_____

_____

_____

_____

_____

_____

_____

_____

_____

_____

_____

_____

_____

_____

_____

_____

_____

_____

Camping Notes

_____

_____

_____

_____

_____

_____

_____

_____

_____

_____

_____

_____

_____

_____

_____

_____

_____

_____

_____

_____

_____

Camping Notes

Camping Notes

_____

_____

_____

_____

_____

_____

_____

_____

_____

_____

_____

_____

_____

_____

_____

_____

_____

_____

_____

_____

_____

About the Author

Tammerie Spires and her family live in Richardson, Texas, where she is a parent, camper, gardener, and freelance writer.

She has worked in various editing positions for *Third Coast,* the city magazine for Austin, Texas, and for three computer journals. More recently she was a staff writer for Price Waterhouse LLP, preparing books and multi-media for inhouse and trade use.

Tammerie is an active member of Peace Mennonite Church in Dallas, Texas.

When he had grabbed her, she'd no longer seemed like his cousin, but like a woman. She had fallen silent almost immediately, with either a gasp or a sigh escaping her lips. Then her body became limp and he'd stumbled in surprise at its languid heaviness, flopped over his arm, as if the sprite in her had fled. As he slapped her bottom she'd made peculiar noises—little gurgles and moans, ooh's and ahh's, and her bottom cheeks under the tightly stretched shorts seemed to melt, soft and palpable, almost flowing onto his hand.

He wondered at her reaction, and then, with a hot flush of fleeting shame, he noticed his own.

Feeling confused and disconcerted, he returned to work on his car. His thoughts all the while were preoccupied with Patti. He had some thinking to do about her. . . .

Other Books by
Blue Moon Authors

The Reckoning

SELECTED STORIES
OF AN ENGLISH
SCHOOLMISTRESS
BY
RACHEL LANGFORD

BLUE MOON BOOKS, INC.

NEW YORK

Copyright © 1988 by Blue Moon Books, Inc.

All Rights Reserved

No part of this book may be reproduced, stored in a retrievals system, or transmitted in any form, by any means, including mechanical, electronic, photocopying, recording or otherwise, without prior written permission of the publishers.

First Blue Moon Edition 1988
First Printing 1988
Second Printing 1990
Third Printing 1993

ISBN 1-56201-036-0

Published by Blue Moon Books, Inc.
PO Box 1040
Cooper Station, NY 10276

Manufactured in the United States of America

THE RECKONING

Contents

Foreword

Wasn't it the French humorist, Pierre Daninos, who said: "In the depths of every Englishman's subconscious there is a cat-'o'-nine-tails and a schoolgirl in black stockings"?

This anthology of contemporary short stories celebrates the extraordinary mythology that has grown up around corporal punishment and young English ladies in their late teens and early twenties.

I—author of these stories and professional English schoolmistress—first became painfully aware of corporal punishment when I was a young schoolgirl. At the all-girls high school which I attended in Sussex, not only did we receive the slipper on our bottoms for quite trivial misdemeanours such as lateness, but for more serious offences we could expect anything up to six strokes from the headmistress' three-foot-long rattan cane. That this was a fairly typical situation in England, twenty or so years ago, may be illustrated by the following extract from the provincial English newspaper *The Cornishman* of 9 July 1964.

A foot-long clothesbrush which both a Helston headmaster and his school's senior mistress admitted using to beat two sixth form girls on their bare buttocks was produced at Truro Magistrates Court on Thursday.

On the morning of April 29, the headmaster called one of the girls to his study. He told her that the caretaker had observed her "necking" in the Green Room the previous Monday. The girl confessed that she had been necking. He told her that he could not let things like this happen in a mixed school. He could make a public disgrace of the girl in front of the whole school. But this might prejudice her entry into college.

He then told her, "We can keep this private if you agree to be spanked by the senior mistress and me—if you have the guts to take a spanking and keep quiet about it." She told him she was prepared to be spanked as punishment.

The head took her along to the senior mistress's study. He told her to take off her jumper, skirt, and underskirt and to tuck her blouse in her knickers, and pull up her knickers so that the buttocks were exposed. He told her to lean over the narrow end of the table. He held her hand and told her to look at him.

The senior mistress stood behind the girl and started to beat her on both buttocks with the back of the brush. The girl said she hit pretty hard and it hurt. In her statement the girl added, "I don't know how many times she hit me. I counted up to seven and then stopped counting."

The headmaster then made the girl kneel between his knees sideways on, and bend over as though to touch her toes. He got hold of her hands behind her back and started to beat her with the same brush on her buttocks. Afterwards she was allowed to get up and the headmaster said, "She does not look very sorry. Perhaps she had better have some more."

He told her to lean over the table again and once more the mistress beat her with the same brush quite a number of times. The girl said it hurt very much more this time. When the mistress had finished, he put the girl over his knee once more and beat her again, holding her hands behind her back. The girl said this hurt "an awful lot."

He stopped and asked her if she was sorry. She said she was sorry. He told her to stand over the table again. He looked at her buttocks to see how bad the bruises were. He placed his hand on each of the girls' buttocks in turn and asked her if it hurt. She told him it did . . .

For the next few days he called her to his study and made her show him her bruises and he looked at them. The prosecutor added: "I am not suggesting there was anything indecent about this. Probably he realised he had hit the girl too hard and was most anxious to see he had not done any lasting damage which would of necessity have brought the whole matter into the open."

The second girl was dealt with in exactly the same way. To quote the girl's own words, "It hurt terribly. I cried and looked away from him. He said, 'Look at me, please,' and while the mistress beat me with the brush, he held my hands in his."

When the beating stopped, he stood behind and put his hand on both her buttocks, asking if it hurt. He sat down on the chair and told the girl he would spank her over his knee. . . . Afterwards she, too, had to go to the head's study. She said he told her to take down her gym knickers to see if there were any marks on her buttocks. He told her to bend over and said, "Does it hurt?" She said, "No."

The headmaster and senior mistress of this Cornish grammar school both resigned from their posts and were fined £50 and £30, respectively, for common assault. But at no stage during the court proceedings was it ever suggested that the two teachers had had no right to administer corporal punishment to the girls. They were only prosecuted because it was felt the punishment had been unduly harsh—the medical report on the first girl had discovered bruising over an area of 72 square inches.

In typically English fashion, the "Helston affair" created a major sensation. The national newspapers seized on it and gave it front-page headline coverage, as though it were something unique and unheard of in the annals of British educational history. Meanwhile throughout the land it was "business as usual": whole legions of schoolgirls were being spanked and caned in the approved manner—but nobody trumpeted *their* cause.

More contemporary reports suggest that up until fairly recently the caning of English schoolgirls was assuming unparalleled proportions. The *South London Press* of 18 September, 1979, published information which it had, by some means or other, managed to glean from a nearby Church of England secondary school's punishment book. The official statistics were that: "In 1976/77, 18 per cent (84) of the girls were caned on 204 occasions, and 26 of the girls received three or more punishments during the year. During the two terms of 1977/78 covered by the survey, 77 (17 per cent) of the girls had received corporal punishment on 150 occasions."

There was much prurient speculation as to whether the girls in question had received the cane on their hands or across their backsides.

Finally, *Private Eye,* the magazine which has got to the bottom of so many stories skimmed over by the more orthodox press, came up with the answer in its issue of 22 May, 1981: "The girls have been caned on the bottom!" Furthermore, they established that "The chief caner is the headmaster," and spoke of his particular "enthusiasm for caning"—an enthusiasm which "the governors, largely clergy, share."

So the corporal punishment of schoolgirls is not just an Englishman's fantasy—it is very much a reality.

Despite having written these short stories, I must say that on educational and humanitarian grounds I am totally opposed to physical punishment of either sex at school. Brute force settles nothing. It degrades both parties, the one who inflicts, and the one who receives. Giving a teacher the prerogative to cane his pupils is simply giving him license to enact his sadistic fantasies. Likewise, if any of the pupils he beats possess a masochistic makeup, then they will go out of their way to court a beating—as indeed did several of the girls at my old school.

I myself was never physically punished by a male teacher. Yet all through my adolescence I used to fantasise guiltily about just such a situation. Who knows, maybe if I had been spanked or caned by a male teacher, I would never have come to write these stories—for despite all my moral qualms, I must count myself among that increasingly large number of adults who are irresistibly drawn to tales of school discipline involving girl pupils and male teachers.

Corporal punishment is now officially banned in all British schools, and I for one am glad—since I have always been appalled by real cruelty and injustice. Nevertheless, perhaps now that it has been finally done away with, more and more people of both sexes will

13

feel freer to erotically dream about corporal punishment with that peculiarly ambivalent excited trepidation that characterises all lovers of the forbidden fruits of sex.

Certainly for many English men and women such weapons of traditional school discipline as the cane, the tawse, the strap, and the slipper will forever keep their sexual resonance. School canes are still sold in England—but no longer to schools. You can easily pick one up in a sex shop, or send for one through the post.

And as for gym tunics, black stockings, and navy-blue school knickers, if you were to inspect the wardrobe of many a young Englishwoman of today—married or otherwise—you might just be in for a surprise.

Finally, a word about the stories themselves, one or two of which are based on real life experiences.

Nearly all fictional works on "discipline" that I have read, apart from *The Story of O* and one or two others, have been male-oriented. The female victim is perceived as a nebulous shadowy figure who derives no enjoyment whatsoever from being whipped, caned, or spanked. I believe this to be not only unfair, but grossly inaccurate! These stories are an attempt, albeit humble, to redress the balance.

The Reckoning

There is a girl lying on the beach, the sand hot and dry underneath her, moulding gently around her curves as she wriggles now and then into the sharp softness. The beach is deserted; a long pale lip of yellow undulating down to where the sea licks quietly in the distance.

The girl is naked except for two pink triangles knotted sloppily together, which pass for a bikini top, and a pair of shrunken white shorts half undone. Her breasts spill out from the pinkness, nipples tickle the sand.

She lies on her side, her long brown legs stretched straight, one resting on top of the other like a neatly closed pair of scissors. Toes are pointed, too— beautifully symmetrical.

Her shorts are cut high and tight, and they are damp. The dampness makes them cling to her buttocks. They are almost transparent. Each muscular ripple through her round buttocks eddies through the cotton.

Grains of sand chafe under the material at the junction of her thighs. Breathing in deeply, she undoes the zip a little . . . the shorts are so very tight . . . and eases her fingers down to scratch.

The sun makes her careless and she rolls half onto her stomach, stretching her arms above her head, sifting warm sand through her fingers. The shorts undo

15

themselves and crisp curls of hair fluff out in a cocktail-glass triangle above the open zip. Her breasts loll naked on the sand. Her hair, the same colour as sand, is swept over her face obscuring her features except for her lips, which stay caught as if in mid-sigh, slightly apart. In her mind she is being fucked.

The man stops some way off and closes his eyes as soon as he sees her. He has the line and symmetry of her curves, thumping red behind his closed lids, curves like the depth and swell of the sea. Opening his eyes briefly he imprints every detail of her until she is drawn in his head, outlined in silver, like a brand. He can see her with his eyes shut.

He sees the long tanned legs and the crusty patches of sand on her calves which has dried and silvered there; the lines of damp sand in the crook of her knees; the plump brownness of her thighs as their sultry heaviness shifts and rolls itself beautifully into tender wedges of flesh, oozing out from beneath her shorts like crescents of over-ripe fruit. He sighs with a shiver and pauses, some twenty feet away, worming his toes in a rhythmic circle in the sand, tense, hard, and aching inside his shorts. He is a desperate man who will stop at nothing.

Ten feet, and he stops . . . unzips.

A gold chain around her waist winks in the brilliant sun, the thread of it emphasizing the sudden descent of well-fleshed hips into the basin of her waist, tiny and feminine. And now, too, he can see the marks; he takes in the whole of her, to come back to them, like a child saving the best strawberries till last. And he trembles,

16

savours them, jerking all the while.

The segments of buttock below her shorts are a curious pink. Yes, her thighs are a strawberry colour. A curious pink, merging into the honey shade of her legs. He moves silently closer. The details become sharp.

Her shorts are now halfway down her bottom, revealing the dark crack between her cheeks. There are little plum-coloured marks on her skin like thin streaks of lipstick. Aha! So she's been a naughty girl! So that's the reason she can only lie on her side!

The sight of her half-undressed, a mess, dolly-dishevelled, makes him start to pant. With a quick look about him he removes his shorts and lies silently behind her. She doesn't move. A hand flops wantonly through the swirl of blonde hair but this is the only response she makes to his greedy fingers tugging and ripping at the waistband of her shorts. Pulling, jerking at the damp cotton the zip smiles open at last and he takes the shorts down over her passive legs.

She moans softly as if she is dreaming, but that is all, as the male fingers and the grit sandpapers her sore flanks.

"I want your cunt," he says, moving her roughly. His arms grip her waist like tentacles and his fingers pump the round sun-warmed breasts. The faceless man, he enters her from behind as she gives a little shrill cry, half a sob, half joy. At each thrust his naked thighs punish the plum marks still further and her pale pouting lips, the colour of licked ice-cream, twist into the sand.

"I want to know," he says tersely through clenched teeth, "I want to know what happened to you. How did

17

you get those marks? I want to know everything."

How can she tell him? How can she—with the slamming of his thighs and belly against her, his prick like a piston deep inside her—tell him everything?

"Tell me!" he says fiercely and squeezes her breasts, making each nipple painfully hard.

She can't look at him, can't make him stop with her blue eyes. He has her face covered by her hair—no face, no name, no identity. A man's slave. She decides she had better tell him what he demands to know.

"My man did it."

"Go on. Every detail; how you felt—everything!"

The small voice whispers on. He tells her to speak up.

"I was flirting . . . teasing another man. He says I dress provocatively. He says I dress like a tart. I am a hussy." There is a pause before she adds, *"He says it is necessary to punish me."*

"Why?" The thrusts slow down. It is as though he has put a lid on a boiling pan. He waits for her answer.

"Because he wants to. That is the reason."

"Go on," he commands, thrusting even harder.

"He told me to meet him down by the rocks. When I got there he was sitting on a large one which jutted out into the sea. I felt afraid of him.

"Stuck in the sand was a cane with a crooked handle. I thought how incongruous it was—a school cane, a thin stick of rattan quivering in the sea breeze. I stood beside it as though it might devour me, I couldn't quell my fear. Within moments I would be its

18

victim. The roar of the incoming tide filled my ears so that I thought I would faint.

"He leant back against the rock with arms folded like a God. I must be submissive to whatever he desired. I tried. I tried to please him. I knelt in the wet sand at his feet and took his prick in my mouth, thinking that was what he wanted. The cane whined in the wind and I got to my feet. I did not know what he wanted.

"I was frightened, yet it was delicious. I suddenly became aware of my body as a whole extra-sensitised being. I tasted salt on my lips like I had never been aware of it before. I felt grains of sand stab in the corners of my eyes, felt it irritate under my fingernails and rub inside my shorts. My feet felt cold and hot at the same time. I felt ridiculously alive.

"My eyes were fixed on his feet. I could not look at his face. Then, when he gestured with his hands and spoke to me, I became overwhelmed with wild impulses: to run, sing, lie down in the path of the incoming tide and let the sea wash over me.

"He came up to me, ran his hands over every inch of my body, kissed me until I trembled. Then he took down my shorts and let them flop onto the wet sand.

"He said I must place my hands on the rock a little below breast height and bend over—keeping my knees straight—into the shape of an arch. He called it the mouth of a secret cave and laughed to himself. He put one hand flat up against my stomach and the other in the small of my back, pushing me gently into the exact position he wanted. The arc of submission. The buttocks must be deliberately and vulgarly prominent. I thought that flirting with other men wasn't such a good idea. This time, he meant business.

"Pulling the cane from the sand he brought it down immediately on the crown of my buttocks. I cried and hung my head. He did not hear me because of the seagulls overhead. They mocked me.

"Again he brought that cane down—always the same amount of strength behind each descent, never increasing in severity or mercy, or visiting the same place twice. Yet it was severe enough to make my fingers scrabble into the granite and my groomed nails chip and fall off in fragments.

"Do you know that I love him? . . ."

The girl stops her tale as the gulls' screams above her drown her pleasure-pain sobs as she comes. Now, she thinks, now he has got what he wanted: the true story of her humiliation with her lover and the collusion of her orgasm. Now has he had enough? . . .

"There, I have told you everything," she says tonelessly, *as though all her emotion has drained away into the sand.*

He flops back into the warm hollow made by their coupling and then raises himself up to plant kisses on the marks of his ownership.

"Next time . . ." *his tone is teasing,* "next time you want to flirt I shall whip you. Then you will cry like a seagull . . ."

Patti—A Story of the Sixties

John found Patti where he least expected to find her—at the top of the garden sitting on a low bough of the old apple tree, swinging her legs in an urgent little rhythm. She was munching an apple and reading a book. His book.

"Patti," he called irritably to his young cousin, "have you taken my motor manual? If you have, I'm going to be really angry with you."

John strode through the untidy vegetable patch towards the part of the garden which Patti fondly called "the orchard," although the enormous Bramley was the only fruit tree there.

The first thing he saw were her bare feet and legs, slender and tanned, dangling just above his head. He looked up into the dense green. For a moment his eyes made a slow appraisal of her legs, her plump thighs, and absorbed the little blue shorts she always wore which nicely flattered the roundness of her shapely bottom. He thought he could just make out two interesting crescents of flesh which were squashed out from under the hems of her shorts—two soft white glimpses of her bottom, as it sat firmly planted on a swaying branch.

He sighed and rather lamely grabbed hold of her toes, making her squeal, protest, and laugh all at the same time. He didn't feel in the mood for childish games, but it seemed to him that Patti always did. "Patti, please give me back my book," he said

21

wearily, trying not to let too much exasperation creep into his voice.

She looked down through the apples at his upturned face. Her long ponytail fell over her features like an errant guardsman's plume.

"I shall not," she said firmly, "unless you take me to the hop on Friday. I know you want to go with Pamela Douglas, but you know she can't jive like I can." She paused, her voice becoming like a little girl's, sweet and pleading. "And you know how well we dance together. . ."

John loosed Patti's feet and paced about under the tree. An apple fell on his shoulder. He looked up but it wasn't thrown by Patti. Her elfin face that freckled so appealingly in summer was serious now, and he sighed again. He sat down on the grass under the tree and absentmindedly began throwing half-rotten apples at the trunk.

"I promised to take her. I can't let her down, Patti."

Patti glared at him, swung her ponytail haughtily over her shoulder, and climbed rapidly to the top of the tree where she lodged the desired book firmly between the highest branches.

"There! If you don't take me as well," she called down petulantly, "you won't have your precious manual. And besides, I wouldn't have thought you needed it—you being a teacher now."

John groaned and vented his impatience by lunging at the trunk and shaking the lower branches so vigorously that Patti screamed and begged him to stop.

"I just don't know what to do with you, Patti!" he shouted. "You're a pest and no mistake. What a pity that starting college next month won't do anything to make you grow up. We're not kids anymore!"

She snorted. "Stop looking up my legs then," she

pouted, changing the subject.

She was standing above him with her legs a few feet apart, straddling the gap between two branches, gently shifting her weight from one foot to the other as if she was guarding something special and was considering whether all the effort was really worth it.

Her shorts were of the style that all the young women wore back in the early sixties. They were loose in the leg and John could see right up them.

It fascinated him how her thighs swelled, full and plump, under the shadowy protection of blue cotton, and then abruptly were overshadowed by the pear-drop heaviness of her bottom cheeks—each cheek becoming visible and quivering by turns as her body moved to and fro. That was all he could see from his position— but it was enough to make him realise with a strange lightheadedness that his seventeen-year-old sprite of a cousin wasn't wearing any panties under her shorts.

"What are you looking at?" she snapped, but John detected a tremor of excitement in her voice. She had noticed his open-mouthed stare of rapture.

John suddenly grew red and looked down quickly at the fallen apples, each one with its swollen hemispheres and dark dividing cleft reminding him sickeningly of the vision of Patti's bottom he had just glimpsed. He became even more embarrassed at his thought, clearing his throat several times and trying to dislodge the awful squeakiness that seemed to be stuck there.

The book suddenly landed at his feet with a thud and was followed by Patti, scrambling down through the branches in a fever of haste. She was pink in the face, and her breasts heaved wildly. There were twigs in her hair, scratches on her arms and legs and the little white tee-shirt she wore was no longer white, but stained with green lichen and brown smears from slith-ering down the trunk.

She stood in front of him with her hands planted decisively on her hips and hissed at him like a scalded cat.

"I—I hate you, John Wallace! *There's* your stupid book! And—and you can fall over your *own* clumsy feet at the dance! *I* wouldn't want to go with *you*. Not in a million years! So there!"

John took a step back and stared at her, nonplussed. Suddenly she'd become angry and almost hysterical over nothing at all—or so it seemed to him. Her eyes were brimming with tears and her lips trembled furiously.

John wondered if she was deliberately working her-self up into a rage to hide some emotion she wished to conceal from him.

"Patti."

He felt helpless under her shrieking invective.

"Patti!" Anger, coupled with a dizzy excitement, made him flushed and agitated. He felt a sudden hot irresistible urge to slap her face.

The whole situation was rapidly getting out of con-trol. Instead, he grabbed her impulsively around the waist, turned her, jerked her until her body was bent over and her ponytail brushed the ground, and delivered several sharp slaps to her bottom before she wriggled free and ran, clutching her bottom, down the garden and into the house.

John stood motionless for some time. His hand dropped slowly down to his side and stayed there, warm and trembling against his thigh. He became conscious of the little things about him that one usually takes for granted: the dark unbroken canopy of green above him and the dry rustle of leaves in the wind. An

24

apple falling behind with a startling thud, and the rush of his own breathing. The little scene replayed over and over in his mind.

When he had grabbed her, she'd no longer seemed like his cousin, but like a woman. She had fallen silent almost immediately, with either a gasp or a sigh escaping her lips. Then her body became limp and he'd stumbled in surprise at its languid heaviness, flopped over his arm, as if the sprite in her had fled. As he slapped her bottom she'd made peculiar noises—little gurgles and moans, oooh's and ahhh's, and her bottom cheeks under the tightly stretched shorts seemed to melt, soft and palpable, almost flowing onto his hand.

He wondered at her reaction, and then, with a hot flush of fleeting shame, he noticed his own.

Feeling confused and disconcerted, he returned to work on his car. His thoughts all the while were preoccupied with Patti. He had some thinking to do about her. . . .

Patti had stormed up to her room and slammed the door. She lay on the bed thinking. John, by spanking her, had violated the innocence of their relationship, and although this was very exciting she wasn't sure whether she liked it. She tidied her books and then threw them angrily on the bed, wrote several abominable letters to her cousin which she tore up amid angry sobs, and muttered spiteful resolutions of what she would do to his room. Since he had come to live with Patti's parents, because lodgings were hard to find near the school where he had secured his first teaching post, everything, just everything, she decided, had gone wrong.

She looked moodily out of the window at John, tinkering with his old car. What was the matter with him? He hardly seemed to notice her now that he had started

25

THE RECKONING

to go out with girls, and the teasing games they had always played together had stopped.

Perversely she decided that she would become as aggravating as possible, more mischievous than before, so that he would notice her.

Shyly, although she was alone in the room, she sneaked a hand behind her back where it slid cautiously down to her bottom. She smoothed the area which John had smacked, and then impulsively tore down her shorts to see if he had made any impression. The skin felt warm and she fancied that she could see a faint pink glow over the fullest part of her bottom-cheeks—or was it just her imagination? She cupped her cheeks in both hands and looked at herself in the mirror, circling her hips and pouting at her reflection, like Marilyn Monroe.

When Friday came, John sheepishly asked Patti to partner him at the hop.

Patti's eyes were shining. "I suppose Miss Douglas doesn't like the idea of you treading on her toes," she said unkindly.

"Something like that," John said, looking away. He didn't want to tell her the truth—that he'd politely excused himself from his date with Pamela Douglas on purpose, because he really did want to go with his cousin.

John enjoyed dancing with Patti, who was always the fastest, most energetic girl on the floor. She liked to preen a little and show off, but John didn't mind. She was usually very cooperative when they went dancing, definitely more easy to manage.

Patti flounced into the Palais that evening holding John's arm and being gracious to everyone—especially to the jilted Pamela—much to John's embarrassment.

She looked very fresh and pretty in her plain green

26

dress, with its fitted bodice and full skirt swaying exaggeratedly over the tent of starched frilly cotton petticoats underneath. Her long hair was swept up into a top-knot ponytail tied with a gingham ribbon and on her feet were the obligatory pumps.

The night was Jive Night Special and the floor was packed. Before the dancing the sexes separated into groups: the young men jostling each other, constantly smoothing their Brylcreemed hair and tapping their thick crepe-soled shoes on the floor rather self-consciously as the band warmed up. The girls jittered and prinked in another corner, flying in and out of the cloakroom, flashing their compact mirrors at their pouting reflections and linking arms to try out the latest variation on the very latest dance.

Patti screamed with excitement as Rory Storm and the Hurricanes, spotty-faced and stiff-suited to a man, came on stage.

She danced with John until he was obliged to sit down exhausted. And when Vince Dangerfield, leader of the local Teddy Boy gang, seized Patti's arm and grunted, "Take the floor, chick!" she forgot John entirely. He watched her from the side, her skirts flying wildly as she slid through Vince's legs and spun around. Tantalisingly, each time her skirts rose, her stocking-tops, suspenders, and a large expanse of bare thigh above was revealed as the light-footed Vince threw her about as though she were a rag doll. John hoped fervently that she was wearing knickers this time, and prayed that the opportunity would not occur for her to prove it.

Patti, he thought hotly, needed taking in hand.

"Did you like me tonight?" she asked him when they were sitting at home in front of the fire, drinking cocoa. It was late and Patti's parents had gone to bed.

27

"Yes, you're okay, kid," he said stiffly. With Patti curled up on the hearth rug like a satisfied kitten and staring at him so intently with her wide blue eyes, he found he was chasing his thoughts. He'd never found it difficult to talk to her before.

"Did you notice that I wasn't wearing ankle socks tonight?" she purred, a soft teasing in her voice.

John swallowed self-consciously. "I . . . Well, I suppose I did." How could he erase the unforgettable sight of her stockinged legs so sexily revealed at the mere flick of her skirt?

"I was wearing stockings. They're Mummy's really. Don't tell her, will you?" She leant across to John and touched his knee.

"Would you like to see how I look in them? All grown-up I mean?" she whispered.

John slopped cocoa on his trousers. "Patti!" he pleaded, but she stood up and lifted her dress. The white frilly starched petticoats were startling in the firelight.

"I only want to show you!" It was her turn to plead.

John looked deep in the dying fire and then back at her. "All right then, Patti, show me." He sat back in the chair trying to appear composed and casual—as though he were merely indulging a sudden, provocative whim of his cousin. But how she aroused him!

With a wiggle of her hips, she took off the petticoats and left them like a heap of meringue on the hearth rug. Then she began to lift up her dress slowly, coyly, twisting her body round in a half-circle and raising the skirts high, bunching the fullness about her waist like a can-can dancer bent on temptation.

John stared at her as if his eyes had suddenly become petrified and could move nowhere else.

She wore tan-coloured nylons. There were wrinkles

at the knees and the seams above them were wildly crooked.

"Oh—my seams!" she wailed, blushing that John would guess it was the first time she had worn stockings and hadn't mastered the art of keeping the seams straight.

The white suspenders were so long—probably because she hadn't adjusted them properly—that there was a large area of bare thigh between her white knicker-hems and the ruckled tops of her stockings. The exposed area looked irresistibly smooth and pinchable, so much so that John longed to knead the tender white flesh of her thighs between his fingers. The firelight brought a copper sheen to her skin etching her silhouetted figure against an aura of dim, rosy warmth. Everything else in the room—the dark, sombre-patterned furnishings—faded into the insignificant gloom. There was only Patti in John's eyes.

The innocence of her white aertex knickers did nothing to minimise the provocative swelling curves hidden underneath them. In fact, the deception heightened the desire in John to touch her.

"Beautiful . . ." he murmured unconsciously.

At his words Patti ceased her embarrassed fidgeting. She turned on the spot in a complete slow circle, raising her skirts high, giving him a heart-stopping profile of her pertly prominent bottom as she moved. The unruffled contrast of her smooth knickered bottom stood out in breathtaking relief against the rumpled folds of her skirt clutched tightly to her breasts. Sharp images filled his mind—of her tender young bottom, naked beneath her shorts, being spanked under the apple tree.

"Patti!" John leant forward and sat on the edge of the sofa. He placed a hand on her leg above the knee, and the other on her bottom. Somewhere in between he wanted his hands to slide together and meet—linger in the damp, soft warmth between her tightly pinched thighs, but the onrush of desire was paralyzing. Instead, he circled his fingers uncertainly on the two areas, venturing to slip one hand up to her bare thigh, where it toyed with the tops of her nylons and squeezed the flesh gently on her bottom.

Patti wiggled suggestively, pushing down and back on his hands as if she was carried away in her enjoyment. Then suddenly she turned and cried in a shrieking soprano, "John Wallace, what do you think you're doing?" There was a teasing demon in her voice.

John's arousal evaporated as if she had doused him with cold water. His face darkened with anger.

"You little minx, Patti, to carry on so with me!" He hissed, "What do you mean by leading me on? Yes, that's what you were doing," he added as her eyes widened. "Well, I'll not put up with it, young missy. Come here!"

Patti squealed with sudden fright as John grabbed her arm, her heavy skirts falling down like the descent of a curtain over her figure. He pulled her roughly to him. "I'm going to tan your behind!" he said with a growl.

Patti was halfway down, struggling and kicking, across John's lap. She went rigid at his words. Then with a gasp and a violent jerk, she clawed and rolled ignominiously off his knees and onto the floor. She was up and running for the door before John could catch her. John heard her excited breathing in the doorway, like an animal freed from a trap, hovering for the reappearance of the pursuer. She peeped around the door and giggled nervously, taunting him to catch her again, but John sat staring blackly into the dying fire, unable to follow—suffocated by waves of frustration.

She ran upstairs to bed, paused once to listen, hoping that he would follow, and when he did not she bolted into the sanctuary of her room.

It was Sunday, the day before John was due to start work as Math teacher at Fernlea Secondary School. Patti sat disconsolately in the kitchen, elbows on the table, head in her hands.

"Do you really have to go to work tomorrow?" she demanded when John came into the room.

"Of course I do!" he said exasperatedly. "You're bored, Patti. You ought to get involved in something. What about preparing for college?"

"That's two weeks away," she retorted, frowning.

John pulled up a stool and sat opposite her. "Are you annoyed with me, Patti?" he asked softly.

She looked down. "No-o," she said in a tiny voice.

"Liar."

"Oh, all right then. I *am* cross with you." She threw her head back and met his brown eyes with that old defiant expression of hers. "I haven't enjoyed this holiday one bit," she pouted. "You—I mean we—we've done absolutely nothing together."

"What do you mean, Patti?"

"There's been no fun, no games, no *pranks*—like there used to be when we were younger."

John sighed. He wanted to tell her that she was no longer a child—that she ought to grow up. But then again, he rather wanted her to stay as she was, because the emerging woman in her was proving to be difficult to handle.

"And," she added lamely, "I've got two whole weeks without you."

They fell silent, listening to the rain beating against

31

the windows. Then Patti brightened: "Can't imagine you teaching," she smirked. "That *would* be funny. All toffed up and trying to keep all those girls in order!" She giggled. "Bet you're a fraud, really."

John frowned. "I've been trained for the job, little cousin. I can handle them," he retorted.

"Pooh! I'd like to see *that*. When I was at school—"

"Which was only last year," interrupted John.

"We used to give the male teachers merry hell," she declared proudly, ignoring his taunting interruption. Impulsively she reached across and seized his hand. "I'd give *anything* to see you—as a teacher," she said wistfully . . .

After John came home on the first day at school, Patti quizzed him about his experiences. He looked exhilarated, but tired. "Piece of cake—when you know how!" he said mysteriously.

Patti was intrigued. With so much empty time to kill before the start of college she became absolutely determined to gain access to John's school and observe him at his job.

"John, may I come into school and watch you?" she pleaded.

"No, Patti—you may not," he said starchily.

"Oooh, you *bore!* You've no fun in you at all!" she hissed, her temper rising. "You'll end up like all the other teachers—dead from the neck up!"

"And what did you have in mind?" John inquired mildly, fencing a little under her sharp tongue. He didn't want to wade through an argument. He always seemed to lose.

Patti's face lit up. "I sneak into your classroom," she bent low over the table and her voice dropped to a conspiratorial whisper, "and sit at the back during one of your lessons."

John laughed. "You can't do that. You'd be recognized. You'd stand out like a sore thumb."

"No, I wouldn't. Not if I was wearing school uniform like the other girls," she said with a mysterious wag of her head. "Please John, Pl-ee-ase! It'll be our last prank together. Then I'll grow up—I promise!"

She looked at him, so earnest and pleading that John had no heart to refuse. He lowered his head and nodded wearily. If he didn't agree Patti would only make his life a misery with her taunts and retribution. He agreed a day and time when Patti was to come into school and sit discreetly at the back of the classroom. And he made her promise that she would do nothing to give herself away and put his job in jeopardy.

The evening before the prank was due to be played found Patti hovering furtively outside her bedroom waiting for John to come in. She was wearing her cousin's long woolen dressing-gown and her hair, which had just been washed, hung about her face in long damp tendrils. Patti knew he'd been out with Pamela Douglas on a date, and she was filled with jealous imaginings of what might have happened between them.

The front door slammed and John came in, leaping up the stairs two at a time, whistling through his teeth and removing his tie. The smell of cheap scent met Patti's nostrils. So the lovers *had* been close!

John's lightheartedness was abruptly cut short as he swung around the bannisters and came face to face with Patti. He immediately felt guilty.

She stood huddled in the unbecoming ampleness of his dressing-gown, her arms folded like a washerwoman, hissing with displeasure. He was taken aback but something about her appearance reminded him of an irate landlady, and he began to laugh.

33

"I want you," she hissed. "Come into my room. I've got something to show you."

Feeling intoxicated with his successful evening and by a few glasses of wine, he followed Patti into her bedroom with amused curiosity.

"I've been waiting all evening to show you," she said petulantly.

One the bed lay the complete uniform of Fernlea School.

"I bought it all from the secondhand uniform sale," she added proudly.

"It looks too small to me," John observed.

"Oh for God's sake, don't say that!" she turned to him, "because I'm wearing it, no matter what the size. So there!"

She slumped on the bed, crestfallen. Her big surprise wasn't having the desired effect on her cousin.

"Did you have a good evening?" she said in an off-hand voice.

The dreamy far-away look which had settled on John's features vanished and he came out of his reverie.

"All right, I suppose," he replied, noncommital.

Patti pouted. "You *stink* of perfume!" she said scathingly.

"And you, little girl, are wearing my dressing-gown again!" John retorted with strained good humour.

To his surprise, Patti stood up and with angry haste undid the cord and threw the dressing gown abruptly down on his lap.

She stood before him in a little pink baby doll nightie. It had frilly narrow shoulder straps and a teddy bear motif embroidered on the yoke. The tiny pink matching panties peeped out from beneath the top. The embroidery was repeated on the panties. It was very much a little girl's nightwear. But there the resemblance ended.

Patti's breasts jiggled softly under the thin cotton. He could visualise their roundness, their firmness—detect her budding nipples chafing the soft material.

He noticed the soft swell of her hips; the gentle flaring of her plump bottom straining beneath the fabric. Long legs, smooth and brown. Such tiny feet! And she'd taken her mother's nail polish to varnish her toenails shell-pink.

"Patti." His voice was unintentionally husky as he leant forward, cupping his head in his hands in an expression of rapture.

"What are you staring at?" she retorted shakily, aware all the time of his eyes as she turned coyly away from him.

"You . . . your bottom . . . Mmm! . . ." The words slipped from his thoughts into the embarrassment of consciousness. He reddened.

Patti stood still for a moment, her lips slightly parted; about to say something cutting, but changing her mind.

"D'you want to see me?" Her voice was a dreamy whisper. "I *have* grown up, you know . . ." Blushing and proud, she looked at the carpet between her feet, her bare toes wriggling sensuously in the soft woolly pile.

The situation took her over, and cast her back into the dim recall of childhood, when John had played "Doctors" with her behind the sofa in the front room. Then, the thrill of being caught had added to the excitement. The same tension was present now.

When Patti swiftly took off the little pink nightdress and stood half-turned away from him, John found that the proper cousinly words of reproach would not come. Instead he watched her spellbound. She was wearing only the tiny inadequate panties.

The creamy white full roundness of her breasts, swinging from side to side as the top came over her head, made him swallow audibly. He felt himself stiffen. He had no idea that Patti, the girl he'd grown up with, had metamorphosed into such a curvacious young woman.

She shifted her weight gently from one foot to the other, breasts swaying slightly, bottom shuddering with an eddy of ripples. There was a teasing glint in her eyes that John found irresistible, and she was very well aware of the effect she was having upon her cousin.

"You're Dr. Spicer," she lisped like a little girl, "and I'm Nurse Crumb—remember? And I think I've got something wrong with me. . . ." She advanced towards him, slithering her feet over the carpet, while he nearly lost his balance and fell off the stool, so shocked was he at her seductiveness.

"Go on, examine me please, Doctor," she pouted, leaning forward so that her breasts fell forward like ripe heavy fruits.

The sight of her and the warm musky fragrance of her semi-naked body completely anesthetized his conscience. He placed his hands on Patti's waist and slid them up and down, before gaining courage and moving them slowly up until each breast was cupped firmly in his hands. He stroked and pulled the nipples until they hardened and Patti squirmed in response.

"My, your heart *is* beating fast!" he whispered and added, "let Dr. Spicer have a listen, please." He drew her close and put his head below her breasts, working it slowly upwards until Patti's left nipple was level with his mouth. He licked it.

"Now, Nurse, we must give the rest of you a check-up." His hands slid blindly down over her soft inviting body, following the luscious curve of her hips until they met with the resistance of her baby-doll pants. Still with his head between Patti's breasts, nuzzling into the warm flesh, he put his fingers into the waistband and, smoothing the fragile cotton down over her buttocks, he rolled them down her thighs.

Patti gasped and shuddered as his hands slid over her bare bottom and she clenched her thigh muscles tightly several times, producing a ripple of pleasure between her legs.

John's hands squeezed each bottom-cheek roughly, digging his nails urgently into her skin. Here she was—Patti, his cousin—naked except for her tiny knickers disappearing down her calves. He became aroused to a frenzy. As his hands kneaded each plump, heavy pear-drop cheek, he became overwhelmed by a single unrelenting desire: to up-end her pretty rear over his lap and soundly spank it. He shook at the mere thought. It would of course be impossible to do any such thing with Patti's parents asleep in the next room. The way *he* wanted to spank her bottom would be no light-handed token affair!

Patti was moaning at the touch of John's probing fingers between her legs. She wriggled her bottom in suggestive little jerks. She looked down at John's head cushioned between her breasts, at her wine-red nipples wet from his nibbling and sucking. He was muttering and sighing in the heat of uncontrollable excitement.

Suddenly she became frightened. Things—herself included—were going too far. What on earth was she thinking of? What was she doing?

"Stop it, John!" There was an edge to her voice—harder than she'd intended because of her own

37

excitement.

John pulled back, his fingers still embedded in the heavy crease below her cheeks, pinching their fullness. His face turned flushed and angry.

"What do you mean, 'Stop it?' That's not bloody fair, Patti! Leading me on like this. I want you!"

"Huh!" The word came out in an unpleasant sneer. Patti was frightened in earnest now and didn't know how to handle him, or herself.

"Give me my nightdress. I'm not having you staring at me like this!" she said in a shrill little voice.

"Damn you, Patti! I've bloody well had enough of you and your teasing!" There were tears of rage and frustration in his eyes. "You've ruined things between us!"

"Oh—and why?" Patti demanded, hands on hips. "Because you wanted to have your way with me, I suppose!" she hissed.

He turned on her, "Because you've always got to have things *your* way! Always got to call the tune!" His anger bubbled up within him and he glowered fiercely at her.

Patti stamped her foot defiantly and dropped the nightdress that she had clutched to her breasts. The tiny pants, in a taut tangle around her knees, made her lose balance. Once again her breasts and bottom cheeks wobbled and shuddered with her movement.

John suddenly grabbed her, infuriated by her duplicity. She had the achingly desirable body of a young woman but the face of a spoilt child. If only he could have one or the other, but he couldn't cope with both at the same time!

In blind hurt and anger he dragged her, sprawling and naked, across his lap where desire and anger fused into a burning lust.

38

She struggled and wriggled, clawing at his trousers and humping her bare bottom wildly up and down as it lay over his knees.

"My God, Patti—I'm going to pay you back," he hissed, bending low so that she could hear him above her mews of protest. "I'm going to tan your arse, good and proper!"

At this Patti turned fearfully, "John—you can't! Oh please—you can't—you'll wake up the house! John— STOP IT!"

Again she was telling him what to do. He felt sick with impotent rage and frustration. The sight of her naked rump so gloriously spreadeagled across his lap—so vulnerable and accessible—aroused him unbearably. He'd never have another chance to get even with his troublesome provocative cousin. Here was his chance—and he was wretchedly unable to take it.

He put both hands on her bottom cheeks and squeezed them violently, shaking her body from side to side, causing her buttocks to wobble sexily under his palms.

Then, hot with anger, he picked her up, threw her onto the bed, and went out of the room.

The next morning, to John's fury, Patti was convincingly gay, and behaved as if nothing had happened. The least she could do, he thought morosely, was to stop acting quite so brazen-faced. It was obvious that she had fewer misgivings about the previous night than he had. She'd led him on, broken the intangible respect and trust that had bonded them so close as cousins. He felt that a competitive element had crept into their relationship; a playing of games, where the odds were firmly stacked in her favor.

"Remember this afternoon—last lesson!" she re-

39

minded him importantly as he left the house for work.

John began work with a sinking heart. He knew it was going to be a dreadful day, with the appalling prospect of Patti sneaking into his last class. But there was some consolation. He remembered the Headmistress's words to him at the beginning of term. "We use the slipper or the hand here," she'd told him affably, "and you may apply discipline whenever you think fit." John had had no need to use either yet, but if Patti played up in his lesson, why, he wouldn't hesitate to take advantage of Miss Baker's generous and strong-minded attitude to pupil discipline. It seemed that she positively encouraged corporal punishment, "to keep the gals in line . . ."

John's misgivings about the prank that was no longer a prank were fully justified that afternoon.

The fifth form filed in as usual, giggling furtively while pretending not to notice that a teacher was present. He couldn't spot Patti at first among the green blur of so many uniformed girls. Then he saw her. With a saucy pout and slinky wiggle of her hips, she was making her way down between the rows of desks to the back row—where the "naughty" girls always liked to sit.

He was right about one thing. The uniform *was* too small for her. The straight green skirt finished a good six inches above the knee and was so tight she could only strut rather stiffly, placing one foot directly in front of the other as a model might do on a cat-walk. It made her bottom wiggle.

John frowned as he realised she was wearing stockings. But why on earth did they have to be black? The other girls wore long white socks. Her hair was swept back into its usual ponytail and tied with a green gingham ribbon. On her face she wore an expression of alarmingly sweet devilment.

John removed his jacket, although there was no sign that anyone else in the room was feeling the heat. He refused to look at Patti lest it should prompt her into mischief-making, and after a while he almost forgot she was there.

Then the trouble began.

Patti was taken aback when John refused to acknowledge her presence, and, feeling dismayed, hurt and angry, she decided to draw attention to herself. A desk lid slammed and then a pile of books crashed to the floor. John ignored it. Patti's hand went up. Again he took no notice until a hissing among the girls at the front forced him to speak.

"Yes, what is it at the back?" he snapped.

"May I have the window open, Sir?"

John stared steadfastly at a spot two inches above his cousin's head. He dare not look her directly in the eye.

Patti had to climb up onto her desk and stretch in order to reach the rope that opened the window. With all eyes turned obediently to the front, only John could see the spectacle she made.

She teetered on the slanting desk top, reaching high with one hand and trying to balance herself with the other. Her skirt at this point was working its way slowly up her thighs. It ended up above her bottom-cheeks in a line of tight folds. John had a superb view of her stocking tops and the bare thighs above; her white suspenders travelling up her flanks, which were quite visible through the semi-transparent material of her small white cotton knickers.

Then, as he stood, open-mouthed, mesmerized by Patti's provocative display, there was a loud rip and her skirt seam burst open at one side.

41

Patti turned, gasped and lost her balance. She clawed at the bookcase in her clumsy descent and it toppled heavily down with a thunderous crash onto two empty desks. To make matters worse, Patti fell on Matilda Hyde, whose heavy form puffed up like a cushion as Patti landed awkwardly on her lap.

After restoring calm and order—though shaking with rage himself—he silently conducted Patti to the front of the class where, with extreme reluctance, he sat her directly in front of his desk. Then he set the class written work to do, and sat tight-lipped, breathing heavily, in a strenuous effort to calm down.

Patti sulkily took a bottle of nail varnish from her pocket and began to paint her fingernails. John glowered at her and intimated with a wag of his finger that she'd better be careful.

In response, Patti smiled mockingly and proceeded to adjust her stockings, swinging her legs out into the aisle and pulling the ripped skirt up slowly and suggestively, exposing the delicious white softness of her inner thighs, as she inexpertly fiddled with each suspender button in turn.

John grew hot and, although he tried, he couldn't erase the powerfully arousing image of her young naked body, taunting and teasing him the night before.

Meanwhile, Patti had produced her father's hip flask from her pocket and was sipping from it, puckering her face and lips at the alien taste of the brandy. The smell of alcohol reached John's nostrils and he sat bolt upright. This time, by George, his cousin had gone too far.

"Come here," he bellowed. So she thought she'd make a mockery of his position did she? Thought he'd keep quiet because someone would find out? He'd show her!

He snatched the flask from her lips and placed it on the desk. Patti, who'd crept rather unsteadily from her seat, felt foolish. The brandy was making her face hot and red, and her head dizzy. She stood fidgeting, blushing, now that all eyes were on her guilty face, unable to look John in the eye as she leant unsteadily on his desk.

To Patti's and John's horror, the classroom door swung open at that precise moment to admit the portly perspiring bulk of Miss Claudia Baker, the Headmistress.

Immediately the mature nostrils of the lady detected the noisome fumes of alcohol. Her gaze went from Patti, to the hip flask, and finally to John.

Her lip trembled. "Has this young lady been drinking?" she inquired, hoping that the miscreant had committed such a serious crime as to merit a trip to her study after school.

"Yes, Miss Baker. She has." John gulped, but stood his ground.

The Headmistress carefully wiped her spectacles.

"Do you propose to punish her, Mr. Wallace? Or shall I relieve you of that onerous duty?" The Headmistress was hovering eagerly—intending to whisk the transgressor away to the secret torture chamber of her study.

John knew he couldn't let that happen. Miss Baker might interrogate her and discover that Patti wasn't even a pupil at the school. Besides, here was the blissful opportunity he'd waited so long for. The situation was perfect. He actually had the Headmistress's permission to punish Patti—and punish her he would!

"I shall deal with her myself, Miss Baker," he said evenly. "She's been causing me considerable trouble this afternoon."

The Headmistress looked vaguely disappointed. Patti's bottom and thighs, so tightly fettered by her raised skirt, would have made a splendid target for her new cane which had yet to be christened, but it would be good for the young master to make an example of someone early in the term. With a curt nod she bustled out of the classroom, wishing she could think of an excuse to stay and witness Patti's punishment, but vowing to return later.

"Well?" John's voice shook angrily and a thrill of excitement rippled around the room. All eyes were focused on the lovely girl trembling so tearfully beside the menacing Math master's desk.

"I said, well—*what is the meaning of this?*" He found heady pleasure in making Patti squirm, knowing that for once, the little madam was powerless to answer him back. "We don't let offences like this go unpunished, young lady!" He paused, and then continued with deliberate emphasis. "I propose to give you a sound spanking with the slipper!"

There was a hush, a holding of breath. She was to be spanked—in front of the whole class! Humiliatingly spanked!

John took a man's size 10 carpet slipper from his desk drawer and made preparations. His heavy chair grated across the little rostrum as he positioned it by the side of his desk, facing the class.

"Now, Miss!" he caught hold of the horror-struck Patti's wrists and led her to the punishment chair. With the awful command, "Come across my knee!" he pushed her down by the small of her back. Like a wooden clockwork toy, she lowered herself. She had no voice with which to protest, no strength with which to struggle. Her whole being was numbed with shame.

The class watched, horrified and fascinated. John

44

eased Patti into position, smoothing down the tightness of her skirt and patting her plump bottom so that it bounced a little in response. Then he picked up the slipper from the desk and raised it . . .

SLAP-P-P!!! The dull toneless sound of the soft-soled slipper meeting its target was the only noise in the room. It was a curious disembodied sound, like the thudding echoes heard in an underground cave or dungeon.

Patti's ponytail brushed the floor from side to side as she rose a little with the impact of the slipper. It didn't hurt very much at all and in a strange way she hoped that it would—for the truth of the matter was that Patti suffered much more in trying to fight back the tears of utter mortification. How wrong everything had gone! How *could* John do such a thing? Had he no feelings or respect for her at all?

It appeared not. "Patti, stand up. You'll have to remove your skirt!"

"Why do I have to do that?" she cried hysterically as she wriggled clumsily off his lap.

"Because I say so, Miss!!" he thundered.

Patti's hands flew jerkily to the zip but she fumbled so long with it that John slapped her hands away and promptly undid it himself. Then John looked at her, stonyfaced, as she tearfully began to obey him.

With a sob she lowered her skirt. Due to its extremely tight nature it necessitated a good deal of suggestive writhings to ease the material over her hips. Even the large rent in the side didn't make any appreciable difference.

John told her to face the class as she undressed, ostensibly so they wouldn't be granted a view of Patti's thinly clad bottom, but so that he, of course, could enjoy it all to himself.

Poor Patti! As the skirt inched down so did her white cotton knickers, and with a gasp of horror she realised that in front of her, the entire class had a revealing glimpse of her pubic triangle, while behind her, John was enjoying the sudden revelation of her deep bottom-crack and creamy white buttocks. Awkwardly—and with one hand jabbing at the descending skirt, the other yanking at the waistband of her knickers—she managed to shed the former in an untidy heap at her feet.

"Pick it up!" John commanded, "and face the class while you do so!"

She bent. John stared long and hard as the thin cotton knickers tautened with incredible elasticity over her thrust-out, bent-over buttocks. He held his breath as she stood up and the fullness of her bottom sprang back, filling the white material to bursting point.

Then she lowered herself down over his waiting lap, divested of her skirt and most of her modesty, her trimly up-turned buttocks ready for their second dose of the slipper.

The slippering recommenced, but not without some difficulty. John held her tightly around her waist with one hand because her wrigglings made it difficult for the slipper to make its mark exactly where he desired. He noticed that if the sole of the slipper did not land firmly on Patti's squirming buttocks, it made a peculiar noise which the pupils might even find comical. He didn't want a shred of amusement to reach the grim white-faced girls, so he decided to abandon the slipper and spank her soundly with his hand instead. This was infinitely more satisfying.

John's fierce angry hand spanked her tirelessly. He had been longing for years to do this! Her thighs became red, and stung with pin-prick pain. The skin below the tight elastic of her thin knickers felt deliciously warm to John, as his hand spanked the once creamy half-moons of flesh until they glowed crimson.

Patti had stuffed her hair messily into her mouth to remind her not to make any fuss. If she screwed her eyes tight and remained mute then the shocking experience would soon be over. It was, however, to be her undoing.

Outside the classroom a heavily perspiring Miss Baker was listening for the sounds of distress within—for a moan or a sob. But there was nothing.

"I find it debatable whether the punishment is having any effect at all," she muttered to herself. "The girl should be all contrition and tears by now. . . ." Frowning, she opened the door and marched into the classroom.

"Mr. Wallace," she boomed, taking in the whole scene with one shrewd glance. "I suggest that you continue on the young lady's bare bottom." She paused to wipe her glasses. "I always find that the girls respond more satisfactorily to correction when they are knickerless."

John blinked. To obey the Headmistress's injunction would be like the passport to a dream. He slipped his fingers greedily inside Patti's knickers, savouring every second of their slow descent. Patti made no sound. She had frozen.

Down they came, baring inch by inch her pert round bottom, with all the smoothness of a peach, and the milky paleness of cream. He studied the long dark shadow of her bottom cleft, his eyes craning to see yet more of her precious secrets—secrets that were now clamped tightly between the trembling muscles of her thighs.

Miss Baker stared in amazement and scandalized

disapproval. As Patti's knickers slid down her legs, the Headmistressed noticed a conspicuous damp patch in their gusset. John saw it, too, and, concealing the sticky wet stain with his hand, he removed the knickers quickly and pocketed them.

Patti moaned as John hugged her half-naked body closer to him. She could feel how excited he was.

And why had little Patti got shamefully wet knickers? Could it be that she, too, was deliriously excited by the prospect of a thoroughly humiliating bare-bottom spanking across his knee? The extraordinary revelation made him strain towards her, so that his tumescence began to pump urgently against her bare thigh.

SMACK!!!   SMACK!!!   SMACK!!!   SMACK!!! SMACK!!! SMACK!!!

"OOOOH-H-H!!! OW-W-W!!!"

Patti twisted her head round in anguish, and John caught her agonised expression. Her cheeks were bright red and her eyes were wild, he noted to his immense satisfaction.

Miss Baker stood breathing heavily and murmuring approval as the redness of her naughty pupil's backside rapidly darkened into purple.

SMACK!!!   SMACK!!!   SMACK!!!   SMACK!!! SMACK!!! SMACK!!!

Many of the class were sniffing and crying in sympathy. Miss Baker was well-satisfied that this exemplary punishment was having a salutary effect on the rest of the girls.

It was then Patti found her voice. Her bottom had reached the stage where it was so excruciatingly painful that she had to give vent to her feelings. Loud choking sobs broke free from her lips, accompanied by desperate cries of "Please! Oh ple-e-e-se!!! I'll do anything you say! ANYTHING!!! Please! I've had enough! Oh! Oh! Ooh! Oooooh!!!"

Miss Baker smiled.

John encouraged her wails, pleadings, and tears by undoing the suspenders of her black stockings—which had twisted right round to the back of her thighs—and crimsoning any areas of her writhing buttocks that he had missed. Patti's body rolled and humped against him in her distress—stimulating him to a point where he felt it would be impossible to go on without climaxing. Then he suddenly became aware that the note of distress in Patti's sobbing had changed.

She lay in such a position that with the pressure of each spank her bottom was pushed, firm and hard, down onto John's trousered thighs. To dissipate the pain, and enhance the peculiarly compulsive sensations she felt down between her legs, Patti started to rock back and forth on his knees. She began to moan—each sound a gasping crescendo—much to the horrified excitement of the class. And, amid the folds of her clothes, John had slipped his hand down into the wetness between her thighs . . .

The black stockings had slipped comically down her legs. Her blouse had risen so high that her bare breasts peeped out beneath it. And, drawing shameful attention to itself, was her well-spanked bottom—thrusting up and down in response to every smack. John's hidden finger was working away rhythmically all the while . . .

Suddenly her body grew dramatically rigid, and Patti's cries of pain became mingled with pleasure. Then she went limp and hung across John's lap, quiet, submissive, and utterly humiliated as the class filed out in silence.

Patti, too, was allowed to leave, and she ran out of

the classroom without so much as a glance at Miss Baker or her cousin. Of course she forgot about her knickers in his pocket and had to wait outside the school, shivering until he could come out and drive her home. To add to her shame, a wicked gust of wind blew up her torn skirt, affording a fascinating view of her naked crimson bottom cheeks to passers-by—boys from the nearby grammar school.

John drove home carefully, because Patti couldn't sit in the seat and had to kneel backwards—so painfully was her behind smarting.

The house was empty and John told a strangely quiet and submissive Patti to take off her skirt and walk upstairs in front of him and go into his bedroom. She obeyed without a murmur.

"Well, what have you to say for yourself?" he asked gently as she stood before him, looking down at her feet.

"I . . . I think that was my last p-prank," she whispered, stumbling over the word that reminded her so painfully of another. "And," she paused before daring to glance quickly at him, "I . . . I think I'm not a child anymore. . . ."

John began to undress quickly, pausing now and then to stroke Patti's still warm bottom-cheeks.

"But you're not a woman are you?" he teased softly.

Slowly, Patti began to undo her blouse.

"Not yet," she said. And blushed.

A Reciprocal Arrangement

The sound was unmistakeable, yet Maudie refused to believe what she'd heard. From the open vicarage windows above her the whimpering animal-like cries pierced the September twilight. She stood at the bottom of the steep drive and peered up through the dense pines and larches, fragrantly resinous from the afternoon showers. If she refused to acknowledge what she'd heard, then she had every reason to carry on walking.

The cries reminded her of an incident in her adolescence when she'd overheard a couple making love in a field, and had been overwhelmed with vicarious desire to watch the naked, humping bodies without being seen. She'd stood, aroused by fear yet impotently rooted to the spot. Then, gaining courage by convincing herself that she'd imagined the soft moaning sighs, she'd walked calmly through the long grass and stood watching as the man reached a noisy climax. He saw her. She looked suitably shocked. She apologised profusely, saying she'd no idea what they were doing.

Maudie stood twisting her long fair hair around her finger, feeling the old indecision paralyse her again. Should she go on?

The rectory was half-hidden by the sombre ranks of conifers, but Maudie glimpsed its startling canary-yellow door and window frames through the needled trunks. One window was open and glinted thickly like a blind man's eye. So like the Reverend John Woolley,

51

she thought, to leave his window open in all weathers. She remembered sitting at his Sunday school classes over ten years ago, shivering in her thin gingham dress like the other children—all because the vicar wanted to smell the piquancy of the sharp winter weather.

The shrill cries ceased abruptly and Maudie decided to carry on. She trod carefully, avoiding the loud crunch of fir cones underfoot and the wide areas of gravelly silt that fingered down the grey drive like an enormous slippery stain.

The isolated sounds about her seemed ridiculously magnified: her own breathing that fluttered with a sharp excitement; the sudden staccato thunderings of a branchful of raindrops and fir cones smattering down on the tarmac around her. Her ears strained through the silence to catch the other noise. . . .

At the top of the drive where it forked, Maudie turned right and walked up three slate steps, flanked on either side by the hooded darkness of the aging yews. She emerged some ten feet away from the open study window. It was unfastened and in danger of slamming shut in a sudden violent gust of wind.

The path ran below the study window and along the entire front of the house under the dripping eaves. It was narrow and thick with tell-tale gravel and, not wishing to advertise her presence, Maudie suffered her high-heels to sink ignominiously into the wet grass of the lawn which dropped away sharply into a steep untended slope. She smoothed her hands over the neat grey flannel suit, picking off imaginary wisps of fluff and trying not to notice that the expensive leather heels were rapidly becoming coated with thick wedges of grass and mud and that her feet were now quite unnecessarily wet. Although her ears were straining for the faintest imaginings of a noise, there was nothing. Maudie felt disappointed and ashamed.

She stood still for a moment, her heels sinking deep into the soft wet earth, wondering what to do next. Sighing, she looked over the house, absorbing the old familiar features—her eyes like a cine camera which records but does not see.

Exactly in the middle of the building the ugly grey stone steps, complete with two unfilled concrete urns, rose to the front door. The urns looked odd and out of place, as did the clumsy ornate trellising either side which supported the huge porch canopy. The attempt to instill fake grandeur into a rather spartan, ordinary house hadn't worked. Somebody had intended the steps and porch to be a symbolic bridge between the parish and its intercessor with God. A place where hats and caps were supposedly removed, ties adjusted and children admonished before entering.

Yet the priest who dwelt within these imposing portals was not as lofty and remote from the parish as some would have liked to think—for halfway up the soft yellow stone the Sunday school children had scrawled "I love Bobby" and "Kathleen," amid even cruder graffiti. The vicar had ignored them, and their irreverence was only partially covered by the slow-spreading fish-scale branches of a cotoneaster, bloody with berries.

"I'm out of breath," Maudie panted, defending her behaviour to the crows that cawked mournfully in the darkening woods, "and it's the first time back since—." She glanced down at the reproachful pale band of flesh on the third finger of her left hand. The ring was some-where in her handbag and in a spasm of nervous guilt she searched through its contents. She'd better put it on—after all, it was John Woolley who'd married her to Daniel.

Suddenly the study window swung inwards. The tiny gold ring that Maudie was about to slip on her finger flew out of her hand and landed in the long wet grass. She jerked her head up just in time to see a large grey-suited arm extend through the window, grasp the catch, and close it with ill-judged force. It was as if he knew Maudie was there.

She shut her handbag and sank desperately to her knees, scrabbling among the grass for the missing ring. Her fine shoulder-length hair falling over her face became damp and tangled with grass as she repeatedly swept it back. Cold muddy wetness seeped into her flimsy shoes. She felt a fool. Squatting uneasily on her haunches, her wet skirt hem rising above the tops of her black stockings, she thought with wistful anger about Mona. Mona, her twin, with the crisp boyish hair, her ill-disciplined figure concealed by shapeless but comfortable dungarees. Shamelessly divorced, defiantly feminist. Mona, who in half an hour would expect her back, ply her with home-brewed beer and awkward questions, and tell her that she was a fool to have any conscience at all.

Now she could hear voices in the study. She recognised John Woolley's slow deliberate burr that never altered, even in his sermons. And there was the thin sulky piping of a girl. Maudie detected a self-righteousness in the girls' voice—proud of her wrong-doing. The vicar repeated a command, the words of which were an infuriating blur. Then silence.

Maudie crouched, placing her hands flat among the wet grass, and held her breath. She looked up anxiously at the upstairs windows, scanning them for the face of Mrs. Bunnie, the silent unblinking housekeeper whose presence could always be felt by visiting parishioners, looking down on them, her body swathed

behind the curtains and her small button-bright
peeping over the yashmak edge of the drapery.

Maudie was too agitated to continue her search for
the ring. Besides, it was growing perceptibly darker
by the minute. She would have to return for it in the
morning.

The sounds began again. Maudie almost choked. It
must be Mrs. Bunnie, she thought desperately as sweat
began to trickle under her arms.

It *had* to be Mrs. Bunnie! Nobody could punch pillows into shape, or beat carpets with quite the vicious-
ness of *that* woman, who spent her life doing to inani-
mate objects what she could not do to her fellows.

Yes, Mrs. Bunnie was up there somewhere, even
now, giving the Reverend Woolley's pillows such a
pummelling. WHACK!!! The rugs are getting it now.
One, two, three—WHACK!!! How many carpet beaters
does she get through in a week? Must flay them to
shreds. Bits of wool and tufts torn out, flying all over
the room. Pillows with dents like mine craters in them.
WHACK!!! Ooh, she makes me shudder . . . split
canes, frayed ends, steady dry palm gripping tight . . .
I've never heard anything like—

Maudie's head was spinning, her body was weak
with fear and excitement. She lost her balance as her
muddy high heels caught one another. She swayed and
fell, nose-diving into the wet luscious grass. The wetness soaked through her skirt and stockings, to the
"frilly nonsense," as Mona called them, of her filmy
underslip and little white nylon panties.

The girl was being spanked! Spanked in the
Reverend John Woolley's study!

Maudie felt the cool wetness of the grass on her bare
thighs as she struggled to get up. WHACK!!! She slid

down again and pressed herself hard against the sodden earth. The cries had changed from intermittent pleadings to a continuous wail. Maudie got to her feet and tottered towards the window.

She stood on tiptoe and looked in.

The first thing she saw was the bare bottom of a girl. It was quite a big bottom, heavily built about the hips—but assuming unnatural prominence owing to its almost comically elevated posture, bent shamefully across the Reverend John Woolley's lap.

Her cheap blue dress was neatly folded in a tight roll of material above her waist, and in a pathetic crumple about her ankles lay her faded blue cotton briefs. Her legs were sandwiched tightly together, emphasizing the deep crease below her buttocks which were wobbling obscenely with every resounding blow.

Struggling wildly, the girl twisted her head round and gazed in misery and terror at her chastiser. Instantly Maudie recognized the sluttish features of Angela Gordon, the teenage daughter of one of the village's least well-to-do families, the father of whom was perennially in trouble with the police.

Maudie uttered a wail of disgust. She wanted to blot out everything she'd seen—but she somehow couldn't take her eyes away from that broad powerful hand as, time and time again, it exploded with sickening impact and regularity upon that writhing, crimson behind.

She found it hard to look him in the face. Was this really the man whose Confirmation classes she'd attended? Had he no thought for his reputation—let alone his calling—to leave the study window wide open so that anyone passing could hear? Choking back tears of shock, she forced herself to look at the man she'd known ever since she was a child.

He was somberly dressed as usual, no different in

appearance from the last time she'd seen him about two years ago. Thick hair but greying, large build, glasses—there was nothing remarkable about him at all. Except that he had the kindest, most serene face of anyone she'd ever known.

And he was spanking Angela Gordon's bare backside.

Through the rain-smeared window and her tears, Maudie watched in wretched confusion as his arm rose rhythmically in the air and descended in a blur, his heavy palm flattened deliberately into a thick wedge to more effectively belabour those generous expanses of flesh that were rapidly acquiring a shade of deep purple. Angela's coarse surly face twisted into a grimace of agony, revealing a mouth overcrowded with teeth and a fat pink tongue. She was unashamedly yelling her head off.

Maudie's knuckles grew white as she gripped the window ledge and she tensed every muscle in her body until she ached, in response to each ear-splitting detonation of sound. As she watched, the girl's chubby legs inched apart and she threw her hips from side to side in a clumsy parody of erotic abandonment. The sight of the semi-naked adolescent body was shocking enough in itself—almost rivaling the fascinated horror Maudie felt for the merciless rise and fall of the Reverend Woolley's sinewy right arm. As the unfortunate girl's legs grew wider apart, the thick dark bush of pubic hair fuzzed out from between her thighs. Maudie choked with disgust and slid awkwardly down from the window.

Shaking uncontrollably as if she herself had been struck, she walked quietly down the path. Her legs were heavy with a strange kind of weakness.

"Bloody hell!" It was Mona's usual exclamation. "Whatever happened to you?" She circled around her sister cautiously, as if Maudie's dirty, dishevelled state carried something infectious. "Did someone attack you?"

"No." Maudie's voice was flat and toneless as she walked into the low-ceilinged living room of her sister's cottage. She'd tried to enter quietly, hoping to avoid Mona's sharp critical eyes, but Mona was making a big performance of waiting for her.

"You've been gone ages," she said reproachfully, turning to Maudie who was wearily removing her jacket. "So I simply had to have one of these!" She retrieved a large glass full of yeasty-smelling home-made beer which she'd hidden behind a calendar, in case it hadn't been Maudie.

Maudie said nothing, but looked away as Mona greedily raised the glass to her lips. She knew it would be impossible to escape to her bedroom and change before giving her sister a satisfactory explanation, so she went into the kitchen to make a cup of tea. Predictably, Mona followed her.

"Go on then. Tell me what happened." She placed herself in the way of Maudie's preparations. "And don't say you fell over, either."

"I'm sorry to disappoint you, but that's exactly what did happen." Maudie heaved a sigh and looked directly into her sister's eyes—eyes of intense blue, exactly like her own. But whereas Maudie's shone with an honest, often troubled candour—Mona's had a hard cynicism.

It was difficult to believe they were sisters. Although not identical, they were twins, sharing the same silvery-streaked hair and rather sharp angular features—wide mouths and tip-tilted noses.

"I bet you've been having it off in a field with one of

the village studs—you always were a sly one, Maudie!"
Mona laughed coarsely. Little brown bubbles of beer
twinkled on her upper lip, like a moustache. Maudie
blushed at the accusation, despite her innocence.

"Hasn't Daniel even contacted you once since you
two split up?" Mona inquired, changing the subject
while her sister poured the tea. Maudie shook her head.
Not a word, not a line since he'd walked out of their
South London flat nearly a week ago. She'd sat feverishly waiting by the phone for days and nights on end.
Nothing. She felt sick with worry and guilt. He could
be dead, for all she knew.

"Bastard!" Mona exclaimed, her hands on her hips
as though squaring up aggressively to the entire male
species. "All men are bastards, Maudie, take it from
me."

"Don't you ever miss Mike?" Maudie ventured—
then immediately wished she hadn't said it, since she
knew full well the kind of reaction it would provoke.

Mona laughed bitterly. "Miss Mike? That weak
pathetic little shit? Do you know, Maudie, he was
absolutely fucking useless in bed. Couldn't even get it
up most of the time."

Maudie looked away in embarrassment. She would
never dream of discussing her conjugal sex life so blatantly with anyone—even though Daniel and she had
separated.

"Best thing I ever did was to kick Mike out of the
house. Should have done it years ago," Mona said,
plonking her shapeless buttocks on the kitchen table
and lighting up a cigarette before taking another noisy
swig from her beer. She sniggered self-righteously and
added, "Take my advice, Maudie girl, go get yourself
a vibrator. A portable prick, ever eager to please—
always ready, willing and able! Wanna borrow mine

tonight? Take it to bed with you?" She burped noisily and downed the remainder of her beer.

Maudie shook her head. "No thanks, Mona." How like her sister to reduce human relationships to mere animality. She clearly felt no guilt at all about getting rid of Mike.

But for Maudie, things couldn't have been more different. She blamed no one but herself for Daniel's leaving. They'd rowed horribly that morning, the morning of his birthday. It had been she who started it, over a stupid birthday card one of the girls at his work had sent him. As usual, Maudie had blown her top— raved and screamed at him that he was having an affair with an office tart. Not for the first time, she told him to pack his bags and get out.

But on this occasion he took her at her word. Hastily stuffing a suitcase with clothes, he stalked out of the poky little flat calling her a crazy bitch, and that he wasn't prepared to put up with her pathological behaviour any longer.

Maudie had just stood there, white-faced in dazed disbelief, watching him go. An apology hung about her lips like an imminent shower of rain—but somehow she couldn't frame it into words. When at last she managed to stammer out, "I'm sorry," it was too late. He'd already slammed the outer door and gone.

She tried phoning his office at the time he should have reached there, but they told her he'd already been in touch to say he was sick.

That's why she'd come back here—to the village where Mona still lived in the family cottage and where Daniel and Maudie had grown up, sweethearts ever since they were fifteen.

He must be here, staying at his father's house. There was nowhere else he could be.

She'd thought of phoning from London, but she couldn't face the ordeal of talking to Daniel over the telephone. She'd always hated phones—they made her stammer and forget what it was she had to say.

Instead, she rang Mona to ask if she could put her up, and came down on the next train. Only when she stood face to face with Mona in the cottage doorway did she find the courage to tell her what had happened. Mona's reaction, a violent outcry against the perfidy of men and a convincing display of sisterly tears, had been just as Maudie had predicted.

Mona it was who, after ten minutes' emotional bludgeoning, had bullied her cringing sister into removing her wedding ring. "They symbolize male oppression of womanhood," she'd declared indignantly. "Don't you *dare* let me see you wearing it again!" Maudie had twisted it off her finger and thrust it in a quick guilty movement deep into the furthermost recesses of her handbag.

Now that she'd had the chance to stretch her legs and escape for a while from the ministrations of her sister, Maudie felt a little bit better—in spite of the disturbing thing that had happened during the walk.

Tomorrow morning she would go and retrieve her wedding ring. Then she would seek out Daniel at his father's.

She found the ring next day quite easily. It was glinting in the sun amid the gravel of the path that skirted the house. She bent to pick it up, the narrow skirt of her suit—which she'd lovingly sponged clean and hung up to dry the night before—tightening around her thighs. Then she slipped it back onto her finger and, her high heels tottering unsteadily on the gravel path, made her way round towards the front door. She rang the bell.

Mrs. Bunnie's unblinking button eyes scrutinised her grudgingly. "Oh, so it's you, is it? I suppose you've come to see the vicar. He's in the study working. He won't take kindly to being disturbed at this hour of the morning—but since you're here, best come in."

Maudie edged past her and walked into the gloomy hall. She could sense the housekeeper's cold severity boring into her from behind, frowning at her figure-hugging suit, the tiny jacket with its peplum pleat, the accentuated curves of her buttocks beneath the narrow calf-length skirt, the sheer black seamed stockings—the clothes Daniel loved to see her in, which was why she had worn them today. She caught herself feeling rather as Angela Gordon must have felt yesterday evening when she had been shown into the Reverend Woolley's study by the housekeeper in order to be soundly spanked for her sins. Only Maudie wasn't a snivelling adolescent like Angela, wearing her elder sister's shabby hand-me-downs. She was a grown woman of twenty-five.

The study was exactly as she'd remembered it. Nothing had changed. The old red Axminster carpet looked even more patchy and threadbare, and the bookshelves lining the right hand wall from floor to ceiling sagged in the middle more drunkenly than ever beneath the weight of the dusty old leather-bound volumes. Proudly displayed on the mantelshelf above the empty grate were three small, badly executed watercolours—one of the Tamar Bridge and two of a Cornish fishing village. The man who had painted them was at his desk by the window, sitting on the old upright chair with its frayed, faded green and brown tapestry seat. He was reading *The Diary of Francis Kilvert*.

He jumped up immediately and embraced Maudie in a powerful hug, from which she discreetly tried to wriggle free—for, despite his serenely beatific demeanor, she'd always been secretly afraid of him. And how many other of his parishioners' daughters had he dutifully spanked here, in his study? She remembered how terrified she'd been when, as a young girl, she'd attended his Confirmation classes. If ever a girl was late for class he'd smile benignly—so that no one knew whether he was joking or in earnest—and say: "Why, Sarah, I've a good mind to put you across my knee and smack your bottom," and the poor girl would go pink with embarrassment. Maudie's reaction to such incidents had been one of fearful fascination, and she always made a point of being strictly punctual for the classes. At all other times she gave the Reverend Woolley a wide berth.

But that was no longer possible when she became the girlfriend of his son, Daniel. During their courtship, Daniel's father was always extremely kind to Maudie—in all respects the fond future father-in-law. Even so, there was something intangible about him which made Maudie feel nervous about being left alone in the room with him.

"I've come about Daniel," she said in a quiet flat voice. "He's left me."

"I know, my poor child," he stroked her hair consolingly. "I was going to phone you but then I thought, better to wait and tell you in person. I knew you'd come."

"Tell me what in person? Where's Daniel? Isn't he here?" She looked up at him, fearing the worst.

"He only stayed a couple of days. He's gone to Canada—for good, I'm afraid." Maudie began to cry. "He phoned up David—you know, his old college friend who works in Vancouver. David said he could easily get him a job in his computer firm. He flew from London yesterday."

The tears trickled down Maudie's cheeks; it felt to her as though her heart was breaking. "D-didn't he say anything about me?" she sobbed.

"Only that he was sure it was all over between you two, and he wanted to begin a new life somewhere far away from you. I told him what a fool he was, what a wonderful girl you are, and that he ought at least to give it another go. Damn it all, it was me that married the pair of you!" He laughed mirthlessly and gazed out of the window at the long grass, dank and glistening from the overnight rain.

"It was all my fault. I behaved abominably," Maudie murmured, drying her tears with a dainty little white handkerchief. Her father-in-law shook his head, his pale blue eyes shining with the light of superior wisdom.

"It's never just one person's fault when things go wrong in a relationship, my child. You were unwise to lose your temper with him the way you did, but you and I both know that Daniel, too, has more than his fair share of faults—the biggest of which is that of running away from a problem." He took her hand and stroked it comfortingly. "Let's hope that in time he'll see what a dreadful mistake he's made. He'll come back—just you wait and see if he doesn't."

He led her over to the chair and made her sit down, for she was numb and weak with shock. "I'll go and get Mrs. Bunnie to make us some tea," he suggested. "Sadly, she'll be leaving me very soon, and then I too will be alone. Her mother is terminally ill and needs constant caring." He uttered a prolonged sigh, as if shouldering all the burdens of the world. Maudie looked at him and saw an isolated lonely man, still young and active despite his middle age. It made what she'd witnessed outside his window last night perhaps a little more understandable—if no less inexcusable.

He returned with the tea and they drank it together in silence. Finally Maudie spoke. "I feel so dreadful, Mr. Woolley, not just about hurting Daniel, but about hurting you, too. The folks in the village, they're such gossips. They'll make such a meal of all this—the vicar's son's marriage breaking up . . . and after he married them, too. It all seems like a nightmare! Oh please help me—it feels like my life's gone all to pieces. There's nothing left to cling on to." She buried her head in her hands and wept silently. When he placed his arm around her shoulders, she felt only relief and gratitude that here at least was someone who understood and cared—Daniel's father.

"Maudie, dear," he spoke tentatively in her ear, "there is something I could do that would maybe help."

"What is it?" she said, raising her head, desperately eager for anything that might soothe the pain inside her.

"When you hurt yourself," he explained, "say you cut your finger or stub your toe, do you ever bite your lip?"

What a strange question, she thought. After a moment's consideration she said, "Yes, I do bite my lip when I'm in pain. In fact," she smiled shyly, "I'm doing it right now." Sure enough, her lower lip looked red and slightly swollen where she'd caught it between her teeth.

"Exactly, Maudie," he went on, "the pain in your lip helps to neutralize the pain in your soul—except that," he smiled sympathetically, "in this instance you need to experience a somewhat stronger pain than just a bitten lip."

With a jolt, Maudie realised what he was about to say. Angela Gordon atoning for whatever heinous crime she'd committed by undergoing physical chastisement—and departing from his study at the end of it with a painful bottom, but with a clean, untroubled conscience.

And, to her amazement, Maudie found herself wishing desperately that the Reverend John Woolley would take a stick to her bottom and beat it black and blue—for whatever offence Angela Gordon had been guilty of, it was surely nothing compared to Maudie willfully wrecking her own marriage beyond repair. What sin could there possibly be worse than that?

"I want you to punish me physically, Mr. Woolley, as severely as you can," she said slowly and deliberately, looking him in the eye.

For a moment he simply stared at her in astonishment, speechless at how uncannily she had read his thoughts, but he thought it best to conceal his surprise in case she changed her mind. He was immeasurably relieved, too, that such a suggestion had come from her. He had been in the process of working his way as tactfully as he could towards it, but now that Maudie herself had become the instigator of the idea, he could in no way be liable for any blame afterwards.

"A rather unusual request for a lovely young woman to ask of her priest and father-in-law," he queried, raising his eyebrows and trying hard not to appear too eager. "But nevertheless I think a perfectly valid one," he added quickly. "Yes," he stroked his chin thoughtfully, as if subjecting Maudie's immensely thrilling suggestion to the most rigorous scrutiny. "Yes, I should imagine that a smarting backside would go a long way to help relieve the emotional anguish of the last few days. In the early days of the Christian Church, flagellation was used to cure all manner of ills and it is still practiced in some monasteries today. As a matter of fact, I have quite an extensive library on the subject," he said, pointing at a section of books on the top-most shelf. Maudie looked at them warily and imagined him poring over them in gloating delight, night after night, into the small hours of the morning.

He removed his spectacles and methodically wiped the clouded lenses with his handkerchief, in an effort to quell his growing excitement. Above all, he had to seem calm and unconcerned. "Would you like to have a few hours to think about it, Maudie," he asked casually, pretending to examine his lenses. "Then come back later this afternoon? Or would you prefer it to be done here and now?" He felt obliged to say this, even though it might place the whole thing at risk.

"I think I'd rather get it over and done with right away, if you don't mind," Maudie said, fiddling nervously with her silver bracelet and recalling her feelings about going to the dentist. The only times she could ever bear to visit him were when she was actually suffering from unbearable toothache. If she went away now she might lose her nerve and not come back. At that moment, she wanted nothing more than for him to whip her to the bone. If she postponed it and later chickened out, she'd never forgive herself.

"You mean strike while the iron's hot? I really do admire your guts, Maudie. I must admit I never thought you had it in you!" He smiled, enormously relieved, then drew the curtains and went over to lock the door. Angela Gordon was a dirty-minded, promiscuous little tart and there were plenty of legitimate excuses for tanning her bottom. But Maudie was a different matter altogether, and if anyone were to find out—even loyal Mrs. Bunnie—he might have to face embarrassing questions.

"What are you going to use to—you know, to. . . ?" She somehow couldn't bring herself to say the actual words. She had a mental picture of a bamboo cane recruited from the garden shed—or maybe his leather belt. Not his hand, for that would be too personal, too intimate. He was going to be, after all, simply the vehicle of punishment—someone willing to carry it out.

"I shall use this." He went over to his desk and from out of the top drawer produced a foot-long wooden clothesbrush which he laid bristle-side downwards on the desk surface. Above its handle, the clothesbrush's back was solid and oval.

As Maudie stared at it she felt her skin prickle in terror. She'd noticed the ease with which the Reverend Woolley had immediately located such an ideal instrument of correction. Obviously, then, she was not the first female whom he had beaten in this way.

Humming cheerfully, he replaced *The Diary of Francis Kilvert* in the bookcase and cleared his desk of all impedimenta. He took off his grey suit jacket and hung it on a nearby hook on the wall. "Please remove your skirt and top, Maudie," he said, calmly rolling up his shirtsleeves.

"What?"

He smiled compassionately. "Please do as I say, Maudie, it's for the best. You wouldn't feel it as much under those layers of clothing—and that skirt you're wearing is far too tight to roll up."

"Daniel loved it," she retorted in defense of it. As she spoke them, she thought how vacuous the words sounded—they were the first words to come into her head.

"I dare say. You look very nice in it—it suits your figure." His eyes lingered over the curves of her hips. "But I'm afraid it will have to come off."

Maudie's cheeks reddened. It hadn't occurred to her that she would have to undress. But it was too late to back out now. She'd given her word.

She took off her dainty little jacket which he whisked from her grasp, folded in two and laid on the seat of the chair. Then she unzipped her skirt at the back and wriggled it embarrassedly down to her ankles. Her cheeks burning with shame, she stepped out of it, picked it up, handed it to him, and he placed it neatly on top of her jacket.

Maudie felt wretched, standing there in just her cream cotton blouse and white nylon underslip. The clothesbrush seemed bigger and heavier each time she looked at it. She couldn't stop wondering how painful it was going to be.

"Take down your petticoat, too, Maudie," she heard him murmur solicitously. "I can't punish you while you've got it on."

"It's an underslip, not a petticoat," she said hastily without thinking—as pedantic as any woman when it came to the technicalities of lingerie.

"I stand corrected, Maudie," he chuckled at the furiously blushing woman. "Well, kindly take it off whatever it is."

"But—" she protested, fighting back the sob in her throat. "It's so dreadfully shameful!" Beneath her slip she was only wearing flimsy panties and a tiny garter belt to hold up her black stockings. She hadn't expected it to be like this—so personal, so degradingly intimate. A series of painful whacks across the seat of her skirt maybe . . . but not this bizarre pornographic slow strip-tease to order . . .

"Come along, my dear, let's get this unpleasant business over and done with, shall we?" He chivvied her along, a trifle impatient now.

Desperately wishing she hadn't got herself into this situation, Maudie reached for the elasticated waistband and peeled down the underslip. Its hem caught beneath her left shoe. She stumbled and almost fell. The garment ripped.

"Oh dear me, now see what you've done, careless girl!" The Reverend Woolley reproved her gently, like a father scolding a fractious child. Maudie stamped her foot pettishly and, picking up the crumpled garment, examined the tear.

"My best underslip—ruined!" she wailed in disproportionate grief.

Maudie possessed excellent legs, and the flawless sheen of her black stockings only emphasised their elegant neatness. Above the stocking tops the flesh was soft yet firm, and white as ivory. Her white nylon panties, flimsily diaphanous, were patently not designed to conceal, for the Reverend Woolley could quite clearly see the little blond hairs around her pubis.

The drama of the torn slip took a minute or two to die down. Maudie clutched it obstinately to her lower regions and showed great reluctance to part with it, but after suitable encouragements and one or two discreetly veiled threats from the Reverend Woolley, she was finally persuaded to do so.

Then he pushed her down across the desk, instructing her to grip the farther edge. Maudie felt horribly uncomfortable, breasts flattened against the desk top, head twisted to one side, strands of hair falling in her eyes, the sharp edge of the desk digging into her thighs above her stocking tops. Above all, her scantily clad bottom was humiliatingly raised and appallingly vulnerable. Her sole shred of comfort was that at least he hadn't made her remove her panties.

Nevertheless he was not satisfied with them as they were. So, to her horror and disgust, he hooked a finger of each hand into the edges of them, just below her seat, then, sliding his fingers slowly up along her bottom crack, he tucked the panties right inside her cleft. His patient fingers teased and stretched the thin nylon into the deep division between her bottomcheeks. Maudie squeezed them tightly together in self-protection.

During this operation—an excruciatingly embarrassing one for Maudie—it was hardly surprising that the Reverend Woolley's fingers encountered not only the tight lips of her sex, but also her delicate little anus. When that happened she let out a whimper of mortification, twisting her head round with difficulty and looking back at him beseechingly.

His task completed, her buttocks were now completely bare: two luscious orbs of firm flesh. Her cleft and all that lay therein was discreetly veiled by the tautly folded nylon strand—yet the total effect was somehow more erotic than if she were completely naked.

He picked up the clothesbrush from the desk and moved into position behind her. "Relax your bottom, Maudie," he said, frowning at the clenched, dimpling target. Obediently the buttocks slackened into more rounded prominence, and her breathing started to quicken and deepen as if she were gasping for air.

The sight of Maudie's unprotected bottom held him spellbound for a while. It looked so deliciously pert and cheeky—it thoroughly deserved to be taken down a peg or two.

He was going to take his time over punishing it. Begin the beating with judicious moderation to

71

desensitise the flesh—then build up gradually to an almighty crescendo of cruel thudding whacks that would leave Maudie's beautiful bottom blue with bruises for days. . . .

He took aim. Maudie turned, caught sight of the clothesbrush raised behind her, flinched, shut her eyes and quickly turned her head away.

One! Two! Three! Four! Five! Six! Seven!

The clothesbrush attacked Maudie's buttocks with crisp regularity. They flattened and juddered with each loud impact. Maudie greeted each stroke as it landed with a shrill cry of pain.

The Reverend Woolley dealt with each buttock separately, working his way outwards from the cleft, pausing when he reached the outer extremity—only to recommence on the other cheek. He wielded the clothesbrush expertly, not with the full force of his arm but rather with a flicking action of the wrist. He didn't want to bruise Maudie—at least not yet.

In this manner he administered two dozen or so strokes, causing the flesh to redden dramatically. The fiery base of pain he had created on her out-thrust seat made Maudie gasp and squirm frantically.

Pausing for a while to let the pain soak into her cheeks, he walked round to the other side of the desk and faced her.

"Look at me, Maudie," he said, his bright shining eyes, seen indistinctly behind blurred spectacles, betraying his excitement. Maudie slowly raised her head and gazed at him in shameful consternation. Her face, though wet with nervous perspiration, had lost none of its prettiness.

He spoke with infinite concern, almost tenderness, worried that he might already have taken her beyond the limit of her pain threshold. "How do you feel, my poor child? Bottom sore?" She nodded ruefully. "Have you had enough?" he asked her, hoping and praying that she hadn't.

Her lips quivered but she stayed silent, trapped by the look of unspeakable intimacy he was giving her. Unable to tear her eyes away from his keen, omniscient smile, Maudie was like a rabbit caught in the approaching glare of a car's headlamps.

Worse than that, she felt she was actually colluding in his defiling of her—gaining her own perverse satisfaction from it, too, for her sex was starting to dilate and moisten uncontrollably. What crazy lemming-like impulse was it that kept her silent, when just a single word from her would bring the dreadful beating to an end?

"Very well, Maudie, since you wish it, I shall carry on." He could barely contain the jubilance in his voice.

This time he did it differently, removing her pile of clothing from the chair so that he could sit down on it. Then, he held her firmly by the wrist, pulling her across his knee—like he did Angela Richards.

"Please—not like this!" Maudie cried out in alarm, bracing herself with her feet on the floor, her body straight and rigid as an arrow. He clasped her tightly round the waist, pulling her further over his lap until her feet left the floor and began to kick wildly in the air—her face upside down, inches from the threadbare carpet, the blood rushing to her head and her silver-blonde hair dangling in her face.

Snatching the clothesbrush, he raised it at arm's length and brought it down much more heavily than before on Maudie's bottom, directly above the cleft, flattening both cheeks. The impact sounded like a muffled detonation. Maudie howled full-throatedly as the clothesbrush fell again. She tried desperately to wriggle free, but he gripped her so securely round the waist that only her legs and her bottom were able to move.

And when, as a result of her contortions, the flailing clothesbrush missed its intended target altogether and landed inside on the soft vulnerable flesh of her inner thigh—causing her to howl more loudly than ever—Maudie gave up trying to resist and just lay there limply across his lap, allowing the clothesbrush to attack whatever area of her bottom, now visibly streaked with purple blotches and with more than a hint of bruising, it chose to visit.

Years before, in her mid-teens, Maudie had been shown a pornographic magazine by Kerry, her best friend at the time, who'd filched it from her father's bedroom. With feelings of excited disbelief, Maudie had returned over and over again to the page containing a rather crude black-and-white drawing of a woman with ludicrously developed breasts and buttocks being spanked over a man's knee. She was wearing just stockings and garter belt, and her bottom was darkly shaded to depict the effects of the spanking.

What had fascinated Maudie above all else was that the woman was wearing an expression of animal delight. Below on the same page was another drawing—the sequel. The same couple, now standing, she massaging her spanked bottom, gazing coyly behind her at the man, who was eyeing her with a lecherous grin of male satisfaction. The front of his trousers was bulging with his erection. The caption above read: A TEASER TAUGHT!

Only now, while smarting beneath the clothesbrush's blistering assault, did Maudie fully appreciate the bizarre eroticism of those drawings for, although ashamed to admit it to herself, she felt more deeply aroused at that moment than she'd ever done before in her life. As the spanking reached its explosive climax she wriggled frantically and let out a piercing orgasmic scream. Red-faced and sweating with excitement, the Reverend Woolley let the clothesbrush fall to the floor and helped the dazed bewildered girl rise unsteadily to her feet.

There was an embarrassed silence while Maudie got dressed. She was much too sensitive to make any reference to what had happened. All she did know was that for the first time since Daniel had left her she felt at peace with herself. She longed to express her gratitude to him. Perhaps a kiss on the cheek? No, she didn't dare, lest it be misconstrued.

Although hardly an expert in matters pertaining to female sexuality, the Reverend Woolley nevertheless had a shrewd suspicion as to the unforeseen side-effect the spanking had had on Maudie. Although it shocked him beyond words that here was a young woman who actually derived pleasure from having her bottom beaten, it did, however, open up all kinds of interesting possibilities. . . .

As she walked slowly and painfully away from the vicarage, he called out from the doorway, "Remember to phone me, Maudie, as soon as you make up your mind. But don't leave it too long." She turned and gave a shy little wave before disappearing behind the line of conifers that flanked the drive. A pang of sadness overtook him as her neat little bottom finally disappeared out of sight.

Maudie did phone, a week later, from London. What she said brought a rapturous smile to the Reverend Woolley's face that lasted for days. . . .

When Mrs. Bunnie packed her bags and departed from the vicarage for good, Maudie took her place—

for now that Daniel had gone, there was nothing left to keep her in London. True, she was hardly the house-keeping type, but she was willing to learn her duties—and the Reverend Woolley was more than willing to teach her them, and correct her whenever necessary. It was, one might say, a most satisfactory reciprocal arrangement.

And as for the village people, they didn't even give it a passing thought—for after all, she was one of the family.

The Truth Always Hurts

James Langford stood in the garden of his home, contentedly puffing his pipe, savouring the feeling of new ownership. He relished the unaccustomed silence of the country and the privacy which the garden afforded. It was large, partly walled, and the remainder enclosed by a tangled hedge bordering fields that undulated down to the village somewhere below. Wild and overgrown though it was, the garden had transmuted neglect into beauty: clematis and honeysuckle toppling over the crumbling brick walls and a confusion of rampant ivy threatening to smother the orchard.

There it was—the orchard. The cause of his love affair with the house and his commitment to its restoration. There numbered some two dozen mature apple trees, the grey-green flaking lichen on their trunks like a mutant growth on a lizard's scaly fingers. Their branches linked above him as he walked underneath, crunching half-ripe apples underfoot, and looking up with pride at the size of the crop.

A heavy iron greenhouse had been built out from the wall; most of its glass was missing. Inside, a fan-trained peach had gone wild and thrust itself up through the frame. It was covered with ripening fruit: Langford had counted thirty-six, mindful of those which had dropped and were sweet feast for the ants.

With the apples, he mused, he could be generous, but he coveted the peach for himself. And each downy, blush-ripened one would fall into his own cupped hands to eat within moments of its plucking, still sun-warm.

The days passed. He intended to work on the house, but found himself drawn to the garden to explore its labyrinthine paths and hollows.

Plans for re-creating its former glory fermented in his brain, and it was wholly his; and each plant, each tree, would bear the caring touch of his possessive fingers, like a man moulding a young girl until she flushed into womanhood.

Langford visited the greenhouse every morning and many times during the day, waiting to lay claim to the first ripe peach, to feel the softness of its skin and savour its sweet flesh.

Then suddenly there were not so many, so he began counting them again and realised with disproportionate rage that the four ripest ones had vanished, been plucked. It struck him that the culprit had not only stolen his much desired first pickings, but had invaded the privacy of his garden and had no doubt taken similar liberties with it before. It was probably a boy from the village who had skulked around his orchard in the dusk, had marked every tree, every ripening thing. . . . He decided to keep watch for the culprit and catch him red-handed.

There were plenty of canes in the greenhouse, he remembered. Excellent for giving the young rascal a good hiding.

The culprit remained elusive for a few days. Langford rushed down the garden on several occasions at a whisper of a noise, only to find no one, and to suffer the mocking cries of the crows.

It rained for a spell and he relaxed a little, thinking that the audacious thief would be loath to venture out. Evidently not so. One day, in the early afternoon, he heard a crash of glass and a scream. He tore down to the greenhouse, the blood howling in his ears, in time to see a figure running for the hedge with long, slender legs, dressed in a sun-bleached tee-shirt and shorts.

"Stop—you!" he yelled. The boy halted before the hedge and turned round in agitation. For a second their eyes met, both in apprehension. But the surprise was all his. It was a girl.

Before he could speak or move, she was gone, scrambling through the hedge. The last glimpse of her was of her bottom, almost bursting out of the most immodest shorts he had ever seen, wriggling through the hole. He grew hot and angry. If he could catch her, he'd give her bottom such a tanning. . . .

For days Langford dreamed of punishing her, and the desire was at first fed by his anger, but that ebbed away, to be replaced by vague feelings of regret and disappointment. She probably wouldn't come back again, having so nearly been caught.

He answered the door one evening. It was the local clergyman, accompanied by his daughter, inviting Langford to help at the Harvest Festival. Maybe he would like to make a contribution of fruit, or something? He declined, and found himself staring at the daughter. Dressed very modestly in a blue and white skirt which came well below her knees, with a white high-buttoned blouse and gloves to match, she was very much a young woman. A beautiful young thing, with tumbling hair and fresh skin and a mouth that pouted slightly when she nervously smiled. And those eyes . . . the brief scanty shorts, the long tanned length of her thighs, the round cheeks of her bottom on display below sun-bleached shorts that were . . . so . . .

Langford closed his eyes for a second, opened them to fix on the father's mouth, wagging like a gaping fish, and realized that for some time he had not been listening to a word the vicar had said.

"Caught you, young lady!" The triumphant excitement in his voice volleyed round the garden. He'd seen her stealing apples, the brazen cheeky hussy, at the top of a tree, stuffing them hastily into a cradle made by pulling up her skirt. She was barefoot, bare-legged, her bottom squeezed unbelievably into shorts which looked as though they might split down the back at any moment. And from where he was standing, the view up her slender legs to the ripe curve of her bottom was delicious.

The apples fell round him in a heavy shower.

"Come down this minute, Elizabeth, or I'll come up and get you!" He was relishing the spectacle of her, wobbling unsteadily on the branch above, blushing furiously as he stood with arms folded, head cocked, eyes travelling with deliberate slowness over her bottom, neat little waist, the soft swell of her breasts, to her very red face.

"I can't . . ." she stammered in a small voice.

"You will, Miss," he said harshly. "Lost your nerve, have you?"

With purposeful strides he went to the greenhouse and returned with a ladder. Tucked under his arm was a cruel thin cane. Elizabeth watched him from her perch and felt uneasy. A cane! Whatever did he want a cane for? She shut her eyes for a moment and nervously swallowed.

"Now, Elizabeth, I think it's time for us to have a little talk." And he noticed with satisfaction how quickly her face had changed colour from rosy-red to sickly-white. Her eyes were spellbound by the cane. Good! Perhaps she had guessed there was to be more than just talking.

"You may wonder," he went on, as he positioned the ladder and invited her to descend, "how I know your name, Elizabeth." She pouted and he added, "We've met before—remember? Only then you were dressed a little more modestly."

Elizabeth began to blush uncontrollably at this and, rolling her blue eyes skyward, climbed higher up the tree, shrinking from his penetrating stare and her own embarrassment. She began to feel a little dizzy—even though she had a good head for heights.

The birds' singing seemed very loud all of a sudden, and everywhere else was hushed, waiting.

"I've been waiting to catch you for a long time," Langford called out. "I don't like thieves—even pretty ones."

Elizabeth slid her feet along the branch, noticing for the first time how nasty and rough it was.

"That's it, come down. . . ." He was getting a tantalizing view of almost everything that was important to her modesty, and Elizabeth knew it!

Slowly, with trembling legs, Elizabeth began to descend the ladder, trying to position herself this way or that. Oh, if only he wouldn't look at her so intently!

"Elizabeth," he said, when she finally stood before him, digging her nails into her palms, "you're such a pretty little thief, aren't you?" he sighed. "But a thief, nevertheless." Elizabeth was swaying unsteadily, and couldn't look at him.

"I am going to punish you for your childish crime," he said sternly, "and since you are so keen on revealing to all and sundry as much of your bottom as your costume will allow, I think it's appropriate I give it some attention, too."

Elizabeth shrank helplessly against the trunk and

looked frantically about her. She couldn't escape. Being barefoot placed her at a distinct disadvantage. He would easily catch her and the outcome might be worse. She felt like a stricken rabbit caught in a trap. Perhaps she should try a little pleading. With a desperate look of the most appealing contrition she could muster, she fixed her wide blue eyes on his. What a sweet young girl she could be!

"You have every right to be angry with me for taking your fruit," she murmured in a voice which trembled as she caught sight of the cane once more, "but I honestly didn't know at first that you lived here."

Langford looked piercingly at her.

"And when you *did* find out I was living here?" He lashed viciously with the cane at the apples above in a slicing movement, sending several thudding to earth.

Elizabeth flinched. "Then it was j-j-just a t-t-temptation," she blurted out, and looked away miserably. The truth had been told; surely now he'd think what an honest girl she was and relent, let her go. But it seemed to make him more resolute than ever. Langford gripped Elizabeth's arm and led her to the greenhouse.

"What are you going to do to me?" she squeaked in terror, as she vainly tried to wriggle out of his grasp.

"An old-fashioned but appropriate punishment. Short, sharp—and very effective. I am going to give you a sound spanking on your bottom!"

Her mouth dropped open and she froze.

"S-s-spanked! Th-that's the sort of thing you do to children," she squealed, "and I'm *not* a child!"

Langford chuckled, and still keeping hold of the indignant but frightened young girl, he dragged a chair across the tiled floor of the greenhouse. She pushed against him, shook her head ferociously and jiggled about in another attempt to get free. He laughed aloud. Innocent vicar's daughter indeed! He remembered how she'd stood in her demure little outfit, coyly murmuring, holding Daddy's arm, knowing Langford had recognised her. Well, there was no indulgent father to protect her now. She'd have to answer for herself to *him!* He looked at her bare plump thighs and the curve of her cheeks bulging from tight, tight shorts. Provocative young Miss to go flaunting her semi-naked body at him!

He sat down and pulled her arm until she lost her balance and fell awkwardly across his knees.

"No, no-o-o-o-o, p-pl-ee-ase, Ow! No—don't, A-h-hh! She spluttered. He hauled her roughly into a position where her long brown legs dangled down one side, and her tumbling hair swept the floor on the other. Her round wobbling bottom was nicely elevated.

In an unwise flash of indignation she struggled, kicked, tried to bite his leg, and let fly with her fists backwards, catching Langford painfully on the chin. He responded by pushing her further across his lap so that her face was touching the mouldering mushroom-like earth.

"How dare you! I shall tell my father. I shall!—" Her indignant voice trailed away as, with awful shock, she felt the first hard slap on her bottom, heard the "smack" as Langford's hand landed resoundedly on her thighs. She screwed her eyes up tight. It was unthinkable, yet here she was, the vicar's well-brought-up daughter, lying across a man's lap, experiencing the humiliating enormity that she was being spanked like a naughty child. Oh! It couldn't be happening to her!

"You p-p-pig, you bully, you horrible man! Ouch! Ow! you're hurting me. Ow! Piss-piss off—" She stopped, horrified at her profanity, and bit her lip hard.

"What! Elizabeth! Such language from the daughter of the vicar! Get up!" Langford's face darkened.

She stood up, smarting with humiliation more than pain, her hands protectively covering her thighs, her face flushed and excited.

"I can't have this. Take off your shorts, Elizabeth!"

She stared disbelievingly, mouth forming a perfect circle, eyes growing wide in amazement.

Without waiting for her to comply, Langford neatly undid the zipper and tugged at the legs of her shorts. Involuntarily, Elizabeth clutched her hands in front of her, but he roughly swept them aside. He was trembling all over and her eyes were fixed in space.

"Please," she mumbled piteously as the shorts came inching down. Down over flushed pink round flesh. He turned her round, fascinated and excited. So soft her skin, each cheek covered with an almost transparent down. So flowing were her curves, how sensuously the fullness slipped down into the cleft between—into the dark secret recess between her legs.

"Oh, no, no! How could you? How could you?" she wailed.

It was within her character to have slapped Langford hard, but something stopped her. She was very aware of his fingers, indecent though they were, stroking and probing.

"No knickers I see." Langford was breathing heavily. "Back over my knee, young lady." He pulled her down roughly. "Don't tense your muscles like that, Elizabeth, or I shall spank you all the harder till you relax."

Langford was feeling far from relaxed at the picture Elizabeth presented, her naked bottom spread before him so deliciously nubile.

Elizabeth tensed her whole body, waiting for the first

smack. But it didn't come. Perhaps he'd decided that the sheer humiliation was enough.

He sat looking at her bottom as a man might look at a feast when starving. This young hussy was totally in his power. He would spank her when he chose, not when *she* thought he would. Now he was enjoying the warmth of her body against his thighs. Elizabeth wriggled when he touched her, so he began to spank her again, slowly, seriously and much harder this time, covering every part of her bouncing flesh with a red diffuseness. It was like watching a photograph developing, with all the tones of colour appearing in their mistiness, growing clearer and more vivid with every second. It was beautiful, although the restrained mewing noises coming from Elizabeth told him she didn't like it one bit. Langford wanted to punish, hurt, and love her all at the same time.

She had stuffed a fist into her mouth and felt suffocated by the repressed tears that sought release. To cry would be babyish—and surely the object of the punishment was to take it and show how brave she was. She didn't feel sorry—yet.

"Up you get, young lady." Langford put an arm round her naked waist, brushing her little mound of delicate hair, and hoisted her up and over the back of the chair till she lay draped and motionless like a rag doll. Elizabeth's skin prickled with fear.

What was he going to do to her? She was unable to think; her thoughts were paralyzed.

Langford was annoyed by her apparent resistance. Obviously the punishment had made no impact yet. She was showing no signs of contrition although her bottom was really very red. Indeed, he thought, she hung over the chair almost sulkily.

There was no other way—he would have to be more

severe. Almost reluctantly, he picked up the cane, and toyed with it for a while before preparing for the first stroke. He ran the tip of the cane up and down the crack between her cheeks; she wriggled and humped her bottom up and down. It tickled unbearably.

The cane slashed into her buttocks: it was like a shock-wave, piercing through her previously numb emotions. She gasped at the pain which rose to an almost unbearable crescendo, drawing in her cheeks and twisting her body this way and that until the burning eased. Langford ran his hand over the ridge of skin that was swelling and puckering into a plum-coloured weal. Then he brought the cane down smartly again . . . and again . . . measuring each stroke, taking care not to stripe the same place twice. Elizabeth rose after each stroke, clutching her bottom cheeks, her pretty face contorted in agony. She could think or feel nothing but the sensation of heat and pain. As Langford finished one cut, Elizabeth held her breath, curled her toes tight, gripped the chair with whitening knuckles and distorted her lovely mouth into a grimace, in preparation for the next.

Langford paused, panting with effort and excitement. His trousers felt constrictingly tight; the sight of Elizabeth's rubescent rear—rivalled only by his crimson roses—was powerfully arousing. She writhed and bucked, throwing her hips from side to side in futile attempts to ease her sufferings. Her red-blotched bottom shook tantalisingly with each cane-cut as she hopped from one foot to another, curling her free leg tightly around the other one like a tentacle. Apart from strangled gasps and hisses, Elizabeth made little noise, so Langford gave her four quick strokes, one for each stolen peach, on her peach-like bottom. On the last, he uttered her name, "Elizabeth," almost reproachfully.

The resistance in her nature bowed completely at the sound of his voice, and she burst helplessly into tears.

"Oh, oh, I'm sorry! I'm sorry!" And he knew that she was.

Suddenly it was over. He sat down and laid her back over his knees, while she stayed motionless, except for a hiccup and a sigh now and then. His hands smoothed the bottom he had so effectively reddened. His fingers, trickling over her burning skin like cool streams of water, slid down to the dampness between her legs. He squeezed the delicate softness of her inner thighs in a gentle massage, while he battled with the fierceness of his lust.

Finally he let her go and allowed her to pull up her shorts, which made her wince. At his command, she looked shakily at him. He felt very much that she didn't want to go, for she stood before him so quiet and submissive.

"You might as well take what you came for," he said tartly, and gathered the fallen apples. "With my permission, this time."

Langford would dearly have loved to watch the irresistible sight of her red thighs and bottom struggling through his hedge, but he allowed her to leave by the front gate. She walked slowly away. Every cell of his body cried for her to come back.

Would he ever see her again? He thought not.

In fevered realization of what he had done, and with the sudden return of the thudding loneliness which her presence had so joyously driven away, he went back to work with bitter reluctance.

A week went by and there was no sign of her. He was being silly. How could he ever expect the girl to look him in the eyes again?

One evening, after collecting the apple crop into

baskets, he walked in a somber mood to the village.

On returning, he found with some annoyance that the apple baskets were empty. If it was she again . . . surely, she'd learnt?

The back door was open. On the table in the kitchen lay an apple, with one bite-sized piece missing. A little further away lay a long garden cane. He picked them up, wondering.

Upstairs he heard a faint creaking, and—was that the ghost of a laugh? He knew. And sighed. Then picked up the cane.

The bedroom door was open and she was there, sitting on the bed sideways, swinging her legs. Eating one of his apples.

"I'm sorry." She was blushing. "I was tempted again."

Langford sighed. "You'll never learn, will you, Elizabeth?" And flexing the cane rhythmically, added, "Do you know the old saying, Elizabeth, 'the truth always hurts'? I wonder if you would agree with that?"

Elizabeth paled, trembled, and looked away, but obediently began to undo her shorts.

Awaiting Execution

Wednesday, March 21: 9:30 A.M. Morning Assembly has just finished and two fifth-year girls are standing self-consciously outside Mr. Royce's study, waiting their turn for one of his so-called "little pep-talks." A third fifth-former, Carolyn Eglinton, is already inside, being attended to.

Wendy Ferguson bites her lower lip anxiously and whispers in her companion's ear, "We're really for it this time, Lynne! He's in a foul mood—you can tell by the way he glowered at us!"

Lynne Challenor tries to look poker-faced and pretend she doesn't care. Petite, with black urchin-cropped hair, she barely seems old enough to be a fifth-year girl. She has about her an air of sullen insolence that simply invites punishment. Needless to say, this is by no means her first visit to the headmaster's study. Nor, in all probability, will it be her last.

Mr. Royce's study is located at the end of a long, baize-green painted corridor. A deathly hush hangs forever in this corner of the school. The green uniformed pupils avoid it like the plague, never venturing near "Rolls" Royce's somber dark varnished door unless summoned. It's altogether not a healthy place to be in.

"Gives me the creeps, this does," Lynne mutters mournfully, kicking her heels in a little show of defiance.

Wendy nods miserably in agreement. "I'd rather have the school dentist than this, any day!" she says, and is about to say more when Mr. Renshaw, Deputy Head of Burtonwood College for Girls, suddenly appears, as if from out of nowhere, and advances on the girls, eyeing them with prurient interest.

"Oh no—not the Vulture! Just our luck!" gasps Wendy. They call him "the Vulture" not only because of his scrawny birdlike appearance and nervously pecking mannerisms, but also because he's always lurking frustratedly in the background whenever there are girls being caned. Just like a vulture hovering near a lion when it's making its kill.

He asks them why they have been put on "Headmaster's Report."

"Sir," Wendy says blushingly, "it's because we got low marks in our mock O levels." Lynne gazes up at the ceiling, ignoring him.

"Well," Mr. Renshaw wheezes sanctimoniously, "if either one of you girls wants to come and have a little chat about it afterwards, you'll find me in my room. Good counsel is a healing balm, and it's part of my pastoral care duties to attend to the needs of every girl under my wing." He licks his thin lips and gazes longingly at those soon-to-be-caned teenage bottoms. "I'm a very good listener, you know. You need never be afraid of coming to see me!" And with that he walks away reluctantly—because he can think of nothing else to say.

"Kinky old pervert! I know all about him and his jar of cold cream!" Lynne retorts scathingly as Mr. Renshaw disappears round the corner. Wendy shudders at the thought of Mr. Renshaw's wrinkled, claw-like fingers hotly caressing her tender buttocks. "No thanks!" she says.

Then it begins. Those unmistakeable whirring and swishing sounds from within Mr. Royce's study, punctuated by high-pitched girlish yelps. Carolyn Eglinton is being caned.

Wendy and Lynne eye each other in alarm. Lynne is beginning to turn a little pale—not quite so cocky now by half.

SWISH—"Eeow!! Oooh!!"

SWISH—"Aaaaargh!!!"

"God, I was right about him being in a foul mood!" Wendy gasps in terror. Lynne starts to fidget nervously and turns even paler as the ferocious caning nears its climax.

SWISH—THWACK!! "AAAH! OH NO MORE— PLEASE!!!"

Carolyn Eglinton is crying. They can hear her through the door. Big babyish gurgles and sobs.

Lynne looks at Wendy and sees that she's almost near to tears already. Lynne begins to feel distinctly queasy. All her bravado has somehow melted away. She just feels like a frightened little girl.

The dreadful caning sounds have ceased. In their place, faint rustling noises of knickers being painfully pulled up into place around fiercely aching hindquarters . . . elasticated "ping!" of knicker waistband . . . then the muffled buzzing of a zip as the short green pleated skirt is fastened up around hips. A low murmuring of Royce's parting remarks.

The study door opens. Carolyn Eglinton stumbles out into the corridor, her freckled face splashed with tears. Her hands are up under her skirt, trying to rub away the blazing pain. She's a rather pretty, well-developed girl with auburn hair loosely flowing to her shoulders and fringing her pale-blue eyes. "Christ! That was unbearable!" she gasps. "I pity you two— you've both got it still to come!"

"Thanks a bunch!" Lynne snaps acidly.

"Sorry, girls—but don't say I didn't warn you!" Carolyn replies with the wisdom born of painful experience. "What I need now is a lovely cold flannel to put on my poor you-know-what!"

"Watch out—the Vulture's about!" Wendy warns her.

"Gosh, thanks for the tip, Wendy. I could do without being molested in my present condition!" And Carolyn walks slowly and stiffly away.

"Next!" booms the harsh voice from within the study. Wendy and Lynne are rooted to the spot. Both are suffering from the medical condition known to Burtonwood scholars as "jelly-legs"—a recognized symptom of pre-punishment nerves.

The door swings open and Mr. Royce's red-cheeked head juts out like an angry question mark. "Well? Which of you two young ladies am I to have the pleasure of attending to next?" he snaps impatiently, scrutinising the girls with a stare of cold appraisal.

He crooks his index finger at Wendy. "Ferguson, you'll do!"

Wendy is definitely the prettier of the pair: doe-eyed, fragilely lissome, flawlessly complexioned, with long flowing almost saffron coloured hair. It's also patently obvious that she's the more petrified of the two. She's knock-kneed and trembling—whereas Lynne, with her cropped black hair, snub nose, and tomboyish figure, is still desperately trying to look blasé and unconcerned.

Royce scowls malevolently at the dark-haired girl. Her sulky, pouting insolence never ceases to infuriate him. It'll do her good, he thinks, to stew in her own juice a while longer. He's looking forward to dealing with her last of all.

He pokes Wendy in the small of her back and she

walks leadenly into his study. The door slams behind them.

Lynne tries all manner of tricks to fight off the unpleasant images her mind keeps throwing up. A pale shivering Wendy, fingers fluttering at the zip of her skirt . . . the soft "whoosh" as the green pleated garment rapidly descends to her ankles . . . the crimson flush of shame invading her cheeks when Mr. Royce begins to walk round and round her, cane in hand, inspecting her dainty little green-knickered bottom . . . the "target area," as he always jokingly refers to it. Lynne knows full well how skillfully adept Mr. Royce is at spinning out the agonising humiliations, stage by stage and step by step. He knows how to make a girl cry *before* he takes her knickers down—before he even produces the cane from his cupboard.

Minutes go by. Lynne's lurid imagination goes into overdrive.

Then the tell-tale sounds of girlish distress, faintly audible. Morbidly fascinated, Lynne puts her ear to the door just in time to catch Wendy pleading urgently with the Head: "N-not with my knickers down—P-please, not that!"

"Just you take 'em down *this instant,* my girl, or else I'll do it for you!" Royce cuts through Wendy's protests like a knife through butter.

Babyish weeping, accompanied by a muted "ssss" as Wendy despairingly lowers her pants and subjects all her schoolgirl charms, front and rear—to the stern scrutiny of her headmaster.

Lynne, her ear pressed tight against the door, hears Mr. Royce mutter something that sounds like "have to examine you first" and in the silence that ensues, broken only by the childish blubbering of the intensely mortified fifth former, Lynne's imagination again works overtime as she conjures up the appalling scene within. Poor bare-bottomed Wendy being briskly shepherded into punishment position, bottom upwards across the highly polished top of Royce's mahogany desk—where literally hundreds of girls' quaking tummies have lain before.

"Open your legs, girl," Lynne hears him say (she blushes at the awful implications those words contain) followed by a despairing wail from Wendy as she obeys.

Silence again.

Lynne can only conclude that Mr. Royce is at that very moment subjecting Wendy's rear-end to a most minute pre-caning inspection. This is his usual custom. He claims it to be a necessary preliminary in order to determine which grade of cane to apply to the bottom in question.

The data he bases his final decision on include such factors as what he terms "Buttock Resilience" (i.e., is the girl's behind tautly firm or fleshly soft?); "Buttock Dimension" (the bigger the girl's bottom, the more extensively it can be caned); and also "Buttock Sensitivity," which presumably means how susceptible the girl is to being whacked on the arse—although for one or two of the more masochistically inclined pupils (you get them at any school), "buttock sensitivity" can take on a somewhat different meaning.

As Mr. Royce even felt prompted to observe, on page forty-seven of his private memoirs: "Some girls make the very devil of a racket while being caned. One disgustingly perverted 18-year-old moaned and cavorted her way through a 12-stroke caning, which left her well-rounded backside splendidly striped and wealed, and even carried on groaning and wriggling after the twelfth stroke; whereupon I felt urged to administer a further eight hearty strokes to purge her of her sinful excitement. But instead of having that salutary effect, the eight additional strokes only served to inflame her further, with the result that her moans rose to high-pitched shrieks of sado-masochistic ecstasy, and by the time I delivered the twentieth and final stroke she was threshing her purple-striped bottom up and down in utter abandonment, deep in the throes of some highly perverted sexual consummation! Greatly embarrassed, I decided to send the girl straight away to Matron who is, after all, more qualified to deal with female masochism than I am."

Lynne holds her breath and strains to hear even the slightest noise from within the study.

Ominous rattan-rattling signifies that Royce has at last chosen the appropriate grade of cane to use on Wendy Ferguson's bottom. Lynne shudders—not for Wendy's sake but for her own. She prays that when it comes to her turn he won't select a thin swishy rod that bends so readily on impact with her behind that its tip whips spitefully into the tops of her thighs. Cane-marks on thighs are a million times more embarrassing than on the bottom because they're so glaringly visible below the hem of her school skirt.

Mr. Royce is saying something to Wendy. Lynne can't quite catch the exact words, but it sounds like something horribly personal like, "Stick it well up now!" or worse, "Keep it well stuck up and still!"

Whatever it is, Wendy obviously doesn't like it very much because she starts to cry again: a series of poignant little hiccupping sobs that end abruptly in a piercing scream as the first lightning stroke of the cane hums through the air and explodes with a resounding "THWACK!!" against her rudely exposed bottom cheeks.

Lynne's tummy lurches and once more she's beset by a violent attack of "Burtonwood jelly-legs."

"And that was just for starters!" she hears Royce drawling lazily in his well-educated *Daily Telegraph* accent while Wendy blubbers pathetically.

"KEEP THAT BOTTOM OF YOURS STILL, WENDY!" he roars. Suddenly he's as angry as a chafing bull.

That's the trouble with old "Rolls," Lynne reflects bitterly. You never know where you are with him. One moment he's as nice as pie, next moment he's yelling like a madman.

Wendy's blubberings cease momentarily. She's holding her breath, waiting in dread for the next stroke.

Lynne tries to imagine how Wendy must be feeling. All alone in that grim oak-paneled study, green school knickers twisted round her ankles, skirt neatly folded over a chair, bottom vulgarly bare and "well stuck up," just as he likes it—with a thin reddish-purple stripe of throbbing pain imprinted right across the plumpest, rudest part of it.

SWOOOOOSH!! SPLATT!!

Again the cane falls. Again Wendy's voice howls its shrill protest. Again it drowns in a sea of tears.

This arresting sequence of happenings repeats itself six more times. By the end of it all, Wendy is sobbing and mewling like a baby, and Lynne—awaiting her turn for a dose of Mr. Royce's stick—is nearly wetting her pants in terror.

The door opens and a tear-soaked Wendy totters out. She's wearing only her blouse, socks, and sandals. In one had she clutches her skirt and knickers.

"My God!" Lynne thinks in mounting panic as her turn draws near. "She's too sore even to get dressed!"

Wendy manages a wry ghost of a smile. "Your turn

now, Lynne," she murmurs with blessed relief that at least for her it's all over. "Oh, and he told me to tell you he's only been warming up so far—using me and Carolyn as 'target practice.' It's *you* he's really saving it all up for."

Lynne starts to blubber and snivel. No man has ever made her cry before. But then there's always a first time for everything. . . .

"Cheer up, Lynne," Wendy says commiseratingly, "at least you won't have to wait for it any longer. I always think the waiting's the worst part!"

Lynne nods bleakly, ashamedly brushing away the tears.

"I'll be in my dorm if you need a shoulder to cry on afterwards," Wendy adds, "lying on my tummy of course! His Lordship's forbidden me to wear my skirt and knickers for a whole hour—says it'll act as an example to the rest of the school. So I'm going to cut the Biology class and hide in the dorm. I'm blowed if I'm going to let Mr. Forbes feast his eyes on my bare bottom—especially the state it's in right now!"

As she turns to go, Lynne sees for the first time the awful purpling streaks emblazoned on poor Wendy's dainty little rump.

Feeling very alone and vulnerable, Lynne creeps into Mr. Royce's study, dreading every step she takes.

It's quite obvious from the very start that Mr. Royce means business. He has that brisk no-nonsense air about him that the girls have learned to fear.

The first thing he does is to lock the study door and pocket the key. The reason for this is not so much to spare Lynne's blushes as to ensure there are no witnesses as to the manner and the severity of the punishment she's about to undergo.

Next he tells her to undress completely. Lynne

almost faints with shock when she hears this—although he does make a slight concession. She may keep on her socks and sandals.

While the petrified girl divests herself of tie, blouse, skirt, vest, and bottle green knickers, Mr. Royce cheerfully places two upright wooden chairs back to back.

Lynne, halfway through taking down her pants, watches him out of the corner of her eye. She wonders what ordeal awaits her now.

At least she doesn't have long to find out. Once she's naked, save for socks and sandals, Royce impatiently guides her into position by delivering spiteful cane-taps to her thighs. He makes her kneel up on one chair and bend forward across the backs of both chairs until she can support herself by placing the palms of her hands on the seat of the other chair.

Her small round bottom is elevated to an angle of ludicrously obscene exposure. Mr. Royce will now be able to cane not only the crowns of her buttocks, but also the soft delicate undercurve just above her thighs.

Never in all her life has Lynne felt so thoroughly abject—so helpless, so animal-like in dumb subjection. Two big tears trickle slowly down each cheek. She'd do anything not to give him the satisfaction of seeing her cry, but there's no way she can stop herself from bawling her eyes out like a stupid baby.

"Hmm now, let me see," Mr. Royce murmurs, assessing the faint hint of rotundity and fleshiness in Lynne's quivering, cringing buttocks. "I think cane number three will be just right for this little job," and he goes to his cupboard to select the rod in question.

Lynne hears him energetically swishing it up and down. Her heart starts to thump madly and her eyes are misted over with fresh tears. Then she feels the cane's cold caress against her taut, stretched bottomcheeks. And as he slowly raises it to deliver the first stroke, Lynne begins to cry in earnest.

Coping With Jilly

"Look, Jilly, are we going out for this drink or not?" Robert asked her yet again, the irritation rising in his voice.

"Don't care," came the petulant response from the bed where Jilly was lying prone on her tummy, indolently skimming through a *Cosmopolitan*. She had on a pale-blue tee-shirt, tight brown cotton trousers, and white ankle socks that made her look more like an adolescent schoolgirl than a first-year undergraduate at St. Cuthbert's College of Education.

Her long glossy raven hair trailed across her back onto the pink floral bedspread. Robert ached with longing for her. His frustrated gaze travelled up the length of Jilly's shapely, tightly-trousered legs and lingered on her bottom which swayed from side to side—as if to goad him—as she rocked to and fro on the bed, heels scissoring impatiently in the air. The superb division of her buttock crease was dramatically defined by the skin-tight trousers.

Robert grew more and more infuriated as the minutes ticked by. Precious drinking-time going to waste, all because of this maddening, but rather beautiful young woman with whom he was besotted.

Jilly yawned and turned over another page of her magazine. "I'm so bored," she said accusingly. Robert went red, mortified by the implication that she found his company tedious.

He got up from the chair and paced around Jilly's

tiny bed-sit flat. "Oh for godsake come on, Jilly!" he pleaded, looking frantically at his watch. "It's nearly ten. We'll have to get our skates on if we're going!" It was Friday night and there was a disco down at the White Swan in the village. Half the student population of the college would be there living it up. It was the only venue worth going to in that god-forsaken neck of the woods. Robert hated feeling excluded from anything.

"Hardly worth it now. Besides," she murmured indifferently, "I don't really fancy it all that much anyway." She wriggled herself into a more comfortable position on the bed and settled down to read a short story.

Robert scowled and stifled a profanity. It had been *she* who'd suggested going for a drink in the first place! Jilly was the most infuriating girl he'd ever met: capricious, contrary and frequently moody. He'd always treated her with kid gloves, humoured her every whim, done his utmost to please her—yet all she ever did, it seemed, was to throw it all back in his face.

Because he loved her so, he'd kept his feelings of resentment to himself—not wishing to hurt her with words spoken carelessly in anger. But tonight he felt all his repressed annoyance with her, hammering in his brain, demanding to be let out.

The ever-present sexual frustration he felt, too, didn't exactly help matters. Jilly stubbornly refused to go "all the way" with him, even though they'd been going steady now for nearly six months and were even talking of getting engaged. An evening spent with Jilly invariably left Robert feeling like a bomb about to go off. She would allow him to touch her above and below the waist, but that was as far as it went. For some mysterious reason Jilly seemed determined, for the present,

101

to stay a virgin.

There was no doubt that she was passionate—her frantic gasps and moans when they embraced and fondled told him so. But she seemed to have a deep-rooted emotional block about doing "it." Robert lectured Jilly on the dangers of sexual repression until he was blue in the face, but all to no avail—she only got upset, called him cruel and inconsiderate.

He was convinced that if only she'd give in to him, then everything would be fine—even her moodiness would disappear. But she seemed afraid to let him have the mastery, fearful of the maleness thrusting and throbbing between his legs like an angry piston.

Now his months of frustration and exasperation with Jilly welled up uncontrollably into a sudden outburst of temper. "You really are the limit, Jilly," he exploded. "First you say you want to go out for a drink, then you change your mind. I never know where I am with you. I think you do it on purpose, just to rile me!"

Jilly stared up at him in surprise. He'd never lost his temper with her before. This was a new Robert: fiercely glowering, eyes blazing, fists clenched at his sides. She found herself thinking how handsome he looked. She was the kind of girl who thoroughly enjoyed goading her man. She found it great fun to needle him. She decided to push him even further, just to see what he would do.

"Perhaps I only do it because you let me get away with it. Why *do* you let me get away with it, Robert?" she crooned mockingly, kicking her heels in the air as though issuing a challenge. "Aren't you man enough to put your foot down?"

That did it! Robert uttered a sound like an angry bull and advanced threateningly on Jilly. Realising that she'd gone too far this time, she sprang up from the bed and shot across the room towards the bathroom, intending to lock herself in.

But Robert got there first and barred her way. "You've really done it this time, Jilly!" he shouted, quivering with rage. "I've been very patient with you, putting up with all your silly moods and tantrums!"

Jilly gazed at him wide-eyed, with spellbound amazement. Every time he roared at her she blinked and recoiled beneath the fury of his anger. He looked enormously tall and strong. It made her feel weak and helpless, as though she'd become a little girl again.

"Maybe you're right, Jilly," Robert added, pouring out his pent-up feelings. "Maybe it *is* my fault for putting up with all your shenanigans. Maybe I've been *too* patient with you." He gripped her firmly by the shoulders and began to shake her. "You're right about another thing, too, Jilly: I'm not going to stand for it any longer—I *am* going to put my foot down!"

So saying he got hold of her hands and began pulling her back over to the bed.

"Let me go!" she squealed in panic. "W-what on earth do you think you're doing, Robert! How dare you drag me about like this. I won't have it!" She stamped her foot petulantly. How like a little girl she was, Robert thought to himself. And how inexpressibly beautiful she looked, flushed and panting with the exertion of the struggle—stray wisps of dark hair falling over her pretty face.

"I should have done this a long time ago!" he bellowed, pulling her nearer and nearer to the bed.

"Done what?" she cried in alarm. "What are you going to do to me, Robert? You're not—" She saw the bed looming nearer and thought for one dreadful moment that he was going to rape her. Her lovely body tensed itself into an arc of defiance, her feet scrabbling and skittering along the polished parquet floor.

"Oh don't flatter yourself, Jilly. It isn't your precious virginity that's at stake!" He sneered as he sat down heavily on the edge of the bed, holding her at arms length. Jilly gazed at him imploringly through the silky screen of her long raven hair. Had he gone raving mad?

"You said I wasn't man enough to put my foot down. Well, Jilly, I'm going to prove just how wrong you were," he shouted. "You've been asking for this for absolutely ages, Jilly, and now you're going to get it: a damn good old-fashioned spanking!"

"You wouldn't dare lay a—" she began, but Robert didn't allow her to finish her sentence. Instead he gave an almighty tug and there she was: sprawled comically, humiliatingly, across his strong muscular thighs.

Upended, over his knee, her nose practically scraping the floor, Jilly felt a huge pang of mortified self-pity. The blood rushed to her head and made her feel giddy and dazed. She'd never dreamt that Robert had it in him—how wrong she'd been. She'd always thought she could twist him around her little finger.

A wild, god-like elation coursed through Robert. He was determined to tan Jilly's gorgeous backside until his arm ached. He'd never done anything like this before in his life but boy, was he going to enjoy it! He gave no thought to the rights and wrongs of what he was about to do. Jilly had impeached his manhood and by God he was going to make her pay for it! Who did she think she was? A responsible, adult woman? Like hell she was! She hadn't even outgrown her childish tantrums. She was more like a big kid, forever taunting and teasing him. He'd cut her down to size alright—to the level of a grizzling, blubbering little girl who's just had her arse smacked for the very first time.

Robert had always been fascinated by the rich curves, the saucy prominence, of Jilly's rear-end; its sexually provocative little wiggle whenever she walked, as her well-rounded buttocks nudged and jostled each other invitingly.

Now, for the moment at least, Jilly's infinitely tantalizing rear had become *his* property. It was all his to do whatever he liked with, its pert naughtiness spread out across his lap. The thin trousers stretched drum-tight over its appetizing curves, and quite indecently hugged the deep vale of her bottom-cleft.

The sassy little madam had it coming to her. He was so angry he'd made up his mind to spank her until she cried—show her once and for all who was the boss. Then, afterwards, if she told him to get lost once and for all—so what? At least he would have had the satisfaction of teaching her a lesson she'd never forget. And he couldn't imagine a more enjoyable way of doing it than by soundly smacking every inch of that delicious bottom of hers, until its spoilt, pampered owner howled for mercy.

"Robert! Let me up at once!" she cried indignantly. "If you lay as much as a finger on me I'll never speak to you again!" But her protests, muffled by the darkly shimmering mane of hair hanging down over her face, already sounded more plaintive than angry, as if Jilly knew she was in a hopeless situation and that all the power lay with him.

Robert patted Jilly's bottomcheeks tentatively. Their soft fleshy vulnerability delighted and excited him. He smacked her right buttock and it shuddered and wobbled, despite the protective layer of thin trouser-seat. He smacked the left cheek, nestling snugly against his belly, and it yielded to his touch—cushioning and absorbing the slap within its womanly amplitude. He returned to her right cheek and this time smacked it with considerably more force.

"Ouch! Pig!" Jilly declared vehemently, and kicked her legs in mutinous resentment.

"Ever been spanked before, Jilly?" Robert asked her, suddenly curious to know—as well as wickedly determined to exploit her obvious embarrassment.

"I refuse to answer that, you bloody sod!" she gulped, feeling a hot flush of shame suffuse her face.

But Robert was in no mood at all to be trifled with. So far that evening she'd called him a pig and a bastard; he'd make her pay dearly for that.

Gripping her tightly round the waist with his left hand, he began walloping each of Jilly's upthrust buttock cheeks in turn. Robert was no sadist, but he was fully resolved to spank Jilly until she broke down and cried. She thoroughly deserved it, and it would probably do her the world of good.

He spanked Jilly slowly, deliberately, as if deciding what area of her bottom to attack next. Jilly screwed up her face in a grimace of extreme discomfort as a most unpleasant stinging sensation built up in her squirming flanks.

With her right hand planted on the ground to steady herself, and to prevent her humping, bumping body from sliding ignominiously to the floor, Jill thrust her other hand into her mouth and bit it to distract her from the over-mastering feelings of shame and pain raging within her. She swore profanely at Robert—but kept it under her breath, knowing how foolish it would be to goad him any further. She could feel all her resistance, all her stroppy rebelliousness ebbing away with each fearsomely loud wallop he delivered to her bottom.

The mortifying shame, too, was every bit as bad as

the pain. Here she was, a self-possessed attractive young woman of nineteen being treated as if she was a misbehaving ten-year-old. It recalled distinctly unpleasant memories of childhood. Uncle Ralph sternly confronting her with the empty sweet-bag whose contents she'd so unpardonably filched: "Those sweets were meant for *after* tea—not before! Now you've made Auntie and me very cross, so I'm going to have to deal severely with you." Those horrid, painful—yet strangely comforting—punishments that had left an indelible stamp on Jilly's memory. . . .

Robert was really hurting her now. The seat of her trousers felt hot and sore, and each successive time his hand exploded with a resounding SPLAT! on her poor outraged behind, it seemed to inflame the nerve endings and produce an electric shock that made her wriggle like an eel across his lap, and cause her big brown eyes to mist over with tears.

He must have smacked her thus for several minutes—though it felt more like half an hour to Jilly—before he finally stopped. She lay there over his knee—hot, breathless, and panting.

Robert, however, was even more out of breath than Jilly. He made a mental note to spend more time in the gym, since he clearly wasn't as fit as he'd supposed. His right hand ached and smarted every bit as much as Jilly's bottom.

Yet he still hadn't achieved the effect he desired. There were no proper tears—only one or two self-pitying snuffles. He knew if he let her get up now she'd have won the day—and she'd never let him forget it. Things would be back to as they were, with Jilly calling the tune.

No. Since he'd embarked upon such a drastic course of action he'd have to go the whole hog and break her spirit. But how?

Her trousers—that was the answer! He'd make her take them off. It was the taut trouser-fabric that was hurting his hand, as well as providing much too much protection for Jilly's bottom.

"Get up, Jilly," he said brusquely. Thinking it was all over, she lifted herself thankfully off his lap and turned toward him, a sultry pout of derision on her face, as if to say "Didn't *really* hurt—so *there!*"

But when Robert told her to remove her trousers, her face fell and she blushed yet again, more crimson than before.

"Don't say a word, Jilly, just do as I say. If you don't, I'll damn well rip them off you myself!" he snapped, revelling in the power he was wielding over her.

Jilly was about to protest bitterly when she noticed the steely determination in Robert's eyes. He really did mean it, and she'd hate to see her only pair of decent trousers ruined beyond repair. So, for once in her life, she did as she was told.

Jilly was in fact a painfully shy girl, and she'd never done such an intimate thing as take down her trousers in front of a boy before. Her hands shook so much that all sorts of silly little things went wrong. The front button refused to unbutton and she tugged so hard at it that it flew off and nearly hit Robert in the face. Neither of them thought it at all funny. Then the zipper got jammed in a thread of cotton from her tee-shirt, and Robert had to help her free it.

Jilly felt all hot and sticky from nervous perspiration. Her trousers stuck to her legs and she had quite a job peeling them off. She was aware of Robert's eyes watching her every move, eager and possessive.

She felt intensely humiliated that he'd spanked her,

yet mingled with her burning resentment there was also an element of sneaking admiration for Robert that he'd actually been man enough to do it . . . and that he'd conquered and subdued her will so effectively that there she was, standing before him in nothing but her tee-shirt, panties, and socks—fearfully awaiting a further dose of what he'd already given her. Only this time she knew from childhood experience that it was going to hurt a damn sight more in just her knickers. Unaware of what she was doing, she put her hands down the back of her brief white nylon panties and, to comfort herself, began caressing her sore maltreated bottom.

Jilly stood quaking before her angry boyfriend while he glared piercingly at her tanned coltish legs, the erotic swell of her hips, and her neat tiny waist. She went an even deeper shade of red and tried to shield her pubic region with her hands. Her panties, she knew, were embarrassingly diaphanous and he'd be able to see quite clearly all that lay beneath them.

But on the wall directly behind Jilly there hung a large oval, gilt-framed mirror in which Robert could observe a most interesting rear-view of her: the bikini-style panties disappearing into the intriguing valley of her bottom-cleft; her bottom cheeks all pink and blushing from the spanking he'd already given them. They looked almost comical with their hot glowing rubescence—like a clown's make-up—and effectively sabotaged whatever dignity she might have still possessed. Robert suppressed a chuckle, managing instead to turn it into a grunt of severe disapproval.

Then he hauled the crimson-faced Jilly back across his lap and began spanking her all over again.

It soon became apparent to Robert that Jilly's bottom was now extremely sensitive to the loud resonant wallops he was delivering to it. Her panties were so inadequate they left almost the entire area of plump soft buttock cheeks naked and unprotected.

Jilly started to cry out and wriggle agitatedly. Her legs kicked wildly up and down and her bottom jerked convulsively each time Robert's hand attacked it, sending muscular ripples and spasms down the backs of her thighs to her knees. Her frantic cavortings encouraged the skimpy nylon panties to work their way further and further into her deeply inviting bottom-crack until they all but vanished, so that Jilly—much to her bitter mortification—was now receiving every smack on her bare bottom.

Wobbling and weaving beneath the hailstorm of spanks that showed no signs of abating, Jilly's lovely buttocks swiftly reddened and darkened to a rich scarlet. A pair of plump ripe tomatoes, Robert found himself comparing them to, as he steadily worked his way down the length of her right cheek to the tops of her thighs, then back up the left cheek.

Jilly's garbled pleas and protests rose in intensity until they became frenzied cries of distress. Robert noticed that the crowns of her buttocks were taking on a sort of goose-pimpled effect, liberally streaked with wine-coloured finger-marks. So he shifted his assault to the central zone of her bottom, where her luscious cheeks divided.

T,he sheer ignominy of being spanked in such a preciously intimate place as that finally broke Jilly's spirit and she shook with great rending sobs, ceasing to struggle anymore.

"Oh I'm sorry, I'm sorry!" she hiccupped pathetically as the great tears streamed down her face into her hair.

Robert stopped spanking her immediately, lifted her

carefully up from his lap, and laid her down on the
bed. Straightaway she rolled over onto her tummy,
groaning with pain and clutching at her hot stinging
rear.

Now that he'd won the battle Robert felt full of concern for her, worried lest he'd gone too far—punished
her too severely. Would she ever speak to him again?
Would she break it off with him? Even take him to
court?

To his unbounded relief and amazement, Jilly
seemed to bear him no resentment at all. She just lay
face down on the bed, totally preoccupied with her
burning bottom. It felt to her as swollen as a balloon,
throbbing with pain and still radiating the intense heat
Robert's hard male hand had imparted to it.

Robert felt distinct pangs of guilt. Was he, after all,
a brutal sadist who'd inflicted dire punishment on this
sweet innocent girl? He was racked by misgivings, so
much so he barely heard Jilly when she started moaning and crooning to herself in strange baby-like
language.

Then Robert caught the childish sounds. He listened
intently, an anxious frown on his face.

"So bad she was, so wicked . . . oh he *did* smack little Jilly hard! And she deserved every smack," she
whimpered tearfully into her pillow.

Robert bent down and stroked the back of her head,
saying nervously: "Are you all right, Jilly?" But she
didn't answer. She seemed to have lapsed into a childhood world of her own.

"Oh poor Jilly's bottie does hurt so!" she murmured
huskily to herself. "Must have been very naughty to
get smacked so many times . . . on her bare bum
too . . . naughtier even than when she stole the
sweeties . . . I'm glad he smacked me in private, not in

front of Auntie and the others . . . it's so awful when he does it and they're all watching."

Jilly's bizarre soliloquy gradually faded into wordless moans and sighs; and then nothing could be heard but her regular breathing as she drifted off into sleep.

Robert felt completely bemused. Clearly he could do nothing more with Jilly that evening—he'd already done more than enough—so he pulled the quilt up carefully and lovingly over the huddled sleeping form, then quietly let himself out of the room.

His own lodgings lay on the other side of the town. He let himself in, made a coffee, and took it to bed with him.

Jilly's weird verbal outpouring haunted him obsessively. He went over and over it in his mind, looking for clues. Had it been intended for his ears? Had she merely been thinking aloud—or had it been just sleep-talk? What on earth had she meant by "not in front of Auntie and the others?"

Robert was dreadfully worried that by physically punishing Jilly he'd somehow triggered off some inner trauma within her that had lain dormant for years.

He shifted restlessly in his bed. The night air was still hot and stifling. One way or another, Robert knew, he was going to get little, if any, sleep.

One question, above all else, kept repeating itself in his brain: what in God's name was he going to say to Jilly when he saw her next morning at lectures?

As it happened it turned out to be a lot easier than Robert had expected. Jilly greeted him in her customary manner: a languid "Hi," and her usual sulky, reluctant smile. She made no mention of what had taken place the night before, not even when they went for their mid-morning coffee-break in between lectures.

Robert found himself wondering whether he'd dreamt the whole episode.

Yet, as he looked at her across the coffee-table in the bustling college refectory, she *was* different . . . but in an intangible sort of way, calmer, preoccupied—even slightly withdrawn.

They stirred their coffee, and chatted about nothing in particular. Jilly said she'd like to visit Wenlock Edge at the weekend if the weather stayed fine. It was a favourite local beauty spot of hers which she'd been to many times before but never tired of. Robert said it was an excellent idea—he enjoyed going there, too.

Jilly got up to go, planted an impulsive, shy little kiss on Robert's lips, and went off to her lecture. She was wearing a grey cotton straight skirt and white top. Robert watched her trim buttocks sway appealingly from side to side as she walked out through the double doors. Then he gazed thoughtfully into thin air, lost in endless speculation—remembering the night before.

Saturday afternoon saw them strolling happily along a sun-dazed Wenlock Edge. A shimmering heat-haze seemed to enfold the whole world. Jilly had packed a picnic hamper and was wearing the filmy white cotton dress that Robert liked her in best of all. She had on a wide-brimmed straw hat, bedecked with flowers, and looked really radiant.

They walked together arm in arm, stopping frequently to admire the hazy view of the Welsh mountains looming purple on the dim horizon.

Then suddenly, as all lovers do, they quarrelled. Jilly made a tactless, cutting remark about one of Robert's friends. He ignored it and tried to change the subject, but Jilly's comments grew more and more spiteful, to the point of slander. She was like a dog gnawing on a bone—she just couldn't leave the topic alone.

Finally Robert's patience snapped and he told her how stupid she was to carry on so. Next minute they were in the thick of a flaming row. Jilly gave him a far-from-playful push—he stumbled, tripped over a fallen tree and fell flat on his face.

He sprang to his feet in a fury and bore down upon her. "You spiteful bitch!" he shouted.

Jilly stood her ground, defiant, arms akimbo: "Go on then, why don't you *spank* me again?" she sneered tauntingly. It was more than just a jibe—it hurt.

Robert recoiled, as though stung. So she *did* remember after all! He reddened guiltily. She'd hit him below the belt. How typical of her! Well—he'd had enough.

He threw his hands up in the air in a hopeless gesture of resignation and abandonment, turned, and began walking back the way they'd come, towards Wenlock village.

"Hey, where d'you think you're going?" she called after him in a voice full of sudden concern.

"I'm off, Jilly!" he yelled angrily over his shoulder. "That's it! You've done it! I quit! We're all washed-up!" and he continued on his path, ignoring her cries for him to come back. "I just can't cope with her anymore," he muttered to himself. "She's too much of a handful for me—or any man!"

He followed the track as it wound its way through a dense wood of beech trees. But as he emerged at the other end he saw Jilly standing there in his way looking chastened and forlorn. She must have taken a short cut to head him off. She knew those woodland paths a good deal better than he.

"I'm sorry I needled you, Robert," she said sadly. "I

know I am rotten to you sometimes. It's like there's a sort of demon inside me that makes me do it." She was beseeching him with those big sad brown eyes of hers—pleading with him not to leave her all alone.

The truth was that Robert had no real intention of leaving Jilly. He couldn't—she meant everything to him, and he suspected she knew it, too.

But his manhood balked at giving in too easily to her silly moods and tantrums—taking her back without making some reprisal, some show of force.

No, he was damned if he'd let her dangle him on a string like a stupid puppet. He just couldn't let her get away with it.

"All right, Jilly," he said quietly, "I'm prepared to forget about what happened a few minutes ago. But you did behave abominably towards me—and I'm going to punish you for it."

"Are you making conditions, Robert?" Jilly demanded, the demon in her flaring up again.

"Yes I am!" he insisted angrily. "After what you did I think I have every right to! I'm going to take you up on your offer and give you that spanking you suggested!"

Jilly froze. A look that Robert had never seen before came into her eyes: a look of fear mingled with excitement. She dropped the little picnic hamper and backed away from him. "You can't spank me here," she said in a trembling voice. "What if someone came along and saw us?"

Robert indicated the dense woods and foliage either side of the path along which he'd walked. "We'll go down there," he pointed to a secluded spinney over to their left. "Pick up your hamper, Jilly," he said, taking her by the arm.

Jilly felt her legs turn to jelly. She was gripped by a

strange kind of trepidation. Ever since Robert had spanked her last Tuesday night she'd thought of nothing else, apart from secretly hoping that he'd do it again. So she'd set out today deliberately to goad him into doing it a second time—and she'd succeeded.

But now that her plan had worked she was having second thoughts about it. After all, it had hurt terribly and she'd cried. Was she such a masochist as to want to go all through that again, not in the privacy of her bedroom this time but out in the open air, with the very real danger of some rambler—or even a whole party of them—crashing through the undergrowth and catching them in the act? It would be absolutely dreadful if someone saw her being spanked—she'd die of shame.

Yet at the same time every molecule in her body was crying out to be spanked. She desperately needed the security and firm reassurance of Robert's brute male strength controlling and mastering her, punishing her for her flightiness and devious trickery—just like her Uncle Ralph had done years ago.

"Robert, this is crazy. Supposing someone hears us?" Jilly protested weakly as they picked their way carefully over dead branches and clumps of nettles.

"There, look," Robert gestured towards the little clearing ahead. He tugged her by the arm and reluctantly Jilly followed. Her mouth had gone dry with excitement, her heart was pounding and she felt dizzy. Was he *really* going to spank her again? Dare he do it?

The mossy woodland glade couldn't have suited Robert's purpose better. It was a good fifty yards away from the path and more than adequately screened from it by row upon row of densely clustered beech trees.

Robert found a stump just the right height to sit on. He kicked away the fungus from its base, not wishing to spoil Jilly's pretty dress. Jilly stood before him,

116

nervously wringing her hands.

"Come on, over my knee," Robert urged her, hoarse with excitement. For a brief moment Jilly's demon lifted its head again. Why *should* she allow him to spank her? Who did he think he was—God Almighty?

Then she remembered how desolate she'd been when he'd walked away and left her. The little girl inside urged her to obey him: "Take the spanking like a good Jilly, then perhaps afterwards he'll cuddle you and make you feel all lovely and squidgy inside again!"

Shyly, timorously she placed her hands on Robert's muscular blue-denimed thighs. He took hold of her by the waist and pulled her across his lap until her bottom was in the correct position to be spanked.

Jilly found herself staring down at the deep-green carpet of moss which thickly covered the floor of the dimly lit glade. The dense foliage above their heads shut out the hot summer sun. There was a deathly hush, not even the breaking of a twig, which only intensified Jilly's acute embarrassment.

From the branch of a nearby beech a grey squirrel observed the two lovers. It peeped curiously at the dark-haired young girl in the white summer dress, draped submissively across the tall athletic-looking man's knee.

"Hurry up and get it over with please, Robert," Jilly whispered urgently. "I'm dead scared someone's going to come along and see us."

Robert, still angry with Jilly for the scene she'd caused, nevertheless couldn't help but grin wryly to hear her begging him to begin—she was literally asking for it.

In a flash he flipped up her skirt and petticoats at the back, and there was her delicious bottom, chastely clad in plain white cotton panties. Jilly uttered a loud wail of consternation: "Robert! What if someone should see?"

But her objections went unheeded as Robert swiftly applied a furious volley of stinging smacks to her lovely arse. The sounds exploded and echoed through the wooded glade.

Jilly wriggled and kicked like mad, but Robert held her tight round the waist and carried on smacking her wildly cavorting behind until, even through the white cotton panties, a rich carmine hue deepened and spread.

She panted, gasped, moaned, and finally yelled out her distress as the spanking quickly began to take effect. Her pride went out of the window, and all her feelings of stroppy rebelliousness dissolved as if by magic. Once more she became a soundly spanked, thoroughly penitent little girl—concerned only about the awful smarting of her poor punished bottom.

She began to blubber loudly as Robert vented the remainder of his anger on the tops of her nubile thighs—administering a tanning of a very different nature to the rich sun-tan they already possessed.

"Oh no, Robert, *please* don't smack me there—it hurts so. I'll do anything you say. I promise to be good—aaarrgh!"

With that last yell, so vibrant it sent a flock of crows fountaining up from the nearby tree-tops, Jilly arched her body upwards and outwards in a frantic attempt to escape the blistering rain of spanks. Her strength, born of desperation, surprised even Robert. She rolled off his lap and fell with an undignified bump onto the ground a few feet away.

"Ow!" she screeched as her tender bottom hit the ground.

Robert marveled at the sudden change in her. All her

former stroppiness had vanished, and in its place he saw the peaceful passivity, the well-chastised penitence and, above all else, the pleasing dependence of a well-disciplined child who knows she's been naughty and who has at last received the strict, yet loving, punishment she's been craving. Yes, the tear-stained look she gave him was, to his astonishment, one of loving gratefulness.

Robert sighed in mystification. Female psychology was something he'd never, ever understood.

He helped Jilly to her feet and picked up the picnic hamper while she shyly turned her back on him and removed the bits of twig and moss that had stuck to the seat of her knickers when she'd fallen.

Neither of them spoke. Events had taken place between them that seemed too deep for words.

Arm in arm they left the wood and picknicked in a nearby meadow. A deep inner contentment filled them both to the core. Cheese, French bread, and a bottle of red wine had never tasted better. Afterwards they fondled, kissed, and eventually fell asleep in the mellowing afternoon sun.

But that evening, as Robert sat alone in his study-bedroom, his books spread out on the table by the open window, he became once more guilty and troubled. He was a child of the sixties: his mother had been, and still was, deeply involved in the feminist movement. The belief that women should be treated as equals, their dignity not violated—*certainly* not subjected to physical correction—was deeply ingrained in him. If his mother knew that he'd twice put his girlfriend over his knee and spanked her, she'd never speak to him again.

But what made the whole thing even worse was that on both occasions Robert had become highly aroused by the sight of Jilly over his lap, her beautiful bottom reddening beneath his palm. Was there something wrong with him? Was he perverted? Should he see a psychiatrist?

He exacted a solemn promise from himself that on no account would he ever subject Jilly to such barbaric treatment again. He determined to forget the whole matter by immersing himself in his studies.

Jilly, on the other hand, was in seventh heaven. She utterly adored Robert for taking her so firmly in hand—especially as it gave her such exquisitely naughty sensations down between her legs. Well worth a soundly smacked arse she reflected, wriggling appreciatively.

Next time it happened she might even allow him to have his wicked way with her. She couldn't really think of a more exciting way to lose her virginity. She felt so hopelessly vulnerable after he'd spanked her that she was in no fit state to refuse him anything. Nor could she blame herself afterwards for what might occur in the heat of the moment. All in all, she couldn't wait for "it" to happen again . . .

But it didn't. It was Robert who now became strangely withdrawn, as though he was holding himself in check all the time. He continually allowed Jilly to get away with blue murder, with never a hint of a spanking—not even a slap. This infuriated Jilly with the result that she became twice as moody and stroppy as she'd ever been. She made Robert's life pure misery.

Exams had finished and the college year was drawing to a close. Mid-Summer Ball was only a week away, after which the students would disperse for the Long Vacation. By now both Robert and Jilly were feeling thoroughly wretched and ill at ease with each other—to such an extent that they took to avoiding one another's company.

Some weeks ago Robert had suggested that they might hitchhike across Europe during the summer holiday. But he'd made no mention of it since the incident at Wenlock Edge, and now Jilly was having to face the awful possibility of not seeing him at all for twelve weeks, since their respective homes were more than 200 miles apart. She didn't think she'd be able to bear that.

She knew she had to act, and act fast. She had somehow to push him past the limit, provoke him beyond all endurance. So she made her plans.

College tradition decreed that fancy dress be worn to the Mid-Summer Ball and this year the theme was to be "vicars and whores." Jilly decided to go the whole hog with a vengeance. She wrote a begging letter to her mother, and by return of post received a mild ticking-off for extravagence—and a cheque for £40. Jilly kissed it ecstatically, and rushed down to the bank to cash it. She spent the rest of that day shopping in town.

On the night of the ball when Robert called to collect her from her lodgings, his eyes nearly fell out of their sockets. He gaped in amazement at Jilly's bizarre appearance. Instead of the open-air, fresh-faced, demurely dressed girl he'd grown accustomed to, there stood before him a volatile sex-bomb: her long black hair piled on top of her head and cascading vividly down, her bare back in ringlets, a tight black sweater that showed off far too much of her cleavage, and an even more vulgarly tight black straight skirt that ended inches above her knees and which accentuated her shapely bottom to the point of obscenity.

To crown it all, Jilly was wearing black stockings—sheer ones with a seam running up the back of the leg.

Robert knew they were stockings, not tights. Anyone who cared to look could tell, because he could clearly see the outline of her garter belt beneath the drum-tight skirt.

A string of garish purple beads adorned her neck, and her fingers were bedecked with rings. She'd gone to town with make-up, too, especially blusher and eye-shadow. The black stiletto high-heeled shoes Jilly was wearing made her stick her bottom out suggestively, drawing even more attention to it.

All in all, Jilly looked precisely the sort of girl Robert's mother had warned him about consorting with—in a word, devastating.

"You can't go to the ball dressed like that, Jilly!" he gasped.

"Why the hell not? You look pretty stupid yourself, if you must know," Jilly retorted, gazing scornfully at Robert's blond hair plastered down with Brylcreem, his shabby black suit, and the pathetically makeshift dog-collar cut out of white cardboard.

"I didn't mean you looked stupid, Jilly," Robert replied, ignoring her crushing remark about his own get-up. "What I meant was—well, it doesn't look decent. You'll have all the men buzzing round you like bees round a honey-pot."

Jilly made a defiant gesture. "I doubt if *you'd* care a scrap, after all the attention you've been paying me lately—*I don't think!*"

She slung her handbag over her shoulder and set off angrily up the road, with the exaggerated bum-wiggle of a Paris street-walker. Robert stared with morbid fascination at her erotically swaying backside, shrugged his shoulders in resigned despair, and plodded after her.

True to his misgivings, the evening turned out to be

an endless nightmare for Robert. Jilly was constantly surrounded by swarms of admirers, and Robert suffered intense humiliation at seeing his girl groped, pinched, kissed, tweaked, tickled, fondled by all and sundry. Jilly, by nature a rather shy reserved sort of girl, made no effort at all to repel these boorish male advances: in fact she giggled, flirted, and generally gave them all the come-on.

Robert didn't get to dance with her all night. Whenever he asked her she pulled a face and said she was too tired. Yet the moment his back was turned, there she was jiving energetically to the rock 'n' roll music in the middle of the floor with someone else.

The last straw was when he saw Jilly bend down to adjust the strap of one of her shoes—and some beer-swilling yob slapped her hard on the behind, causing everyone around her to laugh uproariously.

That really made Robert see red. Jilly's arse was *his* territory, *his* domain! No one but he had the right to smack it! He waded in, a look of such furious anger on his face that the drunken perpetrator of the act backed away rapidly, a mumbled apology on his lips. His cronies scattered, too, so that for the first time all evening Jilly and he were actually alone.

"You, my girl, are coming home with me—pronto!" he hissed furiously in her ear.

"Oh but darling, the night is still young!" she replied with mocking gaiety and turned to go, but Robert grabbed her by the wrists and practically frogmarched her out of the crowded hall into the cool night air.

"Let me go! Where do you think you're taking me?" Jilly protested indignantly, struggling in his vise-like grip.

"To my place—my landlady's gone away for the weekend and we won't be disturbed," he muttered

123

darkly, the anger seething in his veins. A sense of delicious apprehension at his words made Jilly's legs go weak, so weak Robert almost had to carry her home to his lodgings.

Up in his room she faced him timorously, looking round like a hunted deer for some means of escape while he stood glowering furiously at her.

"I swore to myself I wouldn't do it again, but by God, Jilly, you're enough to try the patience of a saint!" he roared, almost beside himself.

"D-do *what* again, Robert?" Jilly stammered fearfully, no longer the flirtatious belle of the ball she'd been a short while back. She'd never seen him so angry in his life. She had no idea he cared so much about her. That, at least, was terribly reassuring—and terribly, terribly exciting.

"Take that disgusting skirt off *at once!*" Robert yelled in a paroxysm of fury. Too terrified to do anything but obey, Jilly undid the button at the back, unzipped it, and self-consciously wriggled her way out of it—the skirt was much too tight to slip down of its own accord—until at last it lay crumpled at her feet.

Without her skirt Jilly felt exposed and dreadfully vulnerable. Robert's rage was simmering and bubbling, like a volcano about to erupt. He was glaring wrathfully at her knickers. She'd chosen them with great care: exquisitely dainty little French knickers in white combed-cotton, trimmed with a ribbon-bow at the waist, and with deep lacy hems that revealed a lot more than they concealed—especially at the back, where they hugged her bottom cleft quite scandalously. Jilly had begrudged paying nearly ten pounds for a pair of panties, but she'd fallen in love with them the moment she'd seen them hanging on a rack in the lingerie department of the most exclusive department store in town.

As Robert stared in open-mouthed astonishment at Jilly's panties, everything suddenly clicked into place. She's bought those panties deliberately to get spanked in! he thought. The realization struck him like a laser-beam. It opened up all kinds of fascinating speculations. Well, if that's what she wants. But after the merry dance Jilly's led me tonight, she'll find she's bitten off more than she can chew. I'll tan that sexy little arse of hers till she can't sit down for a fortnight! he reflected with grim satisfaction.

He looked at the stockings she was wearing: wicked black stockings clinging to her long shapely legs, and attached to a tiny white satin garter belt. No wonder she'd driven all the men mad that night, he thought, fuming.

"Tramp! Prick-teaser!" he yelled at her. Jilly cowered in a corner, her hands instinctively shielding her pubis from the whiplash of his spleen. "I'll teach you to flaunt yourself like a common prostitute, and make a complete and utter fool of me!" he roared. Tears of rage glistened in his eyes.

Jilly, quaking in her shoes though she was, felt she'd never loved him as much as she did at that moment.

"You belong to *me—me!* D'you hear?" he bellowed. "You're no one else's property but *mine!* Now, sexypants," he went on sarcastically, "you'd better take down those frilly panties of yours, 'cos the way I'm feeling right now, I'm going to spank you so hard I'd probably split them. And we don't want to ruin such pretty pants as those, do we!" he sneered gloatingly.

Jilly felt she was a seething morass of conflicting emotions: intense love for Robert because, at long last, he was showing he really *did* care; an almost embarrassing build-up of longing and sexual desire for what

125

she knew was about to happen; a feeling of complete security and trust in him; and finally, sheer gut-wrenching trepidation and dread of the spanking-to-end-all-spankings he was on the point of giving her.

Then something within her snapped and she started to cry. Whether they were tears of terror, shame, relief, or even happiness, she couldn't say.

"Oh Robert, I *do* so love you!" Jilly sobbed, as she began to obediently pull down her white cotton French knickers. With them clinging round her knees, she started to move awkwardly towards him and the upright wooden chair he was positioning in the centre of the room.

He sat down, stiff and erect, and she went across his knee like a lamb. He ran his hand up and down the silky sheen of her black nylon stockings, and toyed with the ruched straps of her garter belt, making sure they were well away from the area of soft white flesh he was about to spank unmercifully. Her panties slid further and further down her legs until they ended up draped comically around her black high-heeled shoes.

It was the very first time Robert had seen Jilly's bottom completely bare and, furious though he was with her, he couldn't help gazing in wonder at the magnificent ivory orbs of her buttocks, so white and smooth they might have been sculpted from marble. From the deep division of her bum-cleft, they curved outwards and upwards proudly and provocatively, until they reached the full erotic swell of her buttock-crowns—rounded and symmetrical as twin full moons, in dramatic contrast to her slender little waist.

Robert felt his sex stiffen and engorge. He could do nothing to prevent it, yet he cursed himself inwardly for allowing his sexual appetite to rear its head at such an inopportune moment as this.

He gritted his teeth and tried not to look at the delicate wisps of pubic hair shyly peeping out from between Jilly's legs. Yet the more Robert strove to ignore Jilly's blatantly displayed intimate anatomy, the more his penis grew and grew, thrusting up insistently against the yielding female flesh it was nestling against.

Eve! Temptress! It was all *her* fault. Even while she was crying, all helpless and forlorn, she was still unashamedly flaunting her charms and he—like a sucker—was falling for them!

His anger rose again within him and he smacked Jilly hard on the right buttock—then again, and again, and again. The loud fleshy reports seemed to fill the whole room.

He switched to Jilly's other cheek and spanked it fiercely till his hand hurt, and the colour of the left buttock out-rivalled its neighbour in glowing rubescence.

Jilly's pretty face was streaming with hot gushing tears that played havoc with her carefully applied make-up. Her mascara ran in tiny rivulets down her upturned face and into her hair. Her sobs became moans as she rocked up and down on his lap, her bottom rising to meet his descending hand, then slumping back down again after the explosive impact.

Somehow Robert felt that this wasn't enough. Jilly had to be taught a proper lesson—but his hand was aching like fury, and he knew he couldn't keep up the spanking for very much longer.

Then he noticed his clothesbrush, lying on the floor near the chair. Long-handled, with a varnished wooden back to it, it would do perfectly. He leaned over and picked it up.

Robert held it by the handle and tapped the oval-shaped back against the plump centre of Jilly's blazing-red bottom. She stopped wriggling and went

127

rigid immediately she felt the hard back of the brush tap-tapping purposefully against her bottom cheeks.

"Listen to me, Jilly," he said crisply. "I've worn my hand out on your bum, but I still don't think you've been punished enough. So I'm going to use my clothes-brush on you till I think you've had the thorough spanking you deserve. Understand?"

Jilly shifted her position ever so gingerly. Her flanks were already very sore and painful. "Yes," she whispered in that far-away, meek little girlish voice Robert had noticed her use the first time he'd punished her. "Jilly's been ever, ever so naughty, and no one loves her anymore," she lisped in a childlike voice, "so she deserves to get her bottie well and truly tanned. Please, *please* smack naughty Jilly's bottom as hard as you can . . . then she'll be awfully good and do anything you say."

Robert shook his head in bewilderment at Jilly's strange words—actually encouraging him to wallop her bare backside as hard as ever he could. But he refused to listen to whatever his conscience might say about it, and raised the clothesbrush high above Jilly's quivering bottom.

It landed with a dull thud, momentarily indenting the buttock cheek it collided with. Not nearly as spectacu-larly noisy as his hand, but infinitely more painful for Jilly—judging by her reaction. She yelled loudly, drew her stockinged legs up off the ground and likewise raised her head and shoulders until she was as straight as an arrow.

This slackened the muscles in her bottom, making the flesh more yielding and cushiony, so Robert—ignoring her cries of distress—whacked Jilly again and again on the soft round orbs of her buttocks until they took on an angry purple hue.

While belabouring her, he gave vent to the frustration and grief she'd caused him at the ball:

"You're *mine!*"

WHACK!

"Ooh!!" she screeched.

"Mine!"

WHACK!!

"Robert!! Aaargh!!"

"Mine!"

WHACK!!

"Eeeow!! Urgh! Robert, *please* listen!!!" she begged him desperately.

He stopped, the clothesbrush suspended in mid-air.

"Robert," Jilly spluttered, awash with cool purging tears, "I LOVE YOU! I'm yours now, for always. *Please* take me to bed."

He did. And it was perfect beyond belief for both of them.

Afterwards, as they lay together snug and sleepy, they unburdened their consciences to one another.

He told her about his mother's feminism, and how it had rubbed off on him.

"But Robert, just because you spank me, that doesn't make you a male chauvinist pig! I'm sure even feminists get spanked sometimes!" she teased him gently. He grinned and they both began to laugh.

Then it was her turn to be serious. She told him about her Uncle Ralph who used to spank her when she went to stay with him and her aunt years ago. She'd never forgotten the feelings of warmth and security those spankings had given her—especially as her father had been cold and unloving towards her as a child, and had made it no secret that he'd have preferred a son. She looked suddenly sad.

Robert leaned over and gently kissed her. "Jilly," he

said, trying to change the subject, "are you aware of some of the things you come out with while I'm spanking you?"

"No, I didn't think I said anything except 'Ouch! Yarroo! My poor arse!'" Jilly replied impishly. "Why, darling, what *do* I say!"

Robert was about to tell her when he stopped and thought for a moment. Maybe it would worry Jilly if she knew she lapsed back into childhood. Maybe all that would go in time, so he simply laughed and said: "You come out with really wicked things like, 'Robert, please will you fuck me!'"

Jilly blushed and hid her face in her hair. She couldn't believe she could feel so happy.

Tessa and the Archaeologist

For Richard Hankey, history teacher at St. Esmeralda's, the fifth form's weekend field trip that July was a nightmare. At the last minute on Saturday morning when the coach was due to leave, there was an urgent message from Miss Trubshaw, the other teacher accompanying them. She'd gone down with flu and couldn't come. Hankey's heart sank. He would be the only member of staff on the field trip, with sole responsibility for twenty teenage girls.

It was a sickeningly daunting prospect, made worse by the knowledge that Tessa Walker, the fifth form's most troublesome pupil, had decided to join the party. She couldn't possibly be interested in the archaeological "digs" they were to visit, that was for sure, Hankey thought grimly. The only thing she could possibly be interested in was making life miserable for himself.

They boarded the coach, a noisy rabble of excitable jostling girls, followed by the worried young master. Tessa, he noticed, was sporting a positively indecent blue denim mini-skirt. And, heavens, were those stockings she was wearing, too? Hankey forced himself to look away as she wriggled suggestively down the coach to occupy a place in the centre of the back seat.

Tessa Walker was easily the most infuriating girl pupil Hankey had ever taught. She talked non-stop during his classes, fluttering her large heavily made-up eyes at him, and always ready to utter a quip—a witty remark that would send the class into hoots of laughter, completely negating his authority. Though she drove him mad, there was no denying that she was, for her seventeen years, one of the prettiest girls in the school.

Shoulder-length blonde curls framed her face. She had sharp blue eyes full of devilment, freckles that peppered her little snub nose most appealingly, and a pouting mouth that made a perfect "kiss me" rosebud whenever Hankey looked at her. She possessed the maddening ability to be extremely sexually provocative and yet act as though she was completely unaware of it. The almost Pre-Raphaelite innocent face was completely at variance with the precocious sexuality of her lovely blossoming young body.

Hankey watched her shrug off her jacket as it might slip languidly from the shoulders of a model on a catwalk. Sure enough, she wore a white nylon blouse which was semi-transparent, and a see-through bra underneath. He noticed the coach driver goggling in his mirror as she tucked her blouse into her skirt, thrusting her bosom deliberately at her audience who watched unblinkingly as her nipples budded and grew erect like plum-coloured bulls-eyes surrounded by the soft, tender swelling roundness of her breasts.

Hankey sighed in despair. As the coach moved away he saw the driver's eyes remaining fixed on his mirror as Tessa completed her performance, slowly inching up her skirt and adjusting her suspenders with a vexatious pout—displaying to all the world the tight white triangle of her knickers.

Hankey sat down feeling as if he'd overdressed for the very hot July weather. He adjusted his tie and coughed self-consciously. Tessa, he was aware, was watching him.

After an initial spell of high spirits the girls settled down and Hankey dared to relax. This state of affairs, however, was not to last.

A sudden wave of hushed, suppressed excitement rippled through the coach from front to back. Soon several girls had left their seats and formed a crush around the back seat. Hankey looked resolutely forward, flinching from the trouble brewing behind him, feeling his stomach bunching into a painful knot. It had to be Tessa.

Peals of rude laughter broke out and suddenly the impish brunette, Angela Richards, rushed back to her seat in the front with a piece of paper in her hand. A tidal wave of indignant girls surged up the coach aisle and the air became full of shrieks and hysteria. Hankey reluctantly rose from his seat. The driver was mumbling abuse and threatening to stop the coach.

"What's going on here?" snapped Hankey in his best authoritative voice.

"It's *mine!*" shrieked Angela Richards.

"Get back to your seats AT ONCE," he thundered. Still giggling, the girls obeyed. Tessa, her legs crossed provocatively revealing a tantalizing area of her stocking tops, raised an eyebrow at Hankey. He immediately felt his skin prickle.

Turning to Angela he demanded, "What are you hiding down your jumper? Give it to me."

The girl blushed and looked desperately for support among her cronies. Hankey glared down at her all the more fiercely because he could feel Tessa's challenging sarcastic stare at him.

With trembling fingers and a nervous giggle, Angela put her hand down her jumper and withdrew a magazine cut-out picture. She handed it to Hankey amid horrified exclamations and tittering.

He stared at the picture and blinked. It was a picture of male genitalia. A detailed close-up photograph.

Someone sniggered and said cheekily, "Is yours as big as that, Sir?"

He twisted round but could not spot the culprit. Tessa? Her eyes met his, calm and mocking. She appeared so innocent that he was absolutely sure she was involved in some way—but as always he knew it would be hard to find proof.

"This is disgusting," he said tonelessly to the gaggle of tittering girls, "and not in the least amusing." He pocketed the photograph. "I shall deal with this at school on Monday."

There was a hush. Then from the back seat he heard a comment which robbed him devastatingly of his confidence:

"What Angela needs, Sir, is a jolly good spanking, don't you think?" It was the sinuous husky voice of Tessa Walker. The coach lurched and Hankey stumbled wildly into one of the seated girls, grabbing her by the thighs to steady himself. She shrieked loudly.

"That will do, Tessa," he said breathlessly, avoiding her eyes. Sudden heat and anger rose within him; his collar seemed to have an unbearable stranglehold on him. Impatiently he wrenched at his tie. The top shirt button flew off and landed between the slender stocking-clad legs of his tormentor, who calmly and deliberately put her foot over it.

Feeling faint, he slumped in his seat. That damned girl dared to tell him what to do! Spanked indeed! If anyone needed a spanking it was that provocative young Miss. And how he'd love to give her one! He stared with unseeing eyes at the road ahead. Perhaps Tessa had noticed his reaction to her unsettling remark; her eyes had a soul-searching candour and missed little. Nevertheless, he thought consolingly, she did not know about the magazines that lay guiltily hidden under his bed. She did not know about his fantasies. Or did she?

Hankey felt suddenly angry at Miss Trubshaw's ill-timed absence. He was powerless against the scrutiny of so many girls probing and needling him to reveal a chink in his armor. Righteous indignation flared and he crossed his legs assertively in the aisle, visible to every pair of eyes, in an attempt to show his authority.

His composure was uneasy. With sickening unpredictability a sharp vision of Tessa filled his mind. There she was, for a vivid fleeting moment in his imagination, stripped of her blouse and skirt . . . lying across his knees . . . her well-fleshed buttocks sticking vulgarly high up in the air . . . and his hands . . . hotly descending. The thought consumed him so much that he shook, and lest his trembling legs should give him away he abruptly shifted them from the aisle and tucked them tight under his seat.

The coach swerved down a narrow ill-kept lane. Hankey looked out in relief. They must be approaching the first archaeological site whose director was none other than Sir Montague Driver, celebrated authority on all things pre-historic, and famed for his BBC 2 series.

"Girls, girls," he cried excitedly above their chatter, "this is the first site—and we're lucky enough to be invited here by Sir Montague Driver!" He panted as the coach lurched over pot-holes and ruts, coming to an abrupt halt. He clung to his seat tightly, not wanting a repetition of that earlier mortifying incident.

"I need not remind you," he shouted ineffectually as the girls pressed forward like an eager army, "to be on your very best behavior."

They leapt out. Tessa lingered until last, adjusting her stockings again for the benefit of the driver, who grinned lecherously at her in his mirror.

As she passed Hankey's seat she deftly removed her chewing-gum and stuck a huge lurid pink wodge of it on his seat. Hankey could do nothing. Sir Montague Driver was waiting.

Losing the girls like a pack of scattering rabbits, and desperately trying to maintain control, he came face to face with the eminent man who walked briskly towards him brandishing a stick.

"I say, young fellow, are these your lot?" he bellowed. "Kindly control them, sir! The art of centuries could be ruined by all those careless feet!" Sir Montague, dressed in khaki safari jacket and breeches, thick woollen socks and brogues, loomed over the young teacher. Hankey swallowed. Driver was even more formidable in the flesh than on the screen. He had a wild shock of grey hair that blew about in an undisciplined manner, intense pale blue eyes, and a thick bristly nicotine-stained walrus moustache which he smoothed constantly with huge sausage-like fingers.

"I think they're eager to see what's going on here, Sir Montague," Hankey said ineffectually.

"Are they indeed? *Hey, don't drop your litter here, Miss!*" he thundered, waving his stick ferociously in the air at some miscreant who had let a crisp packet flutter onto the immaculate excavation, swept cleaner than the average kitchen floor.

Hankey's eyes were drawn to Tessa, bending over with most convincing interest, innocently unaware that her engrossment in a dry stone bank had caused her skirt to rise well above her stocking tops. He swallowed. If she tipped over any further . . . He caught sight of the brief white panties, the expanse of bare thigh and the full round curve of her cheeks fleshing out beneath their tightness.

Blinking hard, he turned to Sir Montague, who wondered vaguely why the young teacher seemed so flustered and embarrassed all of a sudden.

"If they're here for a conducted tour," Sir Montague rasped, "let's get this rabble of yours organized, sir." He turned to Hankey who was undecided whether to shout at the girls and be ignored or chase after them and appear undignified.

"What they need is a dose of discipline—military style!" grated Sir Montague enthusiastically, and he moved towards the scattered girls, waving his stick in an alarming manner.

"FALL IN, YOU LOT!" he bellowed as if they were a bunch of raw army recruits.

To Hankey's surprise the tactic worked. No one could possibly ignore Sir Montague as he moved agilely among them with the air of a perverse mountain goat, touching heads with his stick to get them into line and shouting in everyone's face. Flushed with the success of his little campaign, the director wasted no time once they were all herded together and started to tell them all about the excavation.

He droned on. Hankey noticed that no one was listening. Tessa was surreptitiously eating her lunch at the back of the group and when she caught sight of him, champed vulgarly on her chicken leg. She slowly stuck out her tongue—ostensibly to lick her lips—but Hankey knew it was done to insult him. He bristled but could do nothing except glare at her. It was fortunate that Sir Montague was oblivious to any distractions. Even the sudden roar of a low-flying army jet ripping across the sky could not quell his sonorous cadences.

Tessa calmly threw her neatly picked chicken bone down into an excavated trench. Hankey's eyes bulged in impotent fury. He tried to slip away and retrieve the offending item, but Sir Montague, borne aloft on the fulsomeness of his own oratory, gripped Hankey by the arm in his fervour, so that he could not move.

A subtle shifting among the girls . . . a ripple of suppressed giggling . . . and Hankey's skin began to prickle in apprehension. Something was about to happen, he just knew it.

Tessa put up her hand. Hankey groaned inwardly. What was the girl getting up to now?

"Sir Montague?" she lisped.

It was a moment before the archaeologist noticed her and when he did he stopped in mid-sentence, his mouth a circle of amazement that someone should dare interrupt him.

"What is it, girl?" he snapped.

Tessa moved slowly forward, lowering her eyes respectfully.

"I've just seen something very exciting." She pointed down into the excavated trench. "Could you tell us what it is, sir?" she asked coyly. "It might be an archaeological discovery."

Sir Montague coughed. He was a little surprised, despite his arrogance, that anyone should find his work of interest. Especially this rabble of precocious females. He moved to where Tessa had pointed and the girls massed round. Hankey followed them uneasily.

"It's down there, sir—right at the bottom of that pit!" She bent over and pretended to lose her balance. Hankey rushed to grab her as her feet scuffed the edge of the director's precious earthwork.

Sir Montague's eyebrows shot up dramatically as Tessa's stocking tops and plump white thighs came into view, and the young master's rescue attempt so clumsily revealed even more of her nubile anatomy. In his panic Hankey lunged awkwardly at Tessa, throwing his

138

arms around her waist. Her skirt shot up in a tangle around her middle revealing her bottom cheeks, threatening to burst from her tightly stretched knickers, and his fingers became embarrassingly entangled with one of her suspenders. Sir Montague, however, was more interested in the possible discovery of skeletons in the earthwork than in the finer points of a young woman's posterior.

He climbed down carefully into the trench, panting with the effort, and for a moment the khaki-clad figure disappeared from view.

Hankey seized the opportunity to deal with young Tessa. He desperately wanted to give her a good shaking—or something. Tell her to behave, and to stop making such a vulgar spectacle of herself every time she bent over—but he couldn't very well do *that*.

"Tessa!" he hissed at the girl, who had slipped unobtrusively to the back of the crowd. "Tessa, for God's sake." But his words choked in his throat as Sir Montague surfaced from the pit, his face an ominous red. Spluttering with anger, he clambered out and walked straight towards Hankey.

"This," he snarled, "*this* is the archaeological discovery, sir!" and he dropped Tessa's chicken bone into Hankey's sweating hands.

It was necessary to appease the archaeologist's wrath, so Hankey drew the girls aside and berated them sternly for what had happened—no easy task with the great man standing behind the master, prompting him at every pause. He felt it unwise to single Tessa out from the bunch for two reasons: she might easily make him look a fool, and he rather wanted to deal with her himself—later.

The next part of the outing was a visit to the Long Man of Warmington, a prehistoric chalk carving which

Sir Montague had discovered and personally restored. It was a short walk from the archaeological site on the top of a steep hill flanking the excavation.

"Up the hill, you lot!" ordered Sir Montague, curling his moustache impatiently and tapping the girls on their bottoms with his stick as if he were herding reluctant sheep. Then he brought up the rear with Hankey, walking at a brisk pace.

Hankey was spared no blushes when Angela Richard's short skirt blew up in a sudden gust of wind and Sir Montague, witnessing the spectacle of her round nubile bottom cheeks so unexpectedly exposed, promptly slapped them hard, making her squeal and jump. She ran ahead, clutching the wayward garment close to her legs, fearful of another assault. Sir Montague obviously knew how to handle them, thought Hankey ruefully.

They reached the hilltop where suddenly the girls, who had been chattering non-stop on the way up, fell silent. They were looking at the Long Man. Hankey, last on the hilltop looked, too—and cringed with embarrassment.

Before them, etched into the chalk, was a huge crude representation of a man, undoubtably male, with an enormously disproportionate erect phallus that stretched almost to his chin.

Sir Montague beamed at the awe-struck girls. At least they were showing some interest in their heritage.

"Girls," he said solemnly to the silent huddle, "you see before you the most enormous prehistoric erection known to man." And he waved his stick up and down the length of the figure. Twenty pairs of eyes swiveled to Sir Montague's face, and twenty mouths slowly, incredulously, fell open.

Sir Montague paused for the impact of his reverently

spoken information to be absorbed—only to realise that he had addressed his unfortunate remark to a silly bunch of indifferent adolescent girls, obsessed with only one thing. Sex. With a pucker and a wince, his ruddy face struggled for composure through the awkward pause. The ends of his walrus moustache disappeared momentarily into the corners of his mouth as he sucked in both cheeks and then blew the wispy hairs out again in an explosive rush of air.

"Hmmm hmm," he cleared his throat loudly and looked away, uncharacteristically lost for words.

The girls circled around the monument in awed silence. Tessa, frowning with concentration, measured the length of the interesting part, pacing around it before conferring with the others.

"Isn't it a bit unrealistic, sir?" she asked Hankey who stood there blushing uncontrollably, not knowing where to look.

"What do you mean?" he stammered, trying vainly to catch Sir Montague's eye for some moral support.

"Well," Tessa paused, curling a lock of her blonde hair around her finger, "it's not like that in real life, is it? I mean a man's . . . his . . . would never reach to his chin, would it?" She looked unblinkingly at Hankey who wondered how he could turn his red embarrassed face into the hot humiliated anger he felt seething impotently inside him. Sir Montague came to his rescue.

"It's a fertility symbol, Miss," he said testily, locking his piercing blue eyes firmly at Tessa's appealingly innocent ones.

"It's time for lunch," interjected Hankey with relief, and the girls dispersed, giggling.

With a critical up-shot of his fearsome eyebrows at Hankey, Sir Montague disappeared and the young master crept halfway down the hill to eat his sandwiches and hopefully enjoy some bird-watching with his new field glasses to calm his nerves. He had no desire to see any of the girls. He hoped he could leave them unsupervised for a short while. After all, he reflected, there was very little they could destroy on the hilltop. The chalk figure seemed immune to their meddling—hadn't it remained unsullied for centuries?

Tessa was lying full length along the fertility symbol in the hot sun. It was wider than her body and much taller.

"Just imagine," she mused to herself, "if he was a real live man. If he walked about like that all the time he'd overbalance." She turned over lazily. "I'm going to sunbathe," she announced, and calmly wriggled out of her blouse and shirt.

Hankey, at that moment, was beginning to feel pangs of unease at leaving the girls, so he reluctantly climbed the hill to spy on them. What he saw made him sink to the ground, spellbound.

Tessa was in the act of removing her stockings like a stripper—much to the delight of her friends. Clad only in her see-through bra and ridiculously inadequate knickers which barely covered her pubic triangle, she danced seductively up and down the Long Man.

Hankey swallowed. He couldn't take his eyes off her.

There came an excited chorus of, "Take 'em off, Tessa—we dare you!" as the girls closed ranks into a circle.

"Where's Wanky Hankey?" she cried in response, writhing her semi-naked body like a snake.

"Down the hill somewhere with his binocs. Wanking, I expect," screamed Angela Richards impatiently.

Tessa looked about her. Hankey and Sir Montague

were nowhere in sight so she began her performance.

To lewd choruses of "The Stripper," she unhooked her bra, shaking her breasts free. The garment fell at her feet and she moved around the circle, wriggling her body so that her firm full breasts wobbled under each girl's nose in the sunlight. There were gasps of excitement. Returning to the centre of the circle, she caressed and squeezed her breasts in front of them all. Pouting in an exaggerated manner, she pinched each nipple until it swelled into a port-wine bud and, sticking her tongue out, ran it salaciously around her provocative rosebud mouth.

Hankey's eyes were watering with the effort of staring at her and he was breathing in little shallow bursts. He couldn't move. He *had* to see what she was going to do next.

Tessa turned away from him, presenting her lovely supple back and curvy rounding of her hips, still swaying rhythmically from side to side. Placing her thumbs inside the top of her knickers over her hips, she inched the nylon down . . . down . . . alternating each deliberate movement with a pronounced jerk and wobble of her buttocks as the knickers strained over their fullness.

"Oh, my God . . ." said Hankey, transfixed and unbearably excited.

The knickers settled in the crease below each cheek, held there deliciously by the weight of curvaceous flesh above, and the plumpness of her thighs.

Hankey's eyes were glued to Tessa's bottom, to the rising and falling of her cheeks, as she undulated like a belly dancer. He was dimly aware of applause from the little group as his eyes roved hungrily over every inch of her womanly, well-developed body, to the dimples halfway down each bottom cheek. "What she needs is—" he murmured, but was unable to finish in his rapture.

Tessa, completely naked, turned slowly around, her arms raised above her head in triumph, before throwing herself to the ground, prostrating herself face down in an act of mock worship along the length of the Long Man.

Hankey moved away, his heart pounding, a sharp image of her in his mind. The hussy, to affect him so! How he dearly wanted to punish her for her very provocativeness—right on her maddeningly saucy backside!

Tessa lay still for a minute after her performance, while her classmates applauded her. Then, suddenly bored, she got up and dressed. It was such a pity, she thought, that Mr. Hankey hadn't witnessed her little drama. After all, in her mind she'd done it all especially for him.

The coach driver had vanished. For a time the girls and their master were abandoned on the hill. Hankey thought it best to turn a blind eye to their indolence as they wandered off in pairs to sunbathe in the hot languid July afternoon.

Tessa returned to her sunbathing on the most coveted part of the Long Man.

She was naked apart from her bra and panties, and she lay spread-eagled on her tummy like an obeisant priestess during a fertility ritual. Her bare bottom-cheeks that bulged out from beneath the taut elastic pinkened a little in the sun, but as the afternoon wore on she began to grow tired of sunbathing and searched for something entertaining to do.

Presently a daring idea struck her and she found a stone and started to scratch away at the grass, exposing the chalk underneath. A wicked gleam came into her eyes. She was going to add her own contribution to history.

Hankey spent a miserable time trying to sustain interest in his hobby while wrestling with his feelings. Try as he might, he could not erase the tantalizing erotic picture of that nubile seventeen-year-old and her powerfully arousing strip-tease. Again and again he saw her bottom cheeks, strokingly round and curvy, humping up and down on the chalk monster in an obvious suggestive manner. Naked . . . bare . . . the small shoulders . . . the hollow in the small of her back. Her buttocks, rising and dividing like twin hills. Her thighs closing tight and contracting. He felt sick with frustration and at the same time furious with himself for allowing a mere slip of a girl to arouse him so.

When the coach driver returned—the worse for drink—Hankey speedily rounded up the girls and marched them back to the coach. They had mostly congregated at Sir Montague's excavation since the arrival of three bronzed young men. He did not notice that Tessa was missing. Sir Montague was trowelling away fiercely on a shard-littered floor, glowering at the noisy girls and bellowing short commands to the three male helpers.

They boarded the coach.

"Where is Tessa Walker?" Hankey asked, noticing the vacant seat in the back.

"Dunno, Sir—haven't seen her," came the unhelpful reply.

Hankey sighed and bit his lip. The coach was stiflingly hot, the driver cross, and the girls all yelling through the windows at the three young men. He saw Sir Montague throw down his trowel in disgust, pick up his tobacco and stick, and stamp angrily away. The minutes ticked by and Hankey became frantic trying to pacify everyone at once. Where the hell was she?

On the top of the hill Tessa Walker stood up and admired her work. Those few finishing touches to the Long Man were a definite improvement. She giggled aloud. "Long Man" he certainly was—and oh, she'd altered him so artistically! The effect now was really quite comical. The enormous phallus, now even longer, extended to the lips of the expressionless monster. It resembled a giant lollipop. Scratching with her stone, she'd removed the turf carefully to extend the monster-organ and skilfully patch up the original end until it was invisible.

She imagined how the next person would react on seeing the masterpiece. Prehistoric pornographia! She laughed delightedly.

To her misfortune, the first person to see it was Sir Montague Driver.

"Oh my God!" she breathed in horror as Sir Montague strode towards her, waving his stick like a belligerent conductor.

"God won't help you now!" he blazed, his watery eyes bulging apoplectically. "What the hell do you think you're doing?" He strode smartly up to her, stopped, and looked down. The defaced organ lay between them.

Tessa, taken completely unawares, lost her usual composure and turned very red. He was ranting at her so dementedly that she feared he might push her down the hill, and he was getting redder and redder by the second. She longed for Mr. Hankey and the sanctuary of the coach. She thought it wise to be as contrite as possible and maybe tell a few lies to get her out of the mess.

"I'm very sorry, Sir," she stuttered when he paused for breath, "but I . . . I didn't mean it. Mr. Hankey says I'm a deprived child, and deprived children—"

"Rubbish!" snapped the archaeologist. "I've never heard such rubbish! The only deprivation you're suffering from, Miss, is an utter ignorance of the fundamentals of good behavior!"

Tessa began to feel uncomfortably vulnerable, perched on the hill with this totally obsessive and wrathful man. It crossed her mind that she might try and run away, but her legs felt so jelly-like she decided not to. She looked at Sir Montague out of the corner of her eyes; he was too formidable to look at properly. She wished she hadn't worn such a short tight skirt. It made her look older than her years and more self-assured. Perhaps if she'd worn her demure little school uniform she'd look pathetic and appealing? Her heavy make-up, sexually provocative skirt and blouse, gave her the appearance of a rebellious troublemaker, and the angry man was certainly treating her like one.

"The Director of Education will have to be informed," Sir Montague was bellowing, "and I shall write to your school and insist on your expulsion!"

Tessa blanched. Expelled! She had no idea that her prank would be viewed so seriously. But it was now apparent that she had irreparably damaged a significant piece of English history.

"Couldn't I—couldn't I patch it up?" she asked tremulously.

"WHAT! How the devil do you think that would look, eh?" He glared brutally down at her. "I've just supervised restoration of this—only to have my work defaced and insulted by a mere slip of a girl! I won't tolerate it!" He grabbed Tessa by the arm.

She quailed. The thought of being frog-marched down the hill to face Hankey made her feel sick. But Sir Montague had no intention of taking the young woman back to the coach—yet. He was a man who firmly believed that the wronged should be allowed their revenge.

"Before you return," he said furiously, "I am going to give you the thrashing you deserve—you young hoyden!"

Tessa desperately tried to wriggle free of his painful grasp. No one was going to thrash her!

"Let go of me, you bloody old man!" she snarled and kicked him spitefully on his shin.

"Oh ho ho! Hoity toity young madam, aren't we!" he hissed. "You either obey me here or," he paused to slash at the turf with his stick, "I shall carry you bodily down that hill—and spank you in front of your master. That'll show him how to deal with the likes of you!"

Spanked! Tessa shrank from the word. To have Hankey and her classmates see her being spanked like a child would be terrible. It would crush her status in the entire school. She knew that Sir Montague was capable of carrying out his word to the very letter, so she decided to cooperate. After all, it was unlikely that they would ever meet again, and nobody else was witness to the event.

"All right," she said sulkily, and dropped her hands to her sides.

"Remove your skirt, Miss," commanded Sir Montague.

Tessa's eyes widened. She didn't expect *this!*

"I SAID REMOVE YOUR SKIRT!" he thundered in her face.

Tessa shook visibly and grappled with the zip. It was a tight skirt and she had to go through quite a performance of suggestive wrigglings and jerks to ease it down over her hips. Eventually it lay in the chalk at her feet. Sir Montague's eyes seemed to hone in on her brief knickers immediately. A little fluff of hair wisped out from the top of the triangle at the front, and the gusset at the back was embarrassingly embedded in her bottom-crack. Tessa didn't know where to put her hands. He was staring so rudely at her stocking tops, bare thighs, and the area not covered by her pants that she felt all her private areas were being scrutinized in scientific detail, the same as afforded to his catalogue of archaeological finds. It seemed so impersonal, so dehumanizing.

Sir Montague hooked up her skirt on the end of his stick and stuffed it inside his khaki jacket.

"Just to make sure you don't bolt away," he said smugly, noticing with satisfaction Tessa's dismayed expression.

A few hours ago Tessa had stood on the same spot—totally naked—with nineteen pairs of eyes staring at her, and had felt nothing but a glorious freedom in her sensual celebration of Eve. Now, this one pair of fiery male eyes made her feel self-conscious and helplessly trapped.

Sir Montague sat down on the chalk carving and abruptly ordered Tessa to spread her semi-naked body across his knees. She couldn't believe him. Frantically she looked about her. If she ran back to the coach now it would leave before the archaeologist could stop it. There would be her missing skirt to account for, of course, but Tessa would say she had lost it after sunbathing and had been trying to find it all this time. Perhaps Sir Montague would forget to phone the school. She clutched at any straw rather than face up to the impending punishment.

As if he could read her thoughts, he calmly grasped her ankle, looking up at her frightened flickering eyes.

Tessa had no choice but to obey him. She crouched

149

awkwardly on her hands and knees over his legs, so far away from his heavily breathing chest as possible. The smell of his grass-stained, nicotined breeches met her nostrils unpleasantly as she wriggled into position.

"I said *lie*, girl—not *sprawl!*" Sir Montague spat savagely.

Groaning with shame, she had to wriggle sideways until her tummy rested on his thighs—in the process elevating her bottom into a vulgar angle, which he obviously approved of, because, with a loud slap, his heavy palm descended on her raised wobbling bottom-cheeks. Her nose cannoned into the chalk, making her cough and splutter and her legs flew wide open with the force of his hand. Fortunately for Tessa there was no one standing behind her to gloat over her deliciously revealing posture at that moment. With her legs spread-eagled, her knickers sucked completely into her bottom-crack, and the other parts of her anatomy between her legs, she might as well have been naked.

Tessa's face was screwed up tight in a mask of expectancy. It was going to hurt, she was sure of that. She felt all the more vulnerable because she couldn't see what was going to happen. She had absolutely no control over the situation and no power to prevent the awful impending punishment.

Sir Montague pulled the seat of her knickers and yanked firmly on the waistband until they were excruciatingly tight. The flimsy nylon bit even deeper into her bottom-crack enhancing the upward curve and plumping out of each cheek. Tessa swallowed. The way he was pulling and tugging on the material made her fear they would suddenly, noisily rip. She tried to prepare herself for that eventuality. She clenched her buttock muscles in and held her breath, hoping this would make her bottom smaller beneath the straining knickers, but it was of little use. Sir Montague pulled more severely, and when Tessa could hold her muscles taut no longer, the relaxing fleshing bottom-cheeks filled the brief pants to overflowing. Delicious ripe crescents of trembling cheek formed beneath the elastic waistband. Sir Montague was very tempted to pinch them.

Tessa felt his hands rove over every inch of her bottom, as if he was getting fully acquainted with the target area before punishment.

SLAP!!!

She twisted around, her face contorted, as the first spank landed on her rear. It couldn't be happening to her! She screamed abuse at him—hardly a wise thing to do under the circumstances. Sir Montague's ample palm stingingly slapped the tender bare skin below her knickers several times in rapid succession. The pain from one smack had no time to dissipate itself before the next one landed neatly in its place.

"Oooh! That hurts—*you!*" she said angrily, scuffing her feet frantically in the grass in a futile reaction to the throbbing soreness.

SLAP!!!

The heavy male hand descended again and again. Tessa tried very hard to think of hateful phrases, but the increasing heat on her bottom destroyed her concentration. She certainly wasn't going to cry. Oh! No! That would be the ultimate degradation. So she champed furiously on her bottom lip and tensed her muscles at every painful spank.

Sir Montague couldn't help but admire such a pretty bottom. It certainly wasn't the first he'd reddened but there was something deliciously individual about them all. Tessa's was quite voluptuous and had a charming dimple on each cheek. He could just see them above her knickers, tiny shadowy hollows that looked as though someone had poked a finger into her creamy flesh, and the impression had stayed.

Her cheeks danced and wobbled entrancingly—as did they all—and they were turning that familiar cherry shade. Quite lovely!

"Right—that's *that* part over," he suddenly announced, and rolled Tessa onto the grass. She glared at him, her face red and streaked with chalk, her mouth a mutinous pout.

Sir Montague's eyebrows shot up involuntarily. That was Stage One, he reflected, and it had had little impression on the defiant young madam. Perhaps Stage Two would break her wayward spirit. It had done so with all the others.

"Take your knickers down!"

Tessa vigorously shook her head. It was one thing to be spanked, but no man was going to feast his eyes on her bare bottom without prior invitation!

"Go to hell!" she blazed.

"TAKE YOUR KNICKERS DOWN, MISS, OR *I* WILL!" he roared implacably.

As before, his deafening command made her tremble with fear. Like an automaton, she obeyed. Sticking her thumbs into the waistband, she pulled them off as fast as she could. If she lingered he might indeed decide to do it himself.

Sir Montague bent to pick up her knickers which he tucked away inside his shirt. As he bent down to retrieve them, wisps of his electrified hair brushed her pubic area. Tessa frantically covered herself with her hands and stepped back.

Sir Montague looked cruelly pleased. The young lady showed all the signs that usually manifested themselves during Stage Two: namely, uncontrollable embarrassment and mortification. He gazed deliberately at her hands covering her pubis. She lowered her head in shame.

To disobey Sir Montague now was impossible: he had her skirt *and* her knickers and she couldn't run away without them. To make matters worse, her blouse was far too short to pull down over her bottom, and it was transparent.

As before, he sat down and told Tessa to drape herself across his legs. Although protest screamed inside her, she nevertheless obeyed, getting into position as quickly as possible with her thighs drawn tightly together.

He commenced the spanking, colouring the previously protected triangle where her knickers had been.

Tessa began to jiggle up and down, unaware of how suggestive she looked, in an effort to dodge the rain of spanks. She clawed the earth with her nails, spluttered as chalk dust blew into her flaring nostrils, and closed her wide staring eyes as the heat fanned out over her bare bottom cheeks like a raging fire. She wouldn't cry. *She wouldn't cry!* All she could think of was how she hated this man and his silly prehistoric obsessions!

Things could hardly get much worse, so she decided to vent her anger.

"You bloody fossil!" she hissed between clenched teeth.

"What did you say, young lady?" demanded Sir Montague.

She repeated her insult, even more vehemently.

Sir Montague frowned. Stage Three was obviously called for.

In the coach, the desperation of Richard Hankey was all too evident. The coach driver was getting abusive and threatening to drive off without the truant. The

girls chanted like a rugby crowd. The sound was split-
ting through his skull. Suddenly it became too much.
He leapt from the coach. He was going to find Miss
Tessa Walker and give her a piece of his mind.

"You unrepentant hussy!" Sir Montague was telling
Tessa, who stood before him cringing. "You're not the
least bit sorry for what you've done. Wipe that defiant
expression off your face!"

Tessa was really frightened by now. What did the
man want of her? If she knew she'd do it. But she had
a feeling that even the most abject apology would not
appease him now.

Sir Montague picked up his stick. For a moment
Tessa thought he was going to march her back to the
coach as she was—half naked.

"Six of the best with this," he told her blandly.

Tessa visibly shrank. "No, n-o-o, *no!* You
wouldn't . . . you couldn't! I . . ." she spluttered and
felt tears welling up inside her.

Sir Montague gripped Tessa tightly around the waist
and bent her over. It was a long time since he'd had to
go this far, but he'd never met anyone so determined to
resist discipline.

He let the stick fall across the fleshiest, fullest part
of her tender, smarting buttocks. She let out an abandoned yell.

Sir Montague had used his stick quite judiciously. It
was more brutal than a cane, so he tempered its use in
relation to its effect. A thick purple weal sprang up
amid the surrounding redness. After five more carefully measured strokes, she'd have a very uncomfortable journey home.

Hankey searched for Tessa in a furious temper, losing his wallet along the way. Always that damned girl
succeeded in making him look a fool. He circumvented

the hill and spiralled up towards the summit. Alien noises met his ears—yells, screams. He went quickly in the direction of the sounds.

There were two figures on the chalk carving. He reached for his binoculars. Sir Montague and Tessa! And she was receiving the caning of her life! He ogled the detail of her ruby cheeks with the binoculars and isolated the area to glorious perfection. Standing astride the archaeologist, she was hunched over his supporting arm while he brought the stick down smartly on her naked rear. Hankey focussed the binoculars leisurely up her body to her face, which had twisted around. It was streaming with tears. Looking down, he noticed Tessa's little contribution to history, and grinned. How appropriate that she should be punished on the very site of her crime!

Tessa's resistance had broken on the second stroke from Sir Montague's stick. She had been spanked, then spanked again, and now this! It was too much to bear, and almost with relief she burst into tears. It seemed to be what Sir Montague wanted because after her first great gulping sobs, the stick descended on her trembling flanks less heavily.

Sir Montague straightened up and backed away, inspecting her bottom with all the scrutiny afforded a prize exhibit.

Tessa was crying softly, a picture of limp dejection, waiting for her clothes so she could run back to the sanctuary of the coach.

Hankey, his eyes fixed lustfully on Tessa's rosy stripy bottom, was in a turmoil of emotion. If this man could spank and cane Tessa Walker with no qualms, why on earth couldn't he? She had been causing him so much trouble that he dearly wanted to punish her. Judging by her tear-blotched face and her palm-blotched bottom, this was an effective and delicious way to accomplish it. He offered up a silent prayer for the opportunity to present itself—soon.

The archaeologist saw Hankey approaching, and after giving Tessa her clothes, walked towards him.

"Here you are, Sir, take your little vandal away from here. I never want to see or hear of her again."

Hankey stared in amazement. "I . . . er suppose you will be sending a full report to the school?" he asked nervously.

"Shan't bother," replied Sir Montague airily. "Rather than waste time with your Board of Governors, I took it upon myself to settle the matter. And it's been to my satisfaction." He paused to take a pinch of snuff, wrinkling his nostrils indelicately at the master. "It lets you off the hook, eh?" he jibed.

Hankey blushed. If Sir Montague *had* informed the school, it would have meant trouble indeed for himself. As it was, Sir Montague seemed well-pleased.

"Never fails," Sir Montague rasped, and Hankey detected the rumblings of a chuckle in the older man's throat. Then, with a final look at Tessa who was shivering and hiccupping, he swished his stick high in the air and loped off down the hill.

Hankey and Tessa were alone on the hill-top. He walked towards her jauntily; his prayer had been answered. Sir Montague had conveniently handed over the reins of power to himself. It was now entirely up to him, Richard Hankey, to inform the school. Tessa Walker was suddenly, delectably, totally, in his power.

"I shall have to inform the Headmistress," he addressed her severely, "and of course your parents."

"But won't Sir Montague do that?" she stammered, sitting on the ground hugging her knees and looking miserably at her feet.

"Sir Montague has decided to let the matter rest. I think he was far too lenient with you," Hankey added cruelly.

Tessa glanced up quickly. She didn't feel he'd been lenient at all!

"But I've been punished, sir," she protested weakly.

"It was fortunate for you that I witnessed the whole thing," he paused, lowering his eyes slightly and crouching down beside her. "And, Tessa, I had no idea your bottom was, shall I say, so chameleonic!" he drawled, savouring every word. "How white it was earlier on this afternoon!" He bent down to see if he could catch her expression. She was flushing a deep miserable crimson, in the awful realisation that he had seen her—completely naked.

"I don't think your father would be too pleased to learn that his daughter is an aspiring stripper," he said knowingly.

Tessa felt completely numb with horror. "What can I do, sir!" she wailed, rocking to and fro on her poor sore bottom. "Please don't tell anyone—the Head, my parents! I know I've been a trial, sir, but I've already been punished dreadfully!" Fresh tears began to run down her cheeks.

"Well," said Hankey graciously, "there *is* a way out for you . . ."

He proceeded to tell her that he would conveniently "forget" about the appalling afternoon's behavior provided that she consented to receive punishment at his own hands the following morning. In short, he would spank her in the same way Sir Montague had done, as it was obviously so effective.

Tessa reacted to his words with a strangled cry of terror. It was blackmail, and she had little choice but to agree.

Following the triumphant master down the hill like a disobedient puppy, she dwelt on her fate. Her bottom was so very sore that she dreaded the thought of yet another assault on it. She'd have to think of some emergency first aid measures to apply to her bruised, burning flesh before morning.

The pupils and their teacher spent Saturday night at a hostel. The girls slept in an ugly plain dormitory while Hankey had a room to himself. He got little sleep.

He cursed Miss Trubshaw's absence, leaving him as the only teacher in charge of twenty girls. It caused him more than a few embarrassing moments.

It was 1:00 A.M. and Hankey had retired as early as he could, to plan and savor exactly what he was going to do with Tessa. A constant high-pitched chatter from the girls' dormitory repeatedly interrupted his reverie.

Forgetting in his annoyance that the girls would be in their nightclothes, he padded barefoot along the corridor to the bathroom. Tessa bumped into him in the doorway, carrying a tube of cream. She was dressed in a pink baby doll nightie and looking very uncomfortable. Hankey caught a whiff of her delicately scented body as she brushed past and, unable to resist, he turned to catch her back view as she slid into the showers. His mouth went slowly dry. Mounds of trembling pinkened bottom-cheek bulged saucily out from under her little panties. A tantalizing glimpse—and she was gone.

In the dormitory the girls were huddled together around a bed, in various stages of undress. Cute baby-doll pyjamas, seductive satin nighties, short thigh-length sleep-shirts and, he gulped—no nighties at all! Feeling that he really shouldn't be there, that this was

Miss Trubshaw's province, he retreated quietly before they noticed him. Unfortunately, he caught his dressing-gown cord in a metal bed-head as he went past. It whipped from around his waist like a snake and his dressing gown flew open. Thank goodness he'd taken the precaution of bringing pyjamas with him. It was obvious, however, to any on-looker, that the peculiar bulge under the loose material was an ill-timed erection.

At that moment Tessa returned, saw the obvious, flushed a deep red and immediately ran out of the room. Simultaneously, the giggling girls noticed him, and there were hysterical shrieks as the naturists among them rushed for their beds. Hankey felt extremely awkward, but managed to utter a lame "Be quiet" before leaving the room as fast as his dignity would allow. The dressing-gown cord remained entangled around the bed frame.

Feeling hot and aroused, he went back to his room and slammed the door. He could cope with *one* girl, he reflected, but not a whole army of seethingly precocious females. Every little incident seemed to add to his frustration. He would symbolically wreak vengeance on them all by punishing their ring-leader— Tessa Walker.

Tessa secreted herself in the showers where there was a mirror. It had been an effort to act like her normal self among her friends. She'd had to plead an upset tummy to explain her reluctance to join them. And of course, she'd avoided Hankey.

She looked in the full length mirror to inspect the state of her bottom, peeling her knickers gingerly down over her sore bottom cheeks. The well-spanked area was a fierce red, blotchy in places, and she gasped in horror at the darker plum-coloured lines of blood-blisters beneath the skin. How could she present herself to Hankey for a similar punishment, looking like that?

How bitterly she regretted wearing such a minuscule baby-doll nightie! The little top barely reached her hips and there was a large gap between it and the brief cotton pants. The latter came so far up her bottom-cheeks it was embarrassing. A substantial pink area billowed out from beneath the elastic, where Sir Montague had angrily spanked her. Luckily the horrid weals were concealed, if she walked carefully and didn't bend over, by the thin cotton—but only just.

She'd told Angela Richards that the redness was merely sunburn, when the other girl quizzed her curiously. Angela had offered her sun-cream and, since she had nothing else with which to soothe her poor burning flanks, she'd gratefully accepted.

Tessa had been walking rather stiffly to the shower room with the cream when she'd bumped into Hankey.

For the remainder of the night Hankey lay sweating in the excruciating sweetness of anticipated excitement. He thought of a plan to make sure he had plenty of time alone with Tessa.

At breakfast the following morning, Hankey announced in a jocular manner that the girls were to go out for a long cross-country run. Tessa immediately brightened. It spelled reprieve for her. So he'd forgotten. He probably didn't have the courage.

The girls dressed in tee-shirts and shorts. Tessa's shorts were decidedly *not* like the school regulation baggy ones. They were predictably as tight as she could squeeze her bottom into, and made from a very thin material. Some of the stitching down the central seam had come undone with the effort of keeping so much voluptuous flesh in restraint. There was barely an inch of gusset between her legs, and they were cut high at the hip so that the crease below each wobbling cheek was clearly visible.

At any other time, Tessa would have been delighted to flaunt her arse in them, but today it was still feeling decidedly tender—and she was worried that the exposed pink parts would invite too much attention. It was, after all, a peculiar place to be quite so sunburnt.

"Aren't you wearing knickers under your shorts, Tess?" asked one of the girls with a sly smile.

"There isn't room," said Tessa somewhat tartly. All allusions to that part of her anatomy today were unwelcome.

Hankey gave them a tortuous route to follow and told them not to return before 12:00 o'clock. They set off in pairs, chattering.

Tessa was very anxious to be away from Richard Hankey. He'd been looking a her rather oddly during breakfast. She preferred not to think of his promise, and the repercussions of her act of vandalism the previous day. She bolted from the doorway. Freedom at last!

"Tessa!"

With an awful sinking feeling she heard her name called over the hubbub of the disappearing girls. Perhaps if she pretended she hadn't heard?

"Tessa!" More authoritative this time. She sullenly came to a halt on the springy grass.

Hankey walked towards her as the last girl vanished from sight.

"I want a word with you," he said menacingly, "and you know what *that* means!"

"But, Sir, I thought you'd—" she protested.

"No, I haven't forgotten. Come on, Tessa, I'm hardly likely to, am I?" he smiled mockingly.

Now that he had the girl in his power again, any

niggling guilty thoughts of the night had disappeared. In their place was a lust and longing that could only be satiated by spanking Tessa Walker's backside.

They went inside the hostel, which was now deserted. Tessa's skin began to prickle as Hankey led the way to his room.

"Please, Sir, do you have to do this?" Tessa pleaded. She looked at him earnestly, eyes wide with fright.

"It's simple," he said blandly. "Either you accept discipline from me—or else you face expulsion."

"But that's blackmail!" she stuttered.

"Blackmail?" He raised one eyebrow, enjoying her discomfiture. "I wouldn't have thought an innocent girl like you would know anything about that," he smirked.

He was sitting on a hard wooden chair, feet placed evenly apart, arms folded, head cocked, revelling in the flustered, blushing spectacle she made.

Tessa looked about her in misery, standing with her legs close together, hoping against hope that he would not insist she expose her more intimate areas.

"I'm going to tan your backside, young lady—good and proper," he said, drawing the words out with great satisfaction.

Tessa gazed out of the window. In the distance she could just make out the bobbing heads of her classmates. How she wished she was with them. Then she lowered her eyes at Hankey, waiting for the inevitable.

He did not speak but gestured with his hand and a swift flicker of his eyes that he wanted her to lie across his lap. Tessa, confused and blushing uncontrollably, clumsily obeyed. Her lovely body lay across his knees. Hankey pulled her closer to his heaving chest until she was horribly aware of the heat from his thighs—and of how very aroused he was.

All Hankey's energy and years of frustration seemed

to burst into sudden life and concentrate in the palm of his hand.

SLAP!!!

With a sigh of release his palm landed explosively on her prominently raised buttocks. There was a slight wobble, a distinct eddying movement of flesh on the crown of her cheeks. He blinked. Was this fantasy or reality? With his eyes closed he raised his hand again and unerringly landed on the luscious segments of arse-cheek that almost oozed from beneath her tight shorts. He felt the warmth his hand had imparted, with sensitive, exploring fingertips, pinching the skin into full, ripe folds. The vibrations of her bouncing bottom-cheeks and his deliciously tingling palm were one.

She *was* real! She was making gurgling noises of protest. He laughed delightedly, giving her three hard slaps on the tenderest part of her upper thighs. She squealed noisily and for a second widened her legs. His fingers descended, feeling around her hot, moist gusset, while she slapped her thighs together and moaned.

Poor Tessa! Two dreadful spankings in one ghastly weekend! She had hated Sir Montague's impersonal vengeance—but to be spanked by a young good-looking master who was so obviously aroused was somehow much worse. Paradoxically she hated and loathed what Hankey was doing to her, yet at the same time she had to acknowledge that somewhere deep inside her was a tiny seed of—could it be excitement? She screwed her eyes up even tighter, feeling dismayed, disgusted with herself, and utterly confused, all at once. Perhaps it would be better if she didn't try to think, but concentrated on making her mind a blank until it was all over. She tried, but she was shamefully aware that Hankey's spanking, and her restrained wriggling in response, were producing peculiar sensations between her legs.

"Tessa," Hankey said huskily, breaking in on her thoughts, "your shorts are quite—er—moist. I think you'd better remove them." So saying, he tipped her off his lap. Her blonde curls hid her face completely so he brushed them aside and peered at her features, which were scarlet with shame.

Dumbly, hardly knowing what she was doing, she put her hands to her zip, when Hankey suddenly slapped them away and stopped her. He had an idea.

"I'd like you to entertain me," he said, rocking back on the chair, "like you did this afternoon—but especially for me this time."

Tessa felt sick. She stood languidly slouching, unable to understand what he meant.

The chair rocked back and landed sharply on the floor.

"Strip!" he commanded. "And you'd better make a good job of it or you can say goodbye to St. Esmeralda's!"

How long would it take, she wondered in a daze, this protracted trial of mortification? He was looking at her with fierce bright eyes and she knew she had no choice.

Fighting back her tears as he goaded and criticised her, she began to peel off her tee-shirt. In the secret depth of her mind, Tessa had always fantasized about Hankey; of making herself a seductive object for his pleasure. Now she had her chance.

She threw the tee-shirt on the floor, standing a few inches from Hankey, in her bra and shorts. Hankey leant forward and began to walk his fingers over her tummy, delighted at her gasp of response. He was aware of her fascinating body-scent. Greedily he wriggled his hand inside her bra and drew out both breasts until they were upthrust globes of firm flesh, hanging out of her bra.

Tessa stood motionless, trying to shrink from his contact. She shut her eyes and recoiled from the insistent circling of his tongue as he teased her nipples.

Hankey's hand undid her bra and wrenched it off, throwing it into a corner of the room. He sat back, red-faced, panting, barely able to restrain himself.

"Go on," he said hoarsely. "Your shorts! Take 'em off, too! I want to see you bare-arsed!"

Tessa had no need to act provocatively. She *was* provocative. Head bent, curls tumbling over her shoulders and covering her bare breasts with a fine curtain of hair, she undid her shorts.

Due to her increasing clamminess, the thin material had stuck to her skin, making it necessary for her to wriggle and writhe indecorously, jerking her hips with a spasm of wobbling bottom-cheek in order to ease them down over her smarting behind.

Her breasts bounced from side to side with the effort. Her bottom-cheeks bounced as they slowly burst free. The shorts slid easily down her supple thighs and sun-tanned legs to the floor where she neatly stepped out of them.

Tessa Walker stood before the delighted history master as naked as the day she was born. The next moments were pure bliss for Richard Hankey.

She draped herself in a submissive arc across his eager, waiting lap. He ran his fingers over her back, her bottom and her thighs. The dull stripes made by Sir Montague's stick were still clearly visible. He traced a finger along them, fascinated. He was going to judiciously add to the picture.

Picking up his large wooden clothesbrush, he tap-tapped it on her jumping quivering bottom. Tessa pressed her body even harder on Hankey's thighs in terrified response, and clutched his legs dementedly.

He lifted his arm high in the air and brought it sizzling down on her dreadfully sore skin. She gave a splattering yell. The brush left a peculiar impression behind. A few minutes more of this, he thought, and her rump would have the appearance of an abstract painting!

With each wooden slap Tessa responded by jerking her head up, her hair wildly flying, and involuntarily widening her legs. After a while she decided that her bottom couldn't feel any worse. The simple fact that she was naked and therefore very vulnerable to this young man's whims was chokingly mortifying. Added to this was the embarrassing knowledge that he was getting a definite kind of pleasure from spanking her. Sir Montague, she knew, hadn't found it arousing.

Soon she was blubbering noisily, clawing at the floor. Hankey had tipped her further over his knee to have a tantalizing view of everything she wanted to desperately to conceal, as her legs and buttocks gyrated vulgarly.

He dropped the clothesbrush and slapped the soft skin of her inner thighs with well-aimed painful precision.

"Oh please stop! Pl-ee-ase!" Tessa cried, sobbing hysterically.

Hankey relented. He felt exhausted with all the determined effort he'd put into her punishment. It was worth it. Tessa's rear was a glorious shade of crimson, beautifully highlighted against the rest of her pale-tanned body.

She climbed tearfully off his lap, rubbing her furnace-hot cheeks in a futile effort to ease the pain. What a picture of womanly subjection she made as she stood before her master so penitently!

Hankey· sat back and ordered her to slowly turn around so that he could feast on every inch of her luscious body. Especially her rubescent rear.

At that moment, as Tessa turned like a pathetic clockwork marionette, there was an imperious tap on the window. Both Tessa and the master looked up in alarm. Hankey's face suddenly became a mask of whiteness, and Tessa's swollen eyes looked anxiously at him. She felt as guilty as he did.

They looked towards the window.

Peering around the side, with an amused expression kindling his cold blue eyes was Sir Montague Driver.

Hankey blushed and Tessa wailed. How long had he been there? By the lop-sided grimace that passed for a smile—obviously quite some time.

Tessa, crying afresh at this double shame, turned her back to the window, incidentally affording Sir Montague a view of the most well-spanked, well-disciplined female bottom he had ever had the pleasure of viewing.

"Found your wallet, Sir," said the archaeologist gruffly, and passed it through the window. Pausing to take a pinch of sniff and sneeze explosively over Hankey, he nodded at Tessa.

"Jolly good show, Sir," and his words drowned amid noisy nose-blowings into a dirty handkerchief. "Never fails, eh?"

Sir Montague turned to go, then swung around abruptly and extended his large calloused hand through the window.

"Glad to know you, Sir!" he said as the dumb-struck Hankey found his spank-warmed palm clasped tight in a vigorous handshake. Then with the beginnings of a twinkle in his eyes, Sir Montague tapped his stick on the ground and set off at a brisk pace.

Tessa was still undressed, submissive—almost waiting for something to happen. Hankey quietly moved up behind her and smoothed her burning flanks with his hands. She showed no signs of recoiling from his touch. Indeed that well-spanked part of her anatomy seemed to press itself into his excited hands. He wondered when the first girl runner would return. Not for some time yet.

Silently he drew the curtain, checked the door. There was something he just had to attend to—with Tessa.

Sunday evening, the end of a very eventful weekend. As the coach left the hostel it passed by the Long Man. Both Richard Hankey and Tessa, sitting quietly on the back seat, looked up at the figure, condemned to frustrated torment for centuries to come. But perhaps not quite.

Standing on the figure, pausing to hold his stick aloft as the coach passed, was Sir Montague Driver.

He'd decided to let Tessa's embellishment remain. After all, he chuckled, even this gaunt pre-historic monster was entitled to some release from his suffering.

The Headmaster Lends a Hand

Lucy Millar's arrival at St. Bede's Boy's Grammar School as the young Biology teacher was as dramatic as suddenly opening the doors of a monastery to women. Among the twenty or so teachers already there, only one was female. She was Miss Arnott, tall, grey-haired with nicotine stains on her gappy teeth, who always spoke in a masculine rumble. She wore mannish suits and brown brogues.

Lucy, fresh from college, was the antithesis of Miss Arnott. She was small, feminine, channelling her enthusiasm for the job into super-efficiency. She wore large glasses with delicate silver frames and had the disconcerting habit of sliding them down her nose to add emphasis to her words. Naked contact with her large intense cobalt-blue eyes had a distinctly unsettling effect on any male who thought he'd like to lose himself for a moment in those mesmeric blue pools.

On the first day of the autumn term, Lucy arrived early to be personally welcomed by the school's Headmaster, George Adams, a tall thoughtful man in his late forties with fair hair liberally streaked with platinum. He had a warm, possessive handshake.

Thus was Lucy Millar greeted as she briskly stepped into Mr. Adams's study and took her seat in front of his old mahogany desk which was dusty and rather neglected in appearance.

"She's very efficient," thought Mr. Adams as Lucy nimbly flicked her hands underneath her slim contour-hugging skirt, smoothing her seat before sitting down with a briskness which amused him.

For a moment both Headmaster and new teacher stared at each other with the cautiously veiled interest that is always present at the meeting of a pretty young woman and a not unattractive man some twenty-five years her senior.

Lucy stared at him, wide-eyed and alert, positively bristling with enthusiasm while he explained the niceties of school policy and administration to her intense, innocent little face.

Mischievously, he tried to distract attention from his words, to make those piercing eyes blink at him—just once. He leant back heavily in his heavy oak chair which creaked lugubriously, but she did not twitch an eyelid, nor was there any sign of a smile. He picked up a ball-point pen and began clicking it loudly and rhythmically on the dull wooden desk top, proceeding with his headmasterly monologue all the while. There was a little crater in the polished wood which suggested that this was a favourite trick to confuse and embarrass his staff. It held implications that he was growing a little impatient, and although he was a gracious man, he had something better to do than pep-talk his teaching force, who after all, were not *that* important.

The effect was lost on Lucy. She had entered the musty chalk-smelling study with the kind of no-nonsense confidence that often frightens men.

George relaxed, feeling wistfully that it was "all down to youth," and studied her closely. Her hair was piled on the top of her head and severely anchored with a good many pins, but George noticed that stray blonde wisps had escaped the tortuous bun, and frothed about her forehead and cheeks quite engagingly. She was, he thought, trying to create the right image, and very successfully, too.

Absentmindedly, he catalogued her other features. Small firm breasts, nicely outlined under a slim-fitting pale blue cashmere jumper, delightfully tiny waist and . . . He leaned forward to complete the picture but the desk blotted his vision. He would fill in the missing detail when she rose to go. At most he could only see her dainty hands crossed tidily in her lap, and the wrinkles of her skirt as it broached into tightness. That was a pity. George always did have a peculiar fondness for the female bottom.

"If you have any trouble with the boys during lessons, let me know," he said.

"I don't foresee any, Sir," she answered him politely and with evident surprise.

George sighed. No, he wouldn't mention the matter of her being an extremely pretty young woman in a school full of adolescent boys. No, he'd decided against it. A few weeks at St. Bede's would soon take the edge off that rather disconcerting confidence.

He found himself thinking that Miss Lucy Millar could be even more formidable than Miss Arnott if she chose. But damned attractive with it.

The assembly bell shrilled in the corridor outside and brought an end to the interview. Lucy rose to go, and the Headmaster was able to complete his appraisal of the young woman. He was quite pleasantly taken aback by what he saw.

She was wearing a thin grey flannel skirt which was so tight that every curvaceous inch of her hips was revealed. As she turned her back on him to leave the room, the most erotic profile was revealed: a round girlish bottom, pertly prominent—even saucy in the obstinate retroussée angle it assumed when she stood up. George's eyebrows rose slowly in delighted surprise.

Lucy had the misfortune at that moment to trip, and George, the fortune of being there to help her. As one of her stiletto heels caught the leg of the chair, she overbalanced all of a sudden and put her hands awkwardly on the chair arm to steady herself. For a brief moment, her body made a perfect arc with her bottom raised vulgarly at its zenith. George, having leapt to her side, felt a barely controllable urge to smack it.

Instead he placed his hands lightly on her hips, while Lucy got to her feet. He noticed she was blushing. He also noticed that her seams were crooked. He looked again at the slender curves. Sure enough, there were tell-tale wrinkles around her ankles and knees. She was wearing stockings.

George found the discovery quite intriguing. Somehow this revelation of secret femininity seemed to be rather at variance with her precise business-like manner. He was puzzled, and excited.

A month passed. Lucy settled in extremely well, proving to be an excellent teacher both in her teaching techniques and the uncompromising method of discipline she employed. The boys adored her, worshipped and fantasized about her—but from a safe distance.

George Adams watched her closely. Somewhere, he decided, beneath that cool unflappable suit of armor she wore so convincingly, was a chink.

One lunchtime, while buying his usual cigar, he bumped into Miss Millar in the newsagent's near the school. She was standing in the corner, head bent, earnestly pouring over a magazine. George approached and tapped her gently on the arm. She reacted as though she had been struck. With a strangled shriek

172

she let the magazine fly out of her hands. It fell to the floor and lay there, open at the center pages.

In full color staring up at them both was an expression of agony on the face of a girl lying upside down across a man's knee. Although dressed in a skimpy school skirt and blouse, she was obviously a grown woman. George blinked and felt beads of tense perspiration breaking out around his collar. The girl in the picture was wearing blue gym-knickers in a tangle about her knees, and she was receiving the spanking of her life.

The Headmaster did not know how to react for a full half-minute. The open magazine seemed to claim all his attention, yet he was aware of Lucy standing next to him, of the flustered distress of her hands, and the fact that she was shaking uncontrollably. He felt the sharp sickness of awakened desire. The poor girl's face was scarlet—she looked as though she had been caught in some criminal act. All her self-composure had vanished.

Mr. Adams decided to save the situation. After all, it seemed to him that it was suddenly, gloriously, in his power to do so. Breathing heavily, he picked up the magazine which flew open embarrassingly in several places before he had command of it.

He cleared his throat. "Dear me, did this fall off the top shelf?" He bent to catch her expression.

Lucy couldn't look at him but muttered a strained "yes" as he put it back.

"They're curious to look at now and again," he continued airily. "Don't be too embarrassed, Miss Millar."

Lucy shook her head, wanly smiled and, after mumbling an incoherent excuse, fled the shop. George stood and watched her go, amazed at the transformation. Far from looking like the assertive young woman he had come to know, she now looked every inch a guilty schoolgirl.

For days after the event Lucy felt her cheeks burn at the mere sound of the Headmaster's approaching footsteps. She felt curiously under his power, knowing he had realized only too well that the spanking magazine she was pouring over had not fallen into her hands by accident. And strangely enough she found the thought of their shared secret very exciting.

Adams noticed a difference in Lucy after the incident. Her once confident walk had shrunk to a guilty scurrying about the school. He even caught her walking on tip-toe to avoid the loud assertive click of her high heels on the hard marble floor. Her hair tumbled down in a loose swirl from the severe little bun, making her look quite beautiful. George found he only had to raise one questioning eyebrow for Lucy to begin to stammer in her replies to him; she blushed and felt helpless under his scrutiny.

One Sunday evening, Adams was walking in his local park, the sad decay of autumn at his feet, when he saw her. Silhouetted on the hill in the dying light, she stood with a dog on a lead, her hair flying madly about her in the determined wind. She wore a short jacket and a figure-hugging pencil skirt.

"Miss Millar?" he shouted into the wind.

She looked up. Simultaneously the mongrel dog wrapped itself about her legs and effectively hobbled her. She couldn't see how to disentangle herself, so George went to help her, crouching down to try to unravel the muddle. She was very embarrassed.

The lead had snaked around her thighs, clipping the skirt to her legs and pulling it furiously tight—drawing compulsive attention to her bottom. Somewhere among the tangle of girl and lead, George found his hands roundly cupping her bottom cheeks over her tight, tight skirt. She squirmed with pleasure.

Her curves were soft and pliant like a young girl's. He could feel the ripeness of each cheek and the intimate crack between them in his exploring fingers. This time his hands wandered uncontrollably down her flannel-clad thighs where he encountered the hardness of her suspender buttons. Feeling her stockinged legs, so slim and so girlish, he suddenly imagined them clad in long white schoolgirlish socks, with little open-meshed sandals on her feet. He grew hot at the thought.

They stood up. Lucy struggled to gain composure as Mr. Adam's hands swept lingeringly around her legs, pulling the lead free.

They parted. She was unable to look at him.

Lucy's work began to suffer. To everyone she appeared in a state of constant agitation. The Headmaster felt she was wrestling with some deep inner problem, but he was reluctant to quiz her about her private life. Pupils were beginning to take liberties with her. Standards had dropped.

Although Adams knew he should confine thoughts about her to the job alone, fantasies filled his mind as to what she did after school. And what he would like to do to her. In his mind, Lucy Millar was the schoolgirl in that magazine centerfold and he, George Adams, Headmaster of St. Bede's, was the strict disciplinarian.

Rothwells department store, one Saturday, found him languidly wandering through the schoolwear department. He hadn't the faintest idea what he was doing, except that a strange wistful longing stirred dully in his mind at the sight of row upon row of schoolgirl gym-slips and blazers.

It was then he saw her. Leaning over the small glass-fronted counter with her now all-too-familiar smackable bottom delicately elevated, she stood on one high heel, curling her other stockinged foot nervously up and down her calf.

On the counter lay a grey pleated gym-slip with a red games girdle, blouse and tie, school cardigan. And, topping the lot, a pair of soft navy blue cotton knickers.

Adams knew instinctively that the uniform was for her, and not some young niece or even for a fancy dress party, although they were probably the reasons she'd given the assistant. The time had come to take the matter of Miss Millar firmly in hand.

That evening he went to the park as usual. He had hoped to see Lucy again, but there was no sign of her. He left in disappointment.

As he neared the park exit, a young woman rushed past him out into the road, with a familiar dog snapping at her heels. It was Lucy Millar, and she was crying.

Forgetting his position, forgetting everything but her, George pursued the hurrying girl along the tree-lined suburban road until she disappeared into a tiny upstairs maisonette. With a thumping heart and his mind in a turmoil, he waited for five minutes before knocking at the door.

Agonising seconds dragged by. It appeared that she wasn't going to answer. Then slowly the door inched open.

Lucy stood, dressed in a pretty white blouse and long tight skirt with fluffy mules on her feet. Her hair was loose around her shoulders, her face streaked and red with crying.

"Miss Millar, is something wrong?"

She stood aside and let him walk into her flat.

"My boyfriend has just left me," she said in between sobs.

George was silent. Suddenly he felt a pang of irrational jealousy. He hadn't known about the boyfriend.

They sat down together on the settee. George looked about him. The room had a chaotic disorder that pleased him. She had a large collection of teddy bears and foreign dolls—little girl's things. Quite at odds with the assertive, brisk young woman he knew at school.

Lucy stood up and went into her bedroom.

"He left me because I bought this." And to Adams's astonishment, she returned holding out the grey pleated gym-slip. She was obviously so upset that she no longer cared what she said, and to whom. Except that she was telling her Headmaster. And he wanted to hear every word.

Standing there in her bedroom doorway with her wet face, was Lucy Millar the teacher, looking every inch Lucy the schoolgirl. Holding out the gym-slip with a pathetic gesture, asking for sympathy . . . asking for approval . . . just begging to be spanked.

A delicious state of arousal flowed through his body, and something of his excited state reached Lucy. She stopped crying and stood wide-eyed, looking at him. Then a blush crimsoned her cheeks.

Adams sat at the edge of the sofa, all the while trying to communicate with his eyes his desire to punish the naughty junior mistress severely. But he couldn't very well just grab the girl and tell her in no uncertain terms, "Lucy Millar, I'm going to give you the spanking you deserve." No, he couldn't do that. He wasn't sure either whether it wasn't just fantasy on her part. How would she feel with his large mature palm

177

descending on her gym-knickered rump time and time
again?

"I don't see what is wrong with you buying a school
uniform," he said as evenly as possible. "There's no
harm in it." He looked down at the space between
them, and then directly into her wide-open eyes.
"Didn't your boyfriend like you in it?" he asked softly.

"No. He said I—" she faltered.

"*I* would have."

Lucy shook. Adams had never seen a girl so visibly
moved. He'd read about it, of course, in magazines.

As Lucy seemed to have lost the power to speak,
Mr. Adams knew this was the moment to take total
supreme control over the young woman. And it was so
easy.

He looked at her and said, as if talking to a little
child, "Now, Lucy, go and put your uniform on for
me. Go on."

Lucy turned obediently and went into her bedroom.
It was as though she had become totally possessed by
Mr. Adams's words.

There was silence, as if for a brief moment she was
thinking about the enormity of what she was doing.
Then a rustle as she took the uniform from the carrier
bag.

Adams removed his jacket and rolled up his sleeves.
He looked around the room for a suitable chair.

"How are you doing, Lucy? Are you ready yet?" he
asked gently, so as not to alarm her.

A muffled voice was his answer. She was pulling on
the jumper.

"Have you any long white socks?"

"Yes, Mr. Adams." There was barely concealed
excitement in her voice.

"Then put them on!" he commanded, and added,

"make sure you're wearing proper sandals, too."

He sat on the chair in the middle of the room, having pushed the sofa back against the walls. He discovered a spotlight which he adjusted so that it would shine on the chair—on his lap—on Lucy Millar's deliciously spankable bottom.

He found in his intense excitement that his eyes kept fixedly returning to trivial details about the room. The pattern-repeats on the wallpaper, the shiny gold hands of the clock. He found himself following each jerky second-hand movement round and round and . . .

She was there. Shy, blushing, treading her way tentatively towards him as if she was temporarily blind and didn't know the room.

Adams's mouth felt sloe-dry. His lips compressed and tightened in excitement.

My God! What a sight she was!

"Stand in front of me, Lucy. I want to inspect your uniform."

As though in a trance, Lucy obeyed him.

Adams's eyes greedily devoured her womanly body, clad so provocatively in schoolgirl clothes. Hair loose, in two bunches. Earrings.

"Take those earrings off!" he snapped. "No jewelry in school!"

Her trembling hands flew to her ears and she removed them, dropping them into his outstretched palm.

"No make-up, I see. Good. One point in your favor—not that it will help you, Lucy Millar!"

She wore a white school blouse and cardigan, which were too small, drawing delicious attention to her breasts. He'd check later whether she was wearing a bra or not. He hoped she wasn't.

The gym-slip ended half-way down her thighs. Nice.

He ordered her to turn around slowly.

"Bend over and touch your toes!" he snapped. "I want to check if you're wearing regulation school knickers!" He drew out the syllables of the word "knickers" with undisguised relish.

Lucy, trembling, did as she was told. Down went her slender little hands, sliding over her long white socks on her calves, until she was touching her ankles. What an excruciating position to be in! And how dreadful to have to do it in front of her Headmaster!

The gym-slip had risen with slow magic. Up, up over the pinchable, squeezable softness of her thighs, bare and talcum-smooth. Up over the crown of her buttocks, thrusting up and over their fullness, until the pleats jutted out like a stage curtain.

George Adams's eyes were greedily focused on the vulgar exhibition of her navy-knickered bottom. There was a dark stain seeping through the gusset already. He leaned forward and tested with a finger. She was wet all right!

"Disgusting," he said throatily, smelling the heat and the juice from her, and enjoying her mortified squirming.

He turned her round again until she was facing him. Her knees touched his knees. Dumbly, her face flushed with shame, Lucy listened to the Headmaster's lecture.

". . . and to crown everything, I catch my young Biology mistress gloating over a pornographic magazine," he paused to add emphasis to his next words. "A magazine where naughty, wicked girls get what they deserve. A jolly good spanking!"

Adams pulled Lucy down onto his wide lap. She, weak from the excitement of being shouted at and lectured, floated down onto his knees like the descent of a feather. She was light and small and schoolgirlish, and she was his very naughty, about-to-be-punished school mistress.

SMACK!!! _____

Lucy's legs and arms flopped onto the floor as she made a perfect arc across his lap. The crisp impact of his decisive palm on her delectable rear sizzled through her body. Her nerves became like telephone wires buzzing with messages.

SMACK!!! SMACK!!! SMACK!!!

She was hardly aware of what was happening. Adams lifted up her gym-slip skirt and neatly laid it back above her waist.

His warm male hands cupped her bottom cheeks, squeezing and kneading each one in turn. His fingers poked indecently into her cleft, forcing the navy cotton into a kind of valley in between. He continued poking and pushing his humiliating finger down, down, into the deep cleft and beyond—massaging the sticky wet cotton stain until she writhed uncontrollably. The hems of her knickers were soaking with perspiration.

SMACK!!! SMACK!!! SMACK!!! Heavier and hard, punishing and determined.

She made no sound. Her face was flushed, her forehead beaded, her ears ringing from the pumping, pumping in them, and from the fly-swatting spanks of her bottom.

"Now I shall really punish you!" he said, his voice rising to an angry crescendo.

Silence.

"Get up, Lucy!" he bellowed.

Lucy awkwardly clambered off his knees, feeling her knickered, spanked bottom gingerly.

"Lucy," Adams's voice rose and fell with subtle sarcasm, "you aren't showing *any* signs of repentance, are you!"

Lucy's toes curled involuntarily. She hadn't the courage to look him in the eye.

"I'm afraid I'm going to insist you take your knickers down!"

Lucy looked at him with enormous eyes. Dare she? Should she? He *was* her Headmaster!

"Mr. Adams—"

"Don't interrupt, girl—do it!" he snapped, taking her hands and placing them on the waistband of her knickers. But the gym-slip was in the way, and it had to come off. Silently, he revolved her like a frozen ballerina and, unzipping the back of the gym-slip, eased it from her shoulders and let it slip into a grey puddle at her feet.

Then he turned her round so that she was facing him, and took her hands, pulling them down to his hot crotch where her fingers closed obediently around his erection.

With her body bent towards him, her hands moving all the while, he lifted his own hands and put them in the waistband of her school knickers, peeling the navy cotton down and away from her beautiful buttocks.

Down they came. He savoured it with a slow deliberate motion, rolling the soft cotton between finger and thumb and then easing it, controlling it down over her nubile pink and white bottom.

Angrily, because at that moment she took her hands away from his trousers, he jerked her down over his knee. Her naked bottom was well stuck-up. The knickers rolled down to her calves of their own accord and stopped there.

Like a hungry man savoring a feast, he looked at every part of her nakedness. The gentle girlish curve of her bottom cheeks, the saucy brown curls of pubic hair peeping from between her tightly closed legs.

Then he began to spank his young Biology mistress on her bare arse.

Lucy had no idea that the punishment would be as painful as her Headmaster seemed determined to make it. He had taken such command of the situation that she felt she could do nothing except obey. "He's feeling my bare bottom," she kept repeating to herself. "He's spanking me!" And with that mnemonic, she forced herself to believe that this was not unreality—that she really was being punished in a thoroughly childish and humiliating manner.

In between the hardest bottom-smacks he could muster, Adams tilted her so that he could rub her pink erect clitoris—already streaming with moisture. As the heat on Lucy's bottom grew, she clenched her cheeks together in an attempt to ease the pain. She began to wish very much that she wasn't being spanked after all. And with that sudden realization—that Adams was spanking her against her will—it became dreadfully humiliating. There was no getting away from it—or from the fire he was stoking on her bottom.

She began to squeal through clenched teeth, but then as the slaps came one after another in the same sore places; she cried out, "Oh! Stop it! Pl-ee-ase!" and screeched in distress.

George Adams was going to do no such thing until he was satisfied she had been punished entirely to his liking.

"Next time I'll bring my cane, young lady—and I'll thrash you with all the strength I have in my body!" he hissed.

"Oh! My poor bottom. Oh! Oooh! Please, I'm sorry!" Lucy yelled, but Adams only seemed to smack her all the harder.

Suddenly there was an explosion of tears. She threw

back her head and sobbed like a baby.

He pushed her off his lap and onto the floor. The schoolmistress lay at her Headmaster's feet.

Still sobbing, Lucy felt his hands lift her up and smooth her well-spanked buttocks. With a voice of acid hardness he told her to take off her jumper and blouse.

She was naked apart from the long white socks. The sweat from her wrigglings mingled with her perfume and trickled down between her bare breasts.

George pushed her over to a corner of the room and positioned the spot-light onto the young woman standing there, rubbing the reddest bottom he'd ever seen.

"Put your hands on your head!" he thundered.

Delicious! The spot-light played up an down the creamy whiteness of her back, the raw rude crimson of her arse. The posture was so like that of a truant schoolgirl made to stand in the corner with her hands on her head.

He stood behind her, smoothing her body and marvelling at the heat coming from her bottom.

Then, like a doll-ballerina, Lucy walked stiffly to her bedroom—propelled urgently by Adams. The Headmaster of St. Bede's Boys' Grammar School had one hand on her burning flanks, the other on the zip of his trousers.

Biology teacher she might be, but that night he taught her a thing or two about Biology she wouldn't find in any science textbook.

A Good All-Rounder

Amelia was, in all outward appearances, the model Head Girl. Her parents were awfully respectable and involved in school affairs; Amelia herself was academically good, articulate, sportive, and very pretty. Eminently suited to represent Normanhurst High School for Girls. Worshipped by first and second years, who found her composure and attractiveness totally awe-inspiring; envied but respected by her contemporaries. A jolly good "all rounder."

Her status was a permit to taking subtle liberties: she always wore the uniform, but had successfully adapted it to be a little more becoming. Her school shirt was more a blouse with a hint of lace around the collar; somehow no one seemed to notice the absence of tie, and the effect was softer, more feminine. Her jumper had an exclusive label and her grey flannel skirt was long, figure-hugging pencil. To complete the picture she wore discreet, slim, high-heeled shoes, tasteful good earrings, and a slim gold bangle adorned each willowy wrist.

Unlike other girls, Amelia was striking to look at even from a distance, identifiable by a turbulent mass of springy fair curls.

The rhythmic rise and fall of her hips as she walked, and the just discernable wobble of her round, plumping bottom beneath a thigh-hugging skirt hypnotised onlookers. In secret she wore stockings and a dainty white cotton embroidered garter belt. Certain male

185

members of staff had noticed the teasing outline of the garter straps beneath her narrow skirt. Whatever else she wore was open to conjecture.

What she *did* wear, in actual fact, were gauzy, lacy, close-fitting French panties, which she sprayed with perfume from her mother's atomiser—hence the aura of elusive scent that was always with her; never obvious, but intriguingly present all the same.

One could easily forgive Amelia's desire to blossom into a woman. The curves of her body made it obvious that no school uniform could disguise her nascent womanhood, because the whole enviable development was somewhat belied by her face and expression. Very much of an innocent, unwordly young girl. Eyes with a sweet and endearing candor, obviously not troubled by silly preoccupations with boys and sex. Baby smooth skin and a full mouth, whose lips were often formed into an engaging provocative pout. Pretty as a picture and probably unaware of it. Unspoilt, unsullied— without a corrupt thought in her head.

Amelia sat on the stage with the staff at morning assembly, listening with admirable concentration to the nasal drone of the headmistress. Unobtrusively, still maintaining the same respectable attentiveness, she put on her tinted glasses and looked at the staff seated around her, who were all trying to look interested, too. She flickered from man to man. In her mind she had been to bed with every one of them.

Passing from one male to the next, she rated each one's sexual performance on a scale from one to ten. Most scored under five.

"Mr. Lines . . . did he make it with his wife last night? Doubt it—his legs are crossed tight . . . bet he's looking at mine." Amelia languorously (but so innocently) uncrossed her legs and crossed them again.

Could he glimpse a stocking top? The victim flushed, fidgeted, and looked down at his knees. "Shame on your dirty mind, Mr. Lines!" Amelia deliberately smoothed down her skirt with delicate, fastidious fingers.

She stared equably over the sea of spotty faces cramped in ragged lines on the floor, wriggling her nose at the omnipresent odor of so many pubescent girls, to the back of the hall where she gazed fixedly at the blank wall. On it projected the camera of her imagination. Her lurid, shameful pornographic fantasies.

"Mr. Marsh . . . sitting directly behind me . . . I know he's aware of me. I can feel him looking at the back of my neck. Let's see. Urgent and athletic (I've seen his cock bulging away under that track suit). Perhaps he'd strip me, rip my clothes, breathing heavily—beads of sweat glistening on his upper arms . . . carry me to bed. Fuck like a maniac. Would he smoke afterwards? Yes. He certainly wouldn't kiss me. Wham, bam, and no 'thank you, ma'am!' Four out of ten. Could do better.

"Monsieur Massot . . . ooh, such slippery hands. A man who knows how to touch a woman—and where! Sweet nothings in French. Body going to seed, though . . . skin smells of garlic and after-shave. Pooh! Still *his* was a nice size and—Wow! didn't he just love what I did with my mouth! Five out of ten for *appreciation!*

"Mr. Finn . . . Mathematics. Calculating prig. Would there be time to squeeze me in before 'Match of the Day'? No score!

"Mr. Raphael . . . my English master. Oooh! I can't think about him. Dark, leonine, and unfathomable. I . . . I don't want to think about him. Help! I'm blushing—and he never misses a thing. Just can't work

him out. I know he's not married—can't imagine why.
He's so good looking. Nearly all the girls have got a
crush on him, but I haven't, have I? No, I'm too old for
that sort of thing. Oh Lord! Mr. Raphael! I've got him
this morning, all morning, for 'Creative Writing.' I'll
be leaving this dump in a few weeks and I think these
filling-in courses are a waste of bloody time . . . Oh!
not another hymn!"

Mr. Raphael always told his students of the Creative
Writing class that he didn't expect them to write anything. He would merely be gratified if they did. If the
creative spirit was not forthcoming that morning, never
mind. A whole morning spent in creative thought was
good enough.

The class arrived late in a mood of sulky resignation.
Mr. Raphael was annoyed and glowered at Amelia,
although she had arrived in time, of course. Amelia
blushed furiously. She had nothing to feel ashamed of,
yet Mr. Raphael usually succeeded in making her feel
vaguely uncomfortable and guilty about nothing at all.
She fingered her earrings to reassure herself that she
was a woman after all.

"Today," began Mr. Raphael, as the class fumbled
to seat itself, "I'm going to change things a little, and
give you a specific subject, as hardly anyone wrote
anything last week. Having the freedom to choose your
own subject seemed to frighten you into producing
nothing at all." He looked accusingly from girl to girl
and then at the pathetically small pile of marked scripts
from last week, lying on his desk. Amelia looked up
brightly and clasped her hands in relief. At least hers
was among them.

"Encounter with a Professional Person," said Mr.
Raphael drily and sat down.

There was a silence, then a faint groan. What a way to bore away a morning! The class, shifting itself like a heaving woman lifting and settling her skirts, slumped into thought—or blankness. Three hours to go with only a short break in between.

Amelia couldn't think of a more uninspiring subject and lamented the hours she had to fill before lunch. Unless . . . she was bold enough to write about. . . ? She looked up, thoughtfully. Yes, she would write a little story—but for herself. A true story about an event which had thrown her thoughts into a fever ever since it happened. But of course she wouldn't hand it in to Mr. Raphael. During the last half-hour of lesson time, she would hastily scribble a token effort for the teacher and add a simpering postscript to the effect that she wasn't well, or inspired this morning. She'd always submitted work on other occasions and Mr. Raphael had praised it. Surely this entitled her to please herself just this once?

"My dentist," she began in her neat precise hand, "is an extremely good-looking man of about thirty-five. Reason enough to pay him a visit!" She paused and caught sight of Mr. Raphael, while smiling to herself, and hastily assumed a studious expression. "He certainly has a way of making one feel at ease," she continued, "an enlightened modern practitioner who dresses casually, has a pleasant chatty manner, and a video in his surgery for his patients' distraction. You can select a short video tape and then lie back for twenty minutes' entertainment!"

Amelia paused, sucking her pen thoughtfully. Again Mr. Raphael looked up at that precise moment and their eyes met. Amelia lowered hers swiftly and he returned to his book. Dare she? Dare she write what actually happened? If Mr. Raphael should see. . .

Feeling excited, she continued: "On a recent visit to this particular 'professional person', something rather extraordinary occurred. I was due for some unpleasant treatment when Mr. Graham, my dentist, suggested I try out his new video. I chose a film called 'Strict Discipline at St. Cecilia's.' Presuming it to be a harmless school comedy, I pushed the cassette into the video player and settled back in the chair to watch the fun. Mr. Graham set to work straight away at his horrible job, humming loudly and concentrating on what he was doing. I supposed he'd seen all the videos before and wasn't interested. He didn't even glance at the screen once.

"The film began with a long line of nubile, grown-up school girls in old-fashioned gym tunics, parading in front of their Headmaster, who was brandishing a cane.

"There was no sound apart from the tap-tapping of the cane on the impatient Headmaster's fingers. It quite heightened the drama not to have any dialogue. Behind the Headmaster stood a small group of other masters positively agog with excitement, all tense and rigid and wide-eyed. The camera passed along the line of girls, noting their woebegone faces (some were snivelling and about to cry) and then travelled along their back view, focusing quite deliberately on their bottoms."

Amelia jerked her head up. Mr. Raphael was deep in his book, so she feverishly resumed her writing.

". . . The dentist was drilling my teeth. It was painful, but the entertainment was *riveting* . . .

"The Headmaster walked slowly along behind the girls and paused before each one to flick up the back of her skirt rather cleverly with the tip of the cane. Each girl was wearing bottle-green panties, horrid thick cotton ones with deep hems like they used to wear years ago. One thing I did notice though was that every girl

190

was wearing a pair that appeared to be several sizes too small for her. This was demonstrated when the Headmaster pushed each girl in the back and made her bend over after he'd lifted her skirt. You could see the stitches around the crotch straining to bursting point. (No wonder I got such funny looks from Mr. Marsh, our P.E. Instructor, when I was playing netball in my gym knickers; I haven't had a new pair since the second year. If I looked like *that* every time *I* bent over .. !) They were also wearing stockings—black ones with seams.

"Mr. Graham's head kept getting in the way. I was desperate not to miss a thing, and as for what happened next . . . it gives me wet panties every time I think about it.

"One master took a couple of girls and, taking a cane out of what looked like a golfing bag, made the girls shuffle over to a corner of the hall. Then a close-up shot. Wow! Dealing with each one at a time, he motioned them to bend over and touch their toes, then promptly whacked them with the cane over their knickers right across the fleshiest part of their bottom. I could just hear a 'hiss' as the cane cut through the air. The dentist was busy singing to himself and the drill was whining so he probably didn't hear it. What a strange choice for a dentist's video selection, I thought. Still it was certainly taking my mind off what was happening in my mouth.

"The next sequence was amazing! One poor girl was led by a master into a back room where he shut the door. She must have done something awful. The other girls were still being whacked in the hall and the camera caught some of their faces—with expressions of pain and horrible grimaces. To return to the poor victim alone with the rather good-looking master—he

191

started to tickle her between the legs with the tip of the cane, causing her to jump about. (If anyone tickled *me* down there it would do more than just tickle!)"

Amelia began to squeeze her thighs together and wriggle her bottom on the chair. She was flushed and quite unaware that Mr. Raphael was quietly observing her.

"The dentist at that point infuriatingly leaned over me, blocking my view, but the next time I looked at the screen I almost choked on that gurgling suction thing I had wedged in my mouth. The girl was taking her knickers down, and the way the master was looking at her bare bottom—I'd give anything to be looked at like that! *Everything* was visible: bottom cheeks all plump and quivering, pubic hair. She'd pulled her plaits over her face so I couldn't see her face, but I should think from the way she was standing, head bent and knock-kneed, that she was terribly embarrassed.

"The master started to run his hands over her bare arse, and then he tipped her over so her bottom was nicely presented to receive the cane.

"She seemed to take it very well, only flinching a little and drawing her buttock muscles in tightly after each stroke. There were red lines appearing on her behind as that thin, whippy little cane landed time after time. The master stopped caning her all of a sudden, grabbed a chair and sat down. She was still, bending over, and the master had a long look at what he'd done. Then he pulled her down so that she was lying across his knees. He started to spank her bottom, already red and stripey, and his hand imparted an all-over red glow to her well-caned bottom cheeks.

"The cameraman obviously got carried away here because he zoomed in on her bottom until it filled the entire screen. I could see the crack between her bottom cheeks and *everything* else, and this male hand coming down on her rosy-red rear. Oooh! To be that close to his cock! And speaking of *that,* the master unzipped himself and lugged his enormous prick out until it rested close up against her thigh. Its knob was purple-red and twitching, and it hovered there with its tip throbbing. A little dewy drop oozed out from it and stayed there like a bubble. The cameraman seemed preoccupied with the master's thing now, and I too couldn't keep my eyes off it. He eased the girl off his lap and while she stood with her back to the camera he squeezed up tightly against her red bum, hot prick rubbing hot skin. Then he pushed her till she was lying across the chair with her naked bottom stuck well up. A shot again of that delicious cock sticking up like a hat-rack. The veins were standing out purple along the shaft—and the master was urgently pushing the skin up and down. There he was, standing over her bum, knees bent, nudging her hot cheeks with his cock, running it along the deep red stripes he'd made with the cane, and lovingly smearing his juice on the marks like it was ointment. The girl must have liked it, because she stuck her ass up even further and wiggled it. I'd have given anything to have been in her place. He moved back and forth, rubbing his red knob against her sore bottom and making weird grunting sounds. His prick grew really huge and purple, and then he came in a lather of goo all over her ass cheeks.

"Yes, I actually saw him coming. I'd never seen that before in my life. The cock grows to bursting—then hunches itself before the spunk shoots out in spasms.

"At that orgasmic moment I nearly fainted and Mr. Graham came out of his daydream and caught sight of the screen. He almost drilled through my gum! He went bright, bright red, stopped drilling, rushed to the video and turned it off. He was panting and embarrassed. 'I'm terribly sorry,' he said, wringing his hands. 'I had no idea *that* was among the videos.' Who's complaining, I thought! '. . . I just don't know how it could have got there,' he stammered.

"Probably part of his private collection, I thought wryly. Kinky tastes. Spanking . . . caning. Exciting! Brings a new dimension to the sex thing. Perhaps he watches it when there are no patients. Perhaps he spanks his dental nurse when she's there."

Amelia had grown very red in the face and was quite carried away with her story; her stockings stuck to her thighs and there were other areas of her which felt uncomfortable, too.

It was nearly lunchtime and Mr. Raphael was not at his desk. Feeling suddenly uneasy, she turned her head, sensing that someone was looking over her shoulder. She was right. Mr. Raphael stood there, an expression of disgust and fascination on his face. He had been reading her last page.

Amelia felt as though she had shrunk to nothingness inside her clothes. The heat of her excitement rapidly turned to clamminess and she swallowed noisily. "Oh my God!" She sat helpless as Mr. Raphael calmly picked up her writing and returned with it to his desk.

"Amelia has finished," he announced to the class. There was sarcasm in his voice. "And I hope you all have, too."

Amelia flung her blonde curls over her face to hide her cheeks; they were burning. The class departed leaving Amelia busy with her bag, still waiting for her face to cool down.

Mr. Raphael sat reading her essay, tapping his teeth with a pencil. Amelia, feeling like a stricken rabbit, caught and unable to run away, made a clumsy movement from her desk. He looked up. His eyes were unfathomable.

"I would like to see you after school, Amelia," he said caustically. "I think we need to have a little talk about this."

The rest of the day passed unendurably slowly for Amelia. She was caught in spasms of panic. Suppose Mr. Raphael had shown her writing to the other staff, or left it lying about in the staffroom? What would he think of her? Now he knew all her private thoughts, knew she wasn't as innocent as she looked.

She rushed into the cloakroom and hid behind the coats when Mr. Raphael loomed out of the staffroom for his lunchtime duty. Deciding that she couldn't face dinner in school, Amelia slipped out and went alone into nearby Reigate to eat in a somber restaurant. She desperately tried to think herself into a state of composure and was puzzled and disconcerted at how fluttery and excited she really felt. Erratically she bought some expensive stockings—fully fashioned ones with seams, nearly purchasing black ones by mistake. She also sprayed herself extravagantly with Je Reviens at the perfume counter, much to the assistant's disapproval.

4:00 P.M. Amelia waited as instructed outside the staffroom. Outwardly she looked calm. Very presentable. Clean stockings (the ones she'd bought specially), a little pale lipstick, smooth shining hair. Standing in front of a mirror she had scrutinized her appearance and picked every speck of fluff, every stray hair from her clothes. She felt as if she were going to a very important interview and had to look her best.

Mr. Raphael emerged from the staffroom long after the other staff had gone home. He was smoking a cigarette and carried a folder under his arm— containing her story, no doubt. He avoided Amelia's flickering glance and walked silently down the dark corridor.

"We'll go to L2 in the annex. The cleaners have finished in that part of school now," he said airily. "Come along, Amelia Rogers."

She followed him like a child, aware of her stockings rustling and chafing her thighs, the pressure of her tight, smooth skirt rubbing and sliding over her hips; the click of her lone high-heels in the echoing corridor and the soft squeak-squeak of Mr. Raphael's suedes.

What was he going to do with her? Should he be seeing her alone like this, so late after school?

He opened the classroom door and Amelia, her eyes downcast, walked past him. She smelled a faint whiff of after-shave as she brushed the softness of his jacket. She could hear his breathing.

He shut the door and moved to the desk where he lit another cigarette. All was silent for a long, electric moment and Amelia shivered.

Mr. Raphael cleared his throat.

"Well, it's disgusting isn't it, Amelia? I don't have to say any more, do I?" He murmured, taking the pages of her work from the folder and shuffling them on the desk. He looked at her laconically.

"I'm sorry, Sir—Mr. Raphael. You weren't meant to see it."

"I know, girl," he snapped, making Amelia jump.

She looked unhappily at the space between their feet.

"But, Sir. It was true—about the dentist, I mean. It *did* happen," she said pleadingly.

He blew smoke from his nostrils in an impatient snort.

"The sexual fantasies of a schoolgirl—the Head Girl," he nodded curtly, "are very interesting . . . and informative . . . but they have no place in school."

196

"Please don't show the Head, Mr. Raphael. Please."
Her voice was barely a whisper.

"I don't know what I should do." He rose and paced
slowly round the desk, loosening his tie. "It's extraordinary," he said at last, "that you find the thought of a
caning so . . . er . . . pleasurable." He paused in front
of her.

Amelia could hear his breathing, quick and shallow.
Like her own.

"I doubt if you would find it so *arousing*," he
pounced on the word with unkind relish, "in real life."

Amelia was mute.

"I think that your appalling little piece of pornogra-
phy should be on the Headmistress's desk. But then, as
she is a lady of some delicacy it would probably make
her sick, Amelia—and you would be in immediate and
everlasting disgrace!" He thumped his fist on the desk.
"I shall therefore take it upon myself to punish you.
Then we shall say no more about the matter to anyone.
Do you agree?" He spoke harshly. Amelia would
readily agree to anything if it meant avoiding disgrace.

"Right!" He sprang from the desk where he had
been sitting and went into the stockroom. He returned
with a thin school cane in his hand.

Amelia's lip trembled. "Please, Sir . . ." she faltered
in a thin voice. She seemed spellbound by the cane
tap-tapping in his hands. There seemed a ghastly inevi-
tability about what was to come.

She felt herself blushing uncontrollably. So the
instrument of her fantasy was going to be used to punish her! She stumbled at this realization, her high-heels
raucously scraping across the floor; the only sound in
the room.

Mr. Raphael paced up and down. He seemed reluctant to look Amelia in the eye.

"It's appropriate, I feel, under the circumstances, to make the punishment fit the crime. I shall in part enact your little fantasy. Only, I think you will find the reality not nearly so pleasant. Amelia, remove your skirt!" He turned his back on her as if he would brook no argument.

Amelia hesitated, then mechanically removed her coat and laid it on the desk. The sound of a rasping zip, the slither of fine nylon against flannel. . . . A sigh of exertion as her hips wriggled free from the clinging material of her skirt.

Mr. Raphael turned. In a brisk glance he noticed her stocking-tops, long bare thighs, the creases in her white cotton French panties—revealing a good deal of her bottom. He looked quickly away again out of the window at the grey afternoon.

He instructed Amelia to bend over and position her rear for the punishment.

With a piteous look she obeyed. Her curls tumbled over her flushed face in a silken stream. Her panties tightened and gradually rose, exposing more and more of her plump ivory cheeks until the cuppable curve beneath each was fully visible. Mr. Raphael stood behind her, unable to take his eyes away from the delectable picture.

"I toyed with the idea of punishing you over your skirt, but I don't think that would sufficiently impress on your mind just how serious the matter is. The Head Girl," he added sarcastically, "needs a humiliating tumble from her lofty position if she is to learn her lesson."

Amelia shuffled and bent over even further. She wanted the whole business finished with as soon as possible. Much of her shame, the gusset of her panties had almost completely disappeared between her cheeks.

Whack! The thin rattan cane cut into her exposed buttocks. Mr. Raphael felt the vibrations travel up the cane into the palm of his hand. His body shook. He saw her bottom cheeks contract and then shudder back into fullness as the pain ebbed away. Another stroke. Amelia bent over even further and stuffed her hair into her mouth to stifle a cry. She had not really believed that the first stroke had happened; was Amelia Rogers, Head Girl of Normanhurst, really being punished by a master with the cane? The second stroke dispelled all her illusions.

Mr. Raphael felt it essential to do the job properly. He did not believe that a few token taps would do any good at all, so he caned her with all the strength in his arm. He noticed that the marks did not appear immediately; the cane left bleached white lines for some time. When the blood returned beneath the skin, the lines fleshed out into rosy stripes bisecting her cheeks.

The proximity of this young woman's semi-naked bottom sticking up so provocatively made his mouth go dry while the rest of him sweated profusely with excitement. As Amelia flinched and wriggled, wisps of hair came into view from beneath the hem of her panties. She had brought her hand low between her thighs and was clutching the gusset. Mr. Raphael unconsciously touched his fly too and was disconcerted by the size of the bulge beneath his trousers.

After the first few strokes, when Amelia had been too shocked to think, the images from the video began to fill her mind. Here she was suffering the most awful humiliation and pain, yet at the same time she felt incredibly excited. It was so much better than fantasy.

A *real*, good-looking man was caning her. She wished that she could see how he was looking at her bottom. Perhaps his cock was unbearably hard, too. She had no way of knowing.

There was something inexplicably delicious in being *made* to appear so sexy and be punished for it at the same time. She had completely forgotten what the punishment was about; the excitement of the fantasy and reality were interwoven.

Mr. Raphael caned Amelia mercilessly. He dared not think what her bottom looked like under those knickers, and he struggled with the desire to pull them down and see for himself.

Suddenly from Amelia came a sound that started as a gasp, like a baby's first cry. Then she hunched, put her hands up to her face and cried loud sobs through her tousled hair.

Mr. Raphael stopped. He was worried. Perhaps he had caned her too hard? While she stood blubbering, he reflected how much she must have hated what he had done. She certainly hadn't found it exciting, had she?

He moved closer to her while she was crying hysterically. She felt weak and, losing her balance, fell heavily against Mr. Raphael's chest. He could smell her hair, feel her breasts squashed tight against him, her tangled fingers clutching his jacket. Red-faced and wildly panting, she pressed her body hard and insistently up against him.

Involuntarily his hands moved over her. Down, down to the fullness of her burning cheeks. She stood on tip-toe, wriggling as his fingers slipped between her legs. He withdrew them quickly, shocked and overwhelmed. They were wet! Her thighs were running with moisture. The cotton gusset of her knickers was wet through!

"Amelia," he said breathlessly, pushing her away

from him, "get dressed at once and go home. You have been—punished. I—" he faltered, unable to speak.

Amelia dressed and ran from the room, flushed and dishevelled. Mr. Raphael stood motionless, distractedly sweeping his hair away from a sweaty forehead, fumbling with his cigarettes; his mind a turmoil.

The days passed and the end of term approached. Both Amelia and Mr. Raphael spent much time avoiding each other. He was preoccupied and short-tempered, she in a dream.

Summer holidays. Amelia was restless. University . . . piano lessons . . . a wedding. But her mind was feverishly obsessed by Mr. Raphael. Night after night in her hot-summer bed she relived what had happened. The undressing . . . the cane . . . Mr. Raphael's fingers. The room was filled with her moaning and her sighs.

She willed that she might see him again. One evening there was a phone call. It was Mr. Raphael.

"I've been looking through your creative writing folder, Amelia," he said, tense and hesitant. "I think it shows promise. I should like to discuss it with you. There is the prospect of publication. Would you like to call on Thursday evening?"

Amelia nearly made herself ill with excitement and anticipation. When Thursday came she bathed and powdered herself like a King's concubine until her skin was sweetly fragrant and baby-soft.

Wearing filmy French panties, a pretty pastel dress, tiny white shoes and ankle socks, with her hair in a cloud about her shoulders, she arrived at Mr. Raphael's house.

"Hello, Mr. Raphael," she said. There was none of the Head Girl confidence in her voice as he ushered her into the sitting room.

He lit a cigarette, offered one to Amelia, paced the room and immediately began to talk very fast.

"You write well, Amelia," he began in a cracked voice, addressing the room. He could not look at her. "However, I think you should pay more attention to colloquial expressions and—"

Amelia sank dispiritedly back into the sofa. The limpid longing in her eyes dimmed, and disappointment clouded her face. What had she expected him to say? Or do? Perhaps she had to learn to accept that he was a schoolmaster, older than herself—and she was sadly trapped in a young girl's fantasy.

To Mr. Raphael a vision of Alice in Wonderland was sitting curled up on his sofa, tanned legs tucked demurely underneath her. She gazed up at him. He stammered over his words.

Amelia could only speak to him with her eyes, and that wasn't enough. He was, after all, a schoolmaster. She meant nothing to him. After a while she stubbed her cigarette out in defeat and rose to go.

"I'm sorry—I can't stay any longer," she said, trying to hide the crushing disappointment in her voice.

Mr. Raphael took her arm urgently and looked into her eyes for the first time.

"Amelia, I've thought of nothing else but our encounter at school since it happened. I am no longer your teacher. I am simply a man who does not understand. I must know. Amelia, did you find my caning you—sexually arousing?" He was breathing in short little gasps.

Amelia went limp and nodded.

Mr. Raphael was exultant. "Amelia, I could say nothing while I was your teacher or I might have lost my job—but I have read that last essay of yours night after night." He began to stroke her throat with trembling fingers. "I confess I enjoyed it very much. I enjoyed caning you very much, too."

"Yes, Sir." Amelia moved closer and whispered into his jacket.

"Amelia, I would like to cane you again. Now. Would you?—" Excitement rendered his words staccato, toneless.

"Yes, Mr. Raphael," the words were simply said.

He moved and went to a drawer where he took out a school cane.

"Sir?"

He turned, the cane shaking in his hands.

"Sir, would you spank me please? Instead of the cane?"

"Yes, Amelia. But why?"

"Because it happened in my story—and because I want to feel the touch of your hands on me," she finished in a shy whisper.

The cane rattled in the drawer as he put it away.

Amelia swept her hair aside and struggled with the zip on her dress, and Mr. Raphael hesitated before helping her.

The dress slid down over her shoulders in one movement and lay in folds at her feet. She stood in her bra and panties—which again had ridden up into the crack of her cheeks and were damp with her own excited perspiration.

Mr. Raphael ran greedy hands over her body in silence. He undid her bra and cupped a hand around each breast, kneading the soft swelling flesh gently. The nipples grew proud under his touch.

He sat down on a chair and struggled with his zip and soon his cock was winking at her through his trousers like a Cyclopian eye. He pushed her hands down onto it. She slid the skin up and down as she'd done so many times in her imaginings, watching him jerk and pant with excitement.

"You can do that again—with your mouth, after I've spanked you, you wicked, wicked girl," he said throatily.

He pushed Amelia away and gazed lustfully at her. Soft hair falling over pink-flushed face, narrow tanned shoulders. Milky paleness of breasts, untouched by the sun.

"I shall spank you, Amelia," he said slowly, savouring every word, "but I shall do it on your bare, naked bottom."

She shuddered, but obediently began to lower her panties.

He turned her to see the round heaviness of her bottom cheeks exposed inch by tantalizing inch. Peach-like bottom, downy, full, and curvaceous. He drew her down on his lap so she was sitting astride him, and he poked her hard on her clit with his cock, nudging deep down into the slipperiness of her aching virgin cunt. She rose up gasping, wanting him to surge like a ruthless piston inside her, but he pulled back.

"No, no young lady. That's for later. I want you over my knee first." He was teasing her cruelly.

Spreading his legs, he laid her across his lap, panties in a creased tangle about her knees. His cock, swollen and angry-looking, twitched between her legs. He told her to hold it during the spanking. Its tip was slippery: it felt like egg-white. Amelia groaned, near to coming from the pressure of her wet thighs against him, and she squirmed in torment.

He raised his hand and brought it down resoundingly, right across the crown of her buttocks.

"Oooh, spank me, Mr. Raphael, spank me *hard*, I'm

such a naughty girl! Oooh!" She was humping and surging against him—and with each spank her fingers jerked spasmodically up and down the shaft of his cock. She moistened the whole knob with his warm viscid juices, and the sensitive flickering motion of her fingertips made his muscles tense and body jerk. He pushed his hard cock up and down in the slippery haven of her young hands.

He gained confidence, and the slaps came measured and heavy. Her round cheeks, dancing under the hot stinging palm, were turning deep pink. She moaned and drew breath, widening her legs until they were restricted by the panties. The fragile cotton began to rip as she strained against them.

He spanked her deep down in the dark furrow between her cheeks, fascinated by the rhythmic contractions of her buttocks. Amelia felt the vibrations travel to her clit like jerky shocks. Mr. Raphael tipped her further over his knee to see the engorged cunt-lips, rude-red and sticky all around. He could see the pink button of her desperate little clit standing proud. He could smell her arousal—and it was driving him mad.

"Naughty, disgusting girl! Wicked Amelia! If you could see what I can seen from here! *You're sopping wet!*—and all because I'm spanking you!" he panted accusingly.

"Oooh, Mr. Raphael—you're hurting me now. Oooh!!!" She clutched her burning cheeks with one hand, but he roughly thrust it aside.

If only he wouldn't spank her down there. Oh! the feeling was unbearable, like a stifled sneeze—only it was spreading all over her bottom from between her legs.

"Mr. Raphael—plee-ase stop! Oh! Oh!" She jerked herself rigid and screamed. Her panties ripped completely. In a mixture of shame and pain, loud sobs broke free and she clutched Mr. Raphael's legs, crying noisily.

Mr. Raphael had Amelia totally in his power. He wanted to do everything all at once: have her suck his cock until he was ready to shudder a fountain of spunk in her wild hair, dress her up in all kinds of sexy and provocative costumes, and cane her hard—stripe her bottom with the marks of his possession.

But there would be plenty of time for that. Right now, he was going to fuck her, with Amelia lying on her sore, red, naughty little bottom.

Mr. Raphael told Amelia's mother that her daughter's creative writing showed exceptional promise, but needed intensive practice. He offered to provide the necessary instruction at his house.

Amelia dutifully presented herself at Mr. Raphael's house every other evening, for most of the summer holidays.

Mrs. Rogers was delighted with Amelia's dedication, and with Mr. Raphael for devoting so much of his valuable time to her. "So thorough and painstaking. Such a charming man!" she said.

Amelia blushed. Painstaking it certainly was. She sat down very gingerly, for a certain part of her was still very tender, due to the previous evening's creative activities.

One thing puzzled Amelia's mother. For all Mr. Raphael's efforts, she had yet to see one single piece of her daughter's creative writing.

SELECTED BLUE MOON BOOKS

_____ Afternoons of A Woman of Leisure (#126)	$5.95
_____ Algier's Tomorrow (#127)	$5.95
_____ Amanda (#131)	$5.95
_____ An English Education (#025)	$5.95
_____ Beating the Wild Tatoo (#132)	$5.95
_____ Bitch Witch (#075)	$4.95
_____ Blue Velvet (#082)	$5.95
_____ The Captive (#043)	$5.95
_____ The Captive II (#098)	$5.95
_____ The Captive III (#123)	$5.95
_____ The Calamities of Jane (#024)	$5.95
_____ Elaine Cox (#056)	$5.95
_____ The Encounter (#078)	$4.95
_____ Fantasy Hunters (#067)	$4.95
_____ Frank and I (#002)	$5.95
_____ The Hidden Gallery (#121)	$4.95
_____ Ironwood (#022)	$4.95
_____ Ironwood Revisited (#046)	$5.95
_____ Images of Ironwood (#063)	$5.95
_____ The Hour of the Wolf (#054)	$4.95
_____ Man With a Maid II (#088)	$4.50
_____ Man With a Maid III (#104)	$4.95
_____ Mariska I (#065)	$4.50
_____ The Merry Order of St. Bridget (#122)	$4.95
_____ Miss High Heels (#020)	$5.95
_____ My Secret Life (#027)	$4.95
_____ Our Scene (#041)	$9.95
_____ Professor Spender and the Sadistic Impulse (#045)	$4.50
_____ Romance of Lust (#116)	$5.95
_____ The Reckoning (#032)	$5.95
_____ The Rites of Sodom (#026)	$5.95
_____ Secret Talents (#005)	$5.95
_____ Sundancer (#125)	$5.95
_____ The Tudor's Bride (#030)	$5.95
_____ The Vicar's Girl (#122)	$5.95
_____ What Love (#117)	$5.95

ORDER FIVE BOOKS RECEIVE ONE BOOK FREE!

Bk#	Title	Qty.	Price
			FREE

Subtotal	
Postage and Handling	
Tax (N.Y. and PA. Residents only add 8.25%)	
Total $	

Signature (I certify by my signature that I am over 21 years of age)

Name

Address

City   State   Zip code

CREDIT CARD USERS CHECK APPROPRIATE BOX

☐ MasterCard   ☐ VISA   ☐ AMEX

Credit Card Number   / Expiration Date

WE ARE NOW ACCEPTING PHONE AND FAX ORDERS!
Call us at 1-800-535-0007 to order by phone or 212-673-1039 to order by fax 7 days a week. We will require your card number, expiration date, name and current mailing address. Include your phone number if possible. If you have any questions about your order please call us. We request a <u>four book minimum</u> credit card order. Forthcoming titles will be shipped as they become available.

Please make all checks payable to Blue Moon Books Inc. in U.S. currency only

THANK YOU!

Postage Information: $1.50 first book $.75 each additional
Canada: $2.00 first book $1.25 each additional
Other foreign: $4.00 first book $2.00 each additional
<u>NO C.O.D. ORDERS</u>

Blue Moon Books Published by: Blue Moon Books, Inc.
P.O. Box1040, Cooper Station, New York, NY 10276
Phone: 212/505-6880 or1-800/535-0007 Fax: 212/673-1039